"With an expert blend of the
clearly explains a deeply syst
Approaching the work with k
in complex intersectional con

empowering school communitie... collaborative skills for addressing today's educational and mental health needs."

Carey Dimmitt, Ph.D., *Professor, UMass Amherst and Director of the Ronald H. Fredrickson Center for School Counseling Outcome Research and Evaluation, U.S.A.*

"An important and necessary text – Drs. Lemberger-Truelove and Bowers Parker are complex thinkers who communicate their ideas clearly. To make real change in students' lives, school counselors must be able to think and act on both an individual and ecological level simultaneously. This text provides practical strategies for school counselors wanting to address the complex challenges today's students encounter."

George McMahon, Ph.D., *Clinical Associate Professor and Associate Department Head at the University of Georgia, U.S.A.*

"Finally, a textbook for school counseling that considers the social determinants of mental health, academic achievement, and the need to modify school environmental conditions inextricably linked to student outcomes! ASE theory can potentially transform how school counselors provide therapeutic interventions in schools, including targeting multiple levels of influence."

Joseph M. Williams, Ph.D., *Professor of Counseling at The University of North Carolina – Chapel Hill, U.S.A.*

AN EVIDENCE-BASED SYSTEMS APPROACH TO SCHOOL COUNSELING

This book presents strategies for using systemic theory and evidence-based practice in schools to support students, the adults in their lives, and their wider communities.

Beginning by introducing and explaining the Advocating Student-within-Environment (ASE) theory, each chapter then addresses a specific school-based issue, such as academic achievement, crisis, trauma, and resiliency, from a systemic and environmental lens. Practical and accessible, the chapters are filled with case examples, evidence-based interventions, and helpful tools to show how counselors can incorporate the approach into their practice. Extending beyond school and student problems, this text also explores greater system functioning, such as community outreach and state level intervention, discussing advocacy and political issues.

This book is essential for school-based professionals who are looking for new ways to work with students, families, and their communities. It will also be of interest to mental health professionals who work systemically, such as marriage and family therapists and community counselors.

Matthew E. Lemberger-Truelove is Professor of Counseling and Higher Education at the University of North Texas, U.S.A. He is the Editor of the *Journal of Counseling and Development* and the Associate Director for the Center for School Counseling Outcome Research and Evaluation. His scholarship includes empirical and theoretical writing. His empirical work pertains to counseling practice with children and adolescents, especially in economically challenged K12 schools.

Hannah Bowers Parker is Associate Professor in the Department of Counselor Education at Florida Atlantic University, U.S.A. Bowers has been working with children and families for over a decade, both as a marriage and family therapist and a school counselor.

Family Systems Counseling: Innovations Then and Now

This series is aimed at both current practitioners and students who wish to learn about the historical power and boldness of the family systems approach, but who also need to see it applied to current problem situations. The books in this series will reflect on the pioneering elements of family systems approaches and how they might have been used previously with a particular issue or population.

Series Editor: Paul R. Peluso, PhD, Florida Atlantic University

Intercultural Perspectives on Family Counseling
Edited by Brian S. Canfield

A Family Systems Guide to Infidelity
Helping Couples Understand, Recover From, and Avoid Future Affairs
Paul R. Peluso

An Evidence-Based Systems Approach to School Counseling
Advocating Student-within-Environment
Matthew E. Lemberger-Truelove and Hannah Bowers Parker

For more information about this series, please visit www.routledge.com/Family-Systems-Counseling-Innovations-Then-and-Now/book-series/FSCTN.

AN EVIDENCE-BASED SYSTEMS APPROACH TO SCHOOL COUNSELING

Advocating Student-within-Environment

Matthew E. Lemberger-Truelove and Hannah Bowers Parker

NEW YORK AND LONDON

Designed cover image: "Kaleidoscope" © Matthew E. Lemberger-Truelove

First published 2024
by Routledge
605 Third Avenue, New York, NY 10158

and by Routledge
4 Park Square, Milton Park, Abingdon, Oxon, OX14 4RN

Routledge is an imprint of the Taylor & Francis Group, an informa business

© 2024 Matthew E. Lemberger-Truelove and Hannah Bowers Parker

The right of Matthew E. Lemberger-Truelove and Hannah Bowers Parker to be identified as authors of this work has been asserted in accordance with sections 77 and 78 of the Copyright, Designs and Patents Act 1988.

All rights reserved. No part of this book may be reprinted or reproduced or utilised in any form or by any electronic, mechanical, or other means, now known or hereafter invented, including photocopying and recording, or in any information storage or retrieval system, without permission in writing from the publishers.

Trademark notice: Product or corporate names may be trademarks or registered trademarks, and are used only for identification and explanation without intent to infringe.

Library of Congress Cataloging-in-Publication Data
Names: Lemberger-Truelove, Matthew E., 1976– author. |
Parker, Hannah Bowers, author.
Title: An evidence-based systems approach to school counseling :
advocating student-within-environment / Matthew Lemberger-Truelove
and Hannah Bowers Parker.
Description: New York, NY : Routledge, 2024. |
Series: Family systems counseling: innovations then and now |
Includes bibliographical references and index. |
Identifiers: LCCN 2023029321 (print) | LCCN 2023029322 (ebook) |
ISBN 9781032321110 (hardback) | ISBN 9781032321103 (paperback) |
ISBN 9781003312871 (ebook)
Subjects: LCSH: Educational counseling. | Educational counseling–Philosophy.
Classification: LCC LB1027.5 .L4184 2024 (print) |
LCC LB1027.5 (ebook) | DDC 371.4/22–dc23/eng/20230807
LC record available at https://lccn.loc.gov/2023029321
LC ebook record available at https://lccn.loc.gov/2023029322

ISBN: 9781032321110 (hbk)
ISBN: 9781032321103 (pbk)
ISBN: 9781003312871 (ebk)

DOI: 10.4324/9781003312871

Typeset in Times New Roman
by Newgen Publishing UK

Matthew's Dedication
For Tamiko, Naarah, and Atom. Thank you for being my "within."

Hannah's Dedication
To Jack and Ava, for teaching me how to advocate.

CONTENTS

FOREWORD BY SERIES EDITOR

This book, *An Evidence-Based Systems Approach to School Counseling: Advocating Student-within-Environment* by Dr. Matthew E. Lemberger-Truelove and Dr. Hannah Bowers Parker, is a truly groundbreaking text that not only addresses an important issue but also forges a completely new theory and approach to working with children in schools. What sets this book apart is that the authors have created an approach to practice, Advocating Student-within-Environment (ASE), that addresses critical issues school-age children facing at every levels. These include academically oriented issues, emotional and behaviorally oriented issues, mental health–related issues, and so on. In addition, they provide meticulous documentation of the evidence base behind their approach. This work is the culmination of years of thinking and refinement, and offers to school counselors, school leaders, and everyone connected with a school community a truly systemic approach. In this text, the authors take the reader on a journey from the philosophical roots of the ASE approach, weaving in the best elements of learning theories and psychological theories, through to practical hands on applications of the ASE approach. Each chapter has case study examples embedded in it, and the book concludes with a detailed case study of ASE in action that provides the reader with a blueprint for enacting the approach immediately in a school setting.

In addition to the myriad ways that this book is transformative for school counselors and other stakeholders, the context that it was written is must be underscored. This book was conceived just prior to the COVID-19 pandemic and written throughout the most significant (and challenging) times that educators have faced. The pandemic revealed the incredible strengths and debts that society owes to its educators, and the tremendous resilience that school personnel went to in order to ensure that students' needs were able to be taken care of, both academic and emotional. From the creativity needed to switch to a completely virtual learning environment, to the almost super-human lengths that some educators would go to travel to student's houses and deliver education materials to children who didn't have them. At the same time, the pandemic revealed the structural and systemic issues that have long-plagued school systems. From inequities across school districts to outmoded methods of instruction, the pandemic pulled back the curtain on the dire challenges that our education system must grapple with. This is reflected in the "pandemic loss" of learning that students today must face (and its implications for the future). However, no single issue has been illuminated more starkly than the mental health crisis that school-age children are facing. It is a crisis of epidemic proportion, and one that is not likely to abate anytime soon. The school is fast becoming the front-line system that must cope with this crisis. As a result, *An Evidence-Based Systems Approach to School Counseling: Advocating Student-within-Environment* with its holistic and systemic approach may be the most important text that has been produced for school counselors to meet this moment head on. It is no hyperbole to say that the future of our children, and our society, may lie in the balance.

Paul R. Peluso, Ph.D.
Boca Raton, FL
May, 2023

FOREWORD BY KAPREA F. JOHNSON

I recall when I received notification that I was accepted into the school counseling master's program at Howard University. I was ecstatic because I secured a spot at my top choice school and I was on my way to meeting my goal, of "supporting, mentoring, and counseling children toward success!" While in the program and through engaging in service-learning opportunities I quickly learned that my goal would need to expand to include supporting children, families, and communities in which they reside. I realized that I could not counsel a child out of food insecurity and that positive behavior interventions were not going to change housing insecurity. My preparation to address systemic injustice was stellar, because of the opportunities to engage with lawmakers in Washington D.C., the faculty's wisdom, and experiential opportunities outside of the classroom. Indeed, these experiences set the foundation for my career as a school counselor and now counselor educator; my expertise is at the intersection of professional school counseling, inter-professional collaboration, and social determinants of mental health. I identify as a professional educator and mental health expert that has worked in school, career, and community-based settings to support the growing and ever-changing needs of children and transitional-aged youth. I use this lens as context for my review of the authors' new book, *An Evidence-Based Systems Approach to School Counseling: Advocating Student-within-Environment* .

Professional school counselors have a responsibility to understand and address systemic factors that impact the lives of the children and families they serve. This includes understanding the social, cultural, and environmental factors that contribute to their successes and challenges, and advocating for policies and practices that promote equity and justice in education. The Advocating

Student-within-Environment Theory book provides an invaluable contribution to this important work. The scope of the text is impressive encompassing chapters that will allow the reader to understand the origins and underpinnings of the theory, which complements the application-driven direction of the latter chapters. The sophisticated structure of the text along with real-world examples and visual cues allows readers at any stage of their professional school counselor identity to latch on, understand the concepts presented, and apply their understanding to address and support the needs of the students and families they serve from a holistic ecological social justice perspective. The approach to this theories book is unique in that it allows the readers to dig deeper than the surface, it breaks free from the standard approach to theory textbooks which provides a brief overview of several different theories but lacks depth on any one specific theory. As the chapters unfold, the reader is taken on a journey that facilitates growth personally and professionally.

Personally, I resonate with the overall approach and application of ASE theory, with my interest gravitating toward the emphasis on professional school counselors intervening with both students and adults within the school ecosystem. This call for "reflexive interventions" in which both the student and adults within the school system are synergistically supported is a strength-based approach that I find truly valuable. Additionally, the authors are very honest in the text, with acknowledgment of potential barriers for professional school counselors in adapting an ASE approach to their practice. As a reader, I appreciate the authors' awareness of the potential barriers or pushback that could be received. Another point of appreciation is the authors' utilization of personal and professional stories from their field experiences, which placed ideas in a broader context and support a deeper understanding of concepts from the theory. As I read through the text, I couldn't help but think how invaluable a guide such as this would have been during my years in Washington D.C.. During my school counselor preparation, I cannot recall a single standalone school counseling theories text, which makes this book about ASE a unique gift to the profession.

My hope for the next generation of professional school counselors is that they will be well-prepared to interrogate systems that cause injustice, continue to meet the evolving needs of students and families, and be visionary leaders in the schools advocating and contributing to education equity. This book is an important contribution to the field of professional school counseling and aligns with my hope for the next generation. The Advocating Student-within-Environment theory provides an invaluable framework for counselors to utilize as they seek to address and support both students and the school system, to advance justice and equity. By understanding and applying the principles of the ASE theory, professional school counselors can help students to develop a sense of agency and advocacy; support adults that work in and around the school eco-system; and build community collaborations to support students and the school community; which all works towards creating a more just and equitable school environment for all. This book provides a comprehensive and accessible guide to understanding and applying the ASE theory and offers practical strategies and tools for empowering professional school counselors to become effective advocates for social change.

Kaprea F. Johnson, PhD, LPC
Associate Vice Provost: Faculty Development & Recognition
Professor of Counselor Education & Supervision
The Ohio State University
April 19, 2023

1

ASE THEORY

Introduction and History

Matthew E. Lemberger-Truelove and Hannah Bowers Parker

School environments are constituted by groups of students, educators, administrators, guardians, policy makers, and other community members. These individuals coalesce in schools as dynamic systems, where each constituent ingredient of the school is affected by the whole, and the whole school environment is affected by each part (Parsons, 1959). In this manner, interventions in schools that are intended to cultivate student development or promote school and societal successes must be performed in ways that are relevant to individuals and the total school system as co-determinants.

School counselors are professional educators and mental health service providers in schools (Levy & Lemberger-Truelove, 2021). Traditionally, many school counselors were trained to use practice approaches primarily concerned with intervening at a student or adult level individually, but not how the various systems affect personal and social co-determinants of experience. In recent years, authors have posited frameworks intended to inform school counseling practices from an ecological or systems perspective (e.g. Bryan & Henry, 2012; Lemberger-Truelove & Bowers, 2019; McMahon & Mason, 2019). Relatedly, several recommendations have been made for school counselors to pursue social justice outcomes, including anti-discrimination and equity praxis (e.g. Griffin & Steen, 2011; Holcomb-McCoy, 2022). One ecological and social justice approach to school counseling is the Advocating Student-within-Environment (ASE) theoretical framework (Lemberger, 2010; Lemberger & Hutchison, 2014; Lemberger-Truelove & Bowers, 2019). ASE has been utilized in several empirical studies, demonstrating desirable outcomes for K12 students and educators (Bowers et al., 2020; Lemberger-Truelove et al., 2021; Lemberger-Truelove et al., in press; Molina et al., 2022; Webb et al., 2019). Adherents of the

DOI: 10.4324/9781003312871-1

ASE approach propound that school professionals intervene with students and adult stakeholders in corresponding ways such that each individual and the total school system ripen into co-regulated experiences and outcomes (Lemberger-Truelove & Bowers, 2019).

The ASE theory of school counseling is patently an ecological-systems approach (see Bronfenbrenner, 1977). Systems approaches are concerned with the influence of various social structures on individuals and groups. Yet ASE is also associated with the various liberation psychologies (e.g. Fanon, 1963; Freire, 1970; Martín-Baró, 1994). Liberation psychologies are dialogical in that they are attentive to societal forces (particularly those that marginalize and oppress) and yet offer insights for how an individual can transcend being entirely consumed by social influence. As a liberatory systems approach to school counseling, the primary concern of ASE practitioners is how one can support the development of students' personal and learning capacities while pursuing more socially just and facilitative environmental conditions.

ASE theory operates from a dialogical epistemological base (Bakhtin, 1973), hence the phrasing of Student-within-Environment. Dialogical suggests that there is some non-reductive concept of a unique self or personal identity that is generally material. At the same time, this concept of self is distributed amongst several social influences and iterations over time and across circumstance, held together loosely by various memories and stories (Hermans, 2014; Hermans et al., 1992). Therefore, the student is wholly constituted by the various systems of influence and yet becomes different as those systems converge into first-person experience. As such, it is reasonable that any intervention in a school must be germane to the student and the features of the school environment as co-determinants of experience.

A school counselor practicing from ASE theory intervenes to help students master aptitudes stifled by restrictive environments (Lemberger-Truelove & Bowers, 2019). Such aptitudes include cognitive abilities, including executive functioning (i.e. self-monitoring, emotional control, task initiation, organizing, monitoring, shifting, and completion), which are regulatory activities necessary to pursue intended goals (Diamond, 2013). By addressing targeted aptitudes, co-regulatory relationships can form between students, school professionals, family members, and members of the broader society. Co-regulation is a term often utilized in traditional family systems work and refers to the bidirectional oscillating of communitive and emotional channels between partners (Butler & Randall, 2013). This co-regulatory relationship begins in infancy between mother and child as they form a relationship through behavioral and emotional synchrony (Butler & Randall, 2013; Tronick et al., 1978). Within the school setting, a co-regulatory relationship occurs as students or members of the school community engage in purposive solidarity intended to co-determine learning and social development (McCaslin, 2009).

Through ASE, students, family members, school professionals, and relevant community members increase awareness of their unique social functioning and create connections with others, feeling as though they are not alone in their unique situations that can otherwise appear extremely isolating. Students that feel more connected to their schools have greater academic outcomes (McClure et al., 2010). Furthermore, those students who feel a greater sense of belonging attribute those feelings to teacher support and positive personal characteristics (Allen et al., 2018; Malecki & Demaray, 2003). At home, students who reported having supportive relationships with their parents were found to have better personal adjustment (Malecki & Demaray, 2003). For parents of school-aged children, interventions that engage families in school activities can result in those parents reporting more educational involvement, greater amounts of parent-teacher communication, and more encouraging parental attitudes towards their children's school environment (Chen, Anderson, & Watkins, 2016). In a similar way, teachers who report feeling connected to their schools have increased job satisfaction, and, in turn, their students generally perform better academically. Together, these studies illustrate how tightly bound school systems affect people's experiences and school-related outcomes.

Approaches to school counseling that focus primarily at the single-student level tend to neglect the profound influences of the various systems that affect students. Conversely, a singular focus on social systems neglects the primary concern of most schooling interventions, that is how one supports the development of the student. The student internalizes the various social forces in and beyond the school environment as the most relevant and viable agent to change the school and other social systems. There are also ethical and pedagogical reasons to support Student-within-Environment. It is entirely laudable for a school counselor to pursue change at the systems level on behalf of students. In so doing, that school counselor inadvertently becomes the arbitrator of what is just and appropriate for that student. Relatedly, the student is not necessarily empowered to define and pursue change, which seems shortsighted given the inevitability of change in the system (e.g. the student will eventually graduate or leave the school, or social forces might evolve over time). The student is not fully responsible for personal or social change, yet the student is always embedded within systems. Therefore, any intervention must engage the student and members of the school environment in appropriate and empowering ways.

A Brief History of ASE Theory for School Counseling

There exist hundreds of approaches to counseling and, across these various approaches, the client outcomes are generally consistent and promising (Laska et al., 2014). Adding one more log to the flame might appear superfluous with such an abundance of helpful frameworks. Yet we (Matthew and Hannah) believe there is a unique urgency for theory specifically tailored to how school counselors support K12 students and other people in school environments.

Across the various theoretical approaches of counseling, select scholars have identified common factors that each contribute to desirable client outcomes regardless of the theoretical orientation (Cuijpers et al., 2019; Wampold, 2015). Given these empirical findings across thousands of counseling studies, one might erroneously assume that theory has little utility in a school counselor's work, especially considering the various educational and mental health roles and responsibilities associated with the profession. Peering into these common factors it becomes increasingly clear that the common factors do not necessarily suggest that one become theoretically agonistic or even a practice chameleon. Instead, the common factors literature suggests that the various approaches to practice can contribute to similar desirable outcomes and that one's choice of theory to inform practice should fit the needs of the anticipated client and setting.

Unfortunately, many school counselors entirely disregard theory, or it only vaguely informs one's preferences as a practitioner (Lemberger-Truelove et al., 2020). It is no wonder that many school counselors and the people we serve are confused about the type and magnitude of mental health service provided by school counselors. In the absence of a clear and germane framework, practice can become ambiguous or even irrelevant. Returning to the common factors literature, qualities such as belief in the capacity of the client to develop in intended ways, the cultural appositeness of the practice approach, and the shared agreements in treatment each indicate that having some theory that is specifically attuned to the client context is vital.

Certainly, each established approach to child development and counseling theory is at least minimally relevant to school counseling (A.S.C.A., 2019). Alternatively, one might question if these classical frameworks provide a thoroughgoing relevance to the school as a setting for treatment, the disposition of students as clients, and the roles and responsibilities of school counselors as interventionists. While classical approaches inform, they might not provide precise insights that capture practice behaviors or empirical scholarship for school counseling. Also, many of the classical theories were developed for clinical settings and greatly influenced by a medicalized way of treating the individual client or patient (Hansen, 2008), which contrasts with the suggested focus of professional counselors who are concerned with development, prevention, wellness, and social justice (Levy & Lemberger-Truelove, 2021; Myers, 1992).

The fitness of theory on practice and professional values also potentially extends to its empirical relevance. Classical theories may or may not necessarily align with the practice language that occurs in schools (e.g. classroom guidance counseling, which includes psycho educational interventions delivered to entire groups of students in classrooms) or all desired outcomes (e.g. academic achievement). For example, students exposed to counseling might experience actualization (person-centered counseling or existential) or develop more adaptive thoughts (cognitive behavioral therapy), but how these concepts pertain to education-specific operations such as a student's executive functioning (i.e. capacities contributing to emotional and cognitive regulation for goal-focused behavior) can be unclear. Furthermore, the language used in counseling or psychological theories might not track on the nomenclature used by educators or other school stakeholders. For these and other empirical reasons (e.g. treatment fidelity in school settings), it is no wonder that school counseling intervention studies only constitute 0.1% of the counseling literature (Griffith et al., 2019).

ASE theory was developed to specifically account for the nuances of school counseling. Each of the concepts found in ASE can be found in the works of other theorists or scholars, yet as they converge into a single kaleidoscopic framework, these concepts manifest into something uniquely fit for school counseling practice. This emergence is consistent with an assumption baked into ASE itself: prior influences come together in ways that both reflect their influences yet the assemblage of these conceptions is altogether unique as they converge.

Matthew and ASE Theory

Akin to many of the historical approaches to counseling, the infancy of ASE theory can be traced back to the personal history and preferences of the initial architect of the theory. For me (Matthew), ASE is undoubtedly related to my personal and professional backgrounds. My father did not make it out of middle school, and my mother struggled with reading and education her entire life. From an early age, I experienced how ruptures in education, social and family strife, and economic struggle affected my personal, social, and learning development. Although I did well during my school years, throughout my life I have often wondered how things might have differed had there been greater educational and personal support.

The influences of my youth certainly catalyzed many of the concepts found in ASE, but there was a single moment when those ideas started to take shape as a formal system. As an undergraduate, I enrolled in a graduate-level course on the philosophy of education. In that course, I was exposed to the ideas of Dewey (1916), Freire (1970), and Vygotsky (1978). I was roused by their ideals but suspicious that their postulates could be vivified in contemporary classrooms. I pondered, "What kind of educator builds the learning and social capacities of the student while challenging the various social structures that limit equitable and just education?" As I reminisce about those questions, I cannot accurately recall the ideas that contributed to my resolve. However, I was convinced that school counselors were these under-utilized educators with the professional dispositions and access to bring life to those philosophers of education. So, I did my best to identify the school counseling professors most closely aligned with my developing values.

Initially, I could not find too many intervention articles in the literature, which I chalked up to my shortcomings as an undergraduate. Undeterred, I continued to probe the literature, and I finally found one article that was published the year I was graduating (Brigman et al., 1999). In the article, Brigman and colleagues discussed findings from an intervention targeting students' attending and self-regulatory, learning, and social strategies. I packed up my modest belongings and relocated to Florida to start a master's program in school counseling under the tutelage of Dr. Brigman.

The timing could not have been more serendipitous as Dr. Brigman was in the early stages of developing a comprehensive manualized school counseling intervention across K-12. I was his first graduate assistant supporting what would become the Student Success Skills (S.S.S.) suite of interventions, which includes small and large group student counseling activities and consultation services to teachers and guardians (https://studentsuccessskills.com). Independent scholars have evaluated S.S.S. and considered it one of the few evidence-based interventions with outcomes specifically attributed to the work of school counselors (Carey et al., 2008).

As a comprehensive theory for school counseling practice, ASE is compatible with the manualized S.S.S. curriculum and yet goes beyond in many important ways. For example, while the authors of S.S.S. suggest that school counselors pursue collaborative and helpful classroom climates, ASE places systemic advocacy as a central value and practice behavior for school counselors. Also, while S.S.S. includes various strategies and practices that can be applied to broader school counseling practice, the intervention is mostly specific to the contents of the various S.S.S. manuals. ASE, on the other hand, is compliant to manualized interventions, including and beyond S.S.S. However, as a comprehensive theory, it includes a distinguishable epistemology, suppositions about student or systemic wellness and deficit, and practice behaviors that are generalizable to various settings and circumstances in school systems.

The first writings about ASE theory occurred during the last semesters of my master's program (circa 2001), but it was not until almost a decade later that these ideas started appearing in published works (e.g. Lemberger, 2010). The initial concern was to highlight the importance of working collaboratively with students and educators, as opposed to one or the other discretely. More recently, most ASE-related publications have been randomized controlled trials considering outcomes for students or their teachers (Lemberger-Truelove et al., 2021; Lemberger-Truelove et al., in press). Looking to the future, there is no intention for ASE to be reified as a stable theoretical approach; instead, the hope is that more individuals will challenge and improve the theory, practice, and empirical investigation of ASE, with the ultimate goal that it can stable enough to provide helpful guidance to practicing school counselors but also prove adaptive enough to continue to support changes in future student and school cultures.

For me (Matthew), the real need for the development of ASE was to provide school counselors with an approach specific to working with children as students in schools. From a young age, school systems did not serve me or many of the people I grew up with in my neighborhood. I wanted to recruit school counselors as allies who could empower students while simultaneously challenging schools to be more relevant and helpful. ASE is intended to be a complete theory for school counselors, and yet it will never be fully finalized; instead, to remain pertinent to complex students and school systems, it is intended to be a framework that evolves with different voices and demands.

Hannah and ASE Theory

My relationship with ASE theory mirrors many of the readers of this text. That is, I joined a movement of thought that transformed my practice personally and professionally. For me, ASE is like putting on glasses that finally have the right prescription, when for years, I had been squinting, trying to read the letters on the page. However, it is all a journey, and I have learned that professional practice often intersects personal experience and genuinely experiencing challenges leads to the most remarkable growth.

I have always been conscious of systemic influences throughout my life. As a young adolescent, I witnessed my mother's transformation as she engaged in personal therapy to better manage relationships. Her therapeutic process began a journey of reflection and transparency of relational patterns, almost to a point where the behaviors of those within my family appeared predetermined. Watching my mother's growth from a co-dependent caregiver to an extremely independent woman, challenging sociocultural norms that defined her generation, was remarkable and awe-inspiring, illuminating the power of the therapeutic process.

While experience led to interest, my master's degree in marriage and family therapy provided a foundation of knowledge about systems, beginning with the basics of scientific thought applied to family functioning from Gregory Bateson (1941) towards pushing the boundaries of how knowledge is constructed by Kenneth Gergen (1985) and the evolution of family therapy as the field transformed through the waves of behaviorism, cognitive, to post-modernism, and social justice. Foundationally, my perspective of the world remained unchanged (if not more post-modern), we are a product of the systems by which we live. While I could see such truths clearly from my own experience, it was not until that first real-world counseling opportunity that I immersed myself in educational disparities.

Working with a group of adolescent males required to complete counseling through the juvenile court system, I felt hopeless. Who was there to help these boys, who often lacked familial support and encouragement, who often expressed that no one cared about them at home or school? While employing evidence-based practices at this level, I wondered if a change would occur for any of these young men. Matthew provided me with a viewpoint, but I was not ready to embrace it at that time.

When I was first presented with ASE, I honestly had to sit with it. Matthew had just successfully published his first conceptual ASE manuscript during my first semester as a doctoral student. I was too novice in my counseling experience and lacked the confidence to challenge what I already knew. However, through continued experiences working with students as a school-based counselor and school counselor, I began to make sense of ASE. I became more mindful of our dialect, seeking to understand the student from their viewpoint and join them in their world. Goals were not directed by the school or parents but rather for themselves. In going a step further, I began attending health and wellness meetings to advocate for the student, engage in conversations with parents from a perspective of curiosity, as well as provide advocacy to encourage dialogue at home. My practice focus shifted, still maintaining a systemic perspective as I moved into the role of a school counselor and eventual school counselor educator, but with a focus more so on advocacy. I wanted students, who often felt so isolated and alone, type-casted into a specific social group, or struggling with symptoms of mental health or neurodiversity, to learn skills to become stronger and to advocate for themselves.

The intersection of experience and knowledge is where ASE lands for me today. While Matthew has provided the foundation, others have contributed perspectives that push ASE to new horizons (e.g. Johnson, et al., in press; Liu et al., 2020; Roche et al., 2020; Zyromski et al., 2022), providing intentionality behind each decision. As a school counselor, ASE is grounded in the mission and vision of a school counseling program, focused on providing all students with the skill sets that promote success in school and life. I embrace ASE not just as a counselor or counselor educator but also as a mother. Advocacy for my neurodiverse children is profound, as well as co-regulating experiences within the home to ensure they can practice and develop the skill sets needed to succeed in their future. While my conscious experience began with systemic awareness, growing into ASE has shifted from theory into a way of being.

The Present Book

The current book intends to provide readers with a basic primer on the assumptions and practice priorities related to the ASE school counseling theory. Chapters 1, 2, and 3 explain some of the most foundational assumptions of ASE and provide some general suggestions for practice. These chapters are mostly organized around the five Cs of ASE theory, a memory device intended to inform how a school counselor assesses students and school systems, pursues practice and advocacy behaviors, and evaluates anticipated outcomes. The five Cs of ASE include curiosity, connectedness, co-regulation, compassion, and contribution. Chapters 4, 5, 6, 7, and 8 include applications to specific educational contexts. These topics are not necessarily exhaustive, but they might provide school counselors with more specific ideas on ASE in practice with certain student or school system concerns. In Chapter 9, we discuss some of the recent empirical studies performed using ASE as the theoretical guide and provide school counseling practitioners and scholars with recommendations for empirical practice as informed specifically by ASE theory. Finally, in Chapter 10 we provide specific examples of ASE practice behaviors that school counselors can use with students and teachers.

This text should elucidate the spirit of ASE. Schools are systems that are influenced by various personal and social forces. Students, educators, and other people affiliated with schools are also systems in that they have been profoundly influenced by external and internal forces. The stance of ASE suggests that the most influential approach to school counseling requires support directly to the student and at the school system levels as co-determinants of experience.

References

Allen, K., Kern, M. L., Vella-Brodrick, D., Hattie, J., & Waters, L. (2018). What schools need to know about fostering school belonging: A meta-analysis. *Educational Psychology Review, 30*(1), 1–34. https://doi.org/10.1007/s10648-016-9389-8

American School Counselor Association (ASCA) (2019). *ASCA standards for school counselor preparation programs.* www.schoolcounselor.org/getmedia/573d7c2c-1622-4d25-a5ac-ac74d2e614ca/ASCA-Standards-for-School-Counselor-Preparation-Programs.pdf

Bakhtin, M. (1973). Problems of Dostoevsky's poetics (2nd ed.; R. W. Rotsel, Trans.). Ann Arbor, MI: Ardis.

Bateson, G. (1941). Experiments in thinking about observed ethnological material. *Philosophy of Science, 8*(1), 53–68. https://doi.org/10.1086/286669

Bowers, H., Lemberger-Truelove, M. E., Whitford, D. K. (2020). Kindergarteners are ready to learn: Executive functioning and social-emotional effects for a pilot school counseling intervention applying Advocating Student-within-Environment theory. *Journal of Humanistic Counseling 59*(1), 3–19. https://doi.org/10.1002/johc.12126

Brigman, G., Lane, D., Switzer, D., Lane, D., & Lawrence, R. (1999). Teaching children school success skills. *The Journal of Educational Research, 92*(6), 323–329. https://doi:10.1080/00220679909597615

Bronfenbrenner, U. (1977). Toward an experimental ecology of human development. *American Psychologist, 32*(7), 513–531. https://doi.org/10.1037/0003-066X.32.7.513

Bryan, J., & Henry, L. (2012). A model for building school–family–community partnerships: Principles and process. *Journal of Counseling & Development*, *90*(4), 408–420. https://doi.org/10.1002/j.1556-6676.2012.00052.x

Butler, E. A., & Randall, A. K. (2013). Emotional co-regulation in close relationships. *Emotion Review*, *5*(2), 202–210. https://doi.org/10.1177/175407391245163

Carey, F., Dimmitt, C., Hatch, T., Lapan, R., & Whiston, S. (2008). Report of the national panel for evidence-based school counseling: Outcome research coding protocol and evaluation of Student Success Skills and Second Step. *Professional School Counseling, 11*(3), 197–206. https://doi.org/10.1177/2156759X0801100306

Chen, M. E., Anderson, J. A., & Watkins, L. (2016). Parent perceptions of connectedness in a full service community school project. *Journal of Child and Family Studies*, *25*(7), 2268–2278. https://doi.org/10.1007/s10826-016-0398-5

Cuijpers, P., Reijnders, M., & Huibers, M. J. H. (2019). The role of common factors in psychotherapy outcome. *Annual Review of Clinical Psychology*, *15*, 207–231. https://doi.org/10.1146/annurev-clinpsy-050718-095424

Dewey, J. (1916). *Democracy and Education*. Teddington: Echo Library.

Diamond, A. (2013). Executive functions. *Annual Review of Psychology*, pp. *64*, 135–168. https:// doi: 10.1146/annurev-psych-113011-143750

Fanon, F. (1963). *The wretched of the earth*. New York, NY: Grove Press.

Freire, P. (1970). *Pedagogy of the oppressed*. New York, NY: Herder and Herder.

Gergen, K. (1985). The social constructionist movement in modern psychology. *American Psychologist, 40*(3), 266–275. https://doi.org/10.1037/0003-066X.40.3.266

Griffin, D., & Steen, S. (2011). A social justice approach to school counseling. *Journal for Social Action in Counseling & Psychology*, *3*(1), 74–85. https://doi.org/10.33043/JSACP.3.1.74-85

Griffith, C., Mariani, M., McMahon, H. G., Zyromski, B., & Greenspan, S. (2019). School counseling intervention research: A 10-year content analysis of ASCA–and ACA-affiliated journals. *Professional School Counseling Journal, 23*(1), 1–12. https://doi.org/10.1177/2156759X19878700

Hansen, J.T. (2008). Neopragmatic thought and counseling values: Reconsidering the role of values in counseling from an alternative epistemological foundation. *Counseling and Values, 52*, 100–112. https://doi:10.1002/j.2161-007X.2008.tb00094.x

Hermans, H. J. (2014). Self as a society of I-positions: A dialogical approach to counseling. *Journal of Humanistic Counseling, 53*(2), 134–159. https://doi.org/10.1002/j.2161-1939.2014.00054.x

Hermans, H. J. M., Kempen, H. J. G., & Van Loon, R. J. P. (1992). The dialogical self: Beyond individualism and rationalism. *American Psychologist, 47*(1), 23–33. https://doi.org/10.1037/0003-066X.47.1.23

Holcomb-McCoy, C. (2022). *School Counseling to Close Opportunity Gaps: A Social Justice and Antiracist Framework for Success*. Corwin Press.

Johnson, K. F., Kim, H., Molina, C. E., Thompson, K. A., Henry, S., & Zyromski, B. (in press). School counseling prevention programming to address social determinants of mental health. *Journal of Counseling & Development*. https://doi.org/10.1002/jcad.12471

Laska, K. M., Gurman, A. S., & Wampold, B. E. (2014). Expanding the lens of evidence-based practice in psychotherapy: A common factors perspective. *Psychotherapy, 51*(4), 467–481. https://doi.org/10.1037/a0034332

Lemberger, M. E. (2010). Advocating Student-within-Environment: A humanistic theory for school counseling. *The Journal of Humanistic Counseling, Education and Development, 49,* 131–146. https://doi.org/10.1002/j.2161-1939.2010.tb00093.x

Lemberger, M. E., & Hutchison, B. (2014). Advocating Student-within-Environment: A humanistic approach for therapists to animate social justice in the schools. *Journal of Humanistic Psychology, 54*, 28–44. https://doi.org/10.1177/0022167816652750

Lemberger-Truelove, M. E., & Bowers, H. (2019). An Advocating Student-within-Environment approach to school counseling. In C. T. Dollarhide & M. E. Lemberger-Truelove (Eds.), *Theories of school counseling for the 21st century* (pp. 266–294). Oxford.

Lemberger-Truelove, M. E., Ceballos, P. L., Molina, C. E., & Carbonneau, K. J. (2021). Growth in middle school students' curiosity, executive functioning, and academic achievement: A theory-informed SEL and MBI school counseling intervention. *Professional School Counselor, 24*(1b): 1–8. https://doi:10.1177/2156759X21 1007654

Lemberger-Truelove, M. E., Ceballos, P. L., Molina, C. E., & Dehner, J. M. (2020). Inclusion of theory for evidence-based school counseling practice and scholarship. *Professional School Counselor. 23*(1_part_3), 1–8. https://doi:10.1177/2156759X2 0903576

Lemberger-Truelove, M. E., Molina, C. E., Carbonneau, K. J., & Smith, M. J. (in press). Effects of a school counselor consultation intervention on middle school teacher-student relationships, student curiosity, and teacher stress. *Professional School Counselor.*

Levy, I. & Lemberger-Truelove, M. E. (2021). Educator-counselor: A non-dual identity for professional school counselors. *Professional School Counselor,* 24(1b): 1–7. https://doi:10.1177/2156759X211007630

Liu, Y., Kim, H., Carney, J. V., Chung, K. S., & Hazler, R. J. (2020). Individual and contextual factors associated with school connectedness in the context of counseling in schools. *Journal of Counseling & Development, 98*(4), 391–401. https://doi.org/10.1002/jcad.12341

Malecki, C. K., & Demaray, M. K. (2003). What type of support do they need? Investigating student adjustment as related to emotional, informational, appraisal, and instrumental support. *School Psychology Quarterly, 18*(3), 231. https://doi.org/10.1521/scpq.18.3.231.22576

Martín-Baró, I. (1994). *Writings for a liberation psychology*. A. Aron & S. Corne (Eds.). Harvard University Press.

McCaslin, M. (2009). Co-regulation of student motivation and emergent identity. *Educational Psychologist, 44*(2), 137–146. https://doi.org/10.1080/0046152090 2832384

McClure, L., Yonezawa, S., & Jones, M. (2010). Can school structures improve teacher-student relationship? The relationship between advisory programs, personalization and students' academic achievement. *Education Policy Analysis Archives, 18*(17). Retrieved from http://epaa.asu.edu/ojs/article/view/719

McMahon, H. G., & Mason, E. C. M. (2019). Ecological school counseling. In C. T. Dollarhide & M. E. Lemberger-Truelove (Eds.), *Theories of school counseling for the 21st century* (pp. 241–265). Oxford University Press.

Molina, C. E., Lemberger-Truelove, M. E., & Zieher, A. K. (2022). School counselor consultation effects on teachers' mindfulness, stress, and relationships. *Professional School Counseling, 26*(1a), 1–9. https://doi.org/10.1177/2156759X221086749

Myers, J. E. (1992). Wellness, prevention, development: The cornerstone of the profession. *Journal of Counseling & Development, 71*(2), 136–139. https://doi.org/10.1002/j.1556-6676.1992.tb02188.x

Parsons, T. (1959). The school class as a social system: Some of its functions in American Society. *Harvard Educational Review, 29*(4), 297–318.

Roche, R., Hutchison, B., & Lemberger-Truelove, M. E. (2020). Historicity in Advocating Student-Within-Environment: Being a socially just school counselor. *The Journal of Humanistic Counseling, 59*(3), 173–187. https://doi.org/10.1002/johc.12143

Tronick, E. Z., Als, H., Adamson, L., Wise, S., & Brazelton, T. B. (1978). The infant's response to entrapment between contradictory messages in face to face interaction. *Journal of the American Academy of Child Psychiatry, 17* (1), 1–13. https://doi.org/10.1016/S0002-7138(09)62273-1

Vygotsky, L. S. (1978). *Mind in society: The development of higher psychological processes*. Harvard University Press.

Wampold, B. E. (2015). How important are the common factors in psychotherapy? An update. *World Psychiatry, 14*(3), 270–277. https://doi.org/10.1002/wps.20238

Webb, L., Brigman, G., Carey, J., Villares, E., Wells, C., Sayer, A., Harrington, K., & Chance, E. (2019). Results of a randomized controlled trial of the student success skills program on grade 5 students' academic and behavioral outcomes. *Journal of Counseling and Development, 97*(4), 398–408. https://doi.org/10.1002/jcad.12288

Zyromski, B., Wolfe, T. E., Choi, J., Shrewsbury, S., & Hamilton, M. (2022). Applying an advocating student-environment lens to foster protective factors: School counselors' role in buffering ACEs. *Journal of Child and Adolescent Counseling, 8*(1), 1–15. https://doi.org/10.1080/23727810.2021.2021052

2

ADVOCATING STUDENT-WITHIN-ENVIRONMENT AS A SYSTEMS THEORY TO SCHOOL COUNSELING

Matthew E. Lemberger-Truelove

Various creatures transmit messages across generations, each intending to prepare the subsequent generation and contribute to their survival and thriving. Although providing guidance and support is not entirely unique to humans, there appear to be no other species that erect enduring buildings of education or scrutinize teaching and learning with similar intention, formality, and duration. The sundry activities in K-12 schools are impressive, as they stretch across histories, disciplines, and cultures that are webbed together into complex systems.

The systems of webs that exist in the school are further tethered to other webs, with students, educators, and other stakeholders coming together as a fulcrum that binds the various external cultural systems to each of the personal and social systems that exist in schools. Each person entering a school carries arrays of prior influences that collide with those held by numerous other groups and persons, culminating in a genuine latticework of perspectives and governors of experience. These webs of experience affect the curricular content and the interpersonal relationships between students and students, students and educators, and students and other social forces extending beyond the school walls.

These systems of webs are incredibly complex to navigate for young students, educators, and other school stakeholders. Even if the complex social forces were consistently apparent and accessible to the players in the school, one could be easily overwhelmed by the sheer complicatedness of a school. Unfortunately, the constituent ingredients across all the personal and social systems affecting schools are not readily perceptible, nonetheless fairly distributed. Instead, baked into these systems are differing agendas, abilities, and histories or trajectories that amplify the complexity and inequalities of opportunities.

DOI: 10.4324/9781003312871-2

Maneuvering the various systems in schools can be challenging and yet critical for schooling success, broadly defined. In this manner, school counselors can be essential allies for students, educators, and stakeholders. A school counselor supports the total school environment and all the participants therein through defining standards of practice, delivering direct and indirect student services, managing programs, and assessing the efficacy of school processes and outcomes (A.S.C.A., 2019). The school counselor reflects a proxy agent in a school as described by Bandura (1986; 1989); that is, when the capacity of one or more individuals in a school is subjacent to others, the proxy can provide the support that is more compatible with the various systems active in the school.

Amplifying the capacity of compromised students, educators, or stakeholders is generally laudable, and yet it can inadvertently contribute to unintended complicity in inimical schooling environments. Education, by nature, oscillates between importing messages from various social institutions and breaking free to new vistas of understanding and functioning. The promise of education suggests that it is insufficient to simply reproduce cultural artifacts and histories into perpetuity (Baudrillard, 1983). Education should incite humanistic innovation and variation that serves the broadest conception of society (Dewey, 1916). Here the potential of the school counselor is again pertinent, as a school counselor moves alongside the various systems in schools while stoking the individual student or educator to forge new meanings, accomplish new ends, and innovate new permutations within the affecting systems.

Unfortunately, the profession of school counseling shoulders a precarious history as influenced by allied mental health professions, educational structures, and even features internal to the profession itself (Borders & Drury, 1992; Levy & Lemberger-Truelove, 2021). School counseling services are often under-utilized and generally misunderstood across school settings, which in turn relegates many professionals to administrative roles (Burnham & Jackson, 2000; Dollarhide, Smith, & Lemberger, 2007). It is also likely that many well-intentioned school counselors have not operated in ways that best support students or their communities.

Formal theoretical approaches to practice are intended to combat against such role ambiguity and resource waste. At best, theory should reflect the systems that manifest them; theories consider said systems, offer parsimonious and effectual descriptions of the past, or make predictions for the future. For school counseling in particular, any appropriate formal theory should be germane to the systems of education and the development of people across the lifespan and yet also embrace these histories enough to encourage new permutations into the future.

Inspired by innovations across multiple academic and practice disciplines, the Advocating Student-within-Environment (ASE) (Lemberger, 2010; Lemberger & Hutchison, 2014; Lemberger-Truelove & Bowers, 2019) theory was explicitly designed for school counselors to work with students, educators, and other school-related persons so that individual capacities ripen into co-regulated experiences and outcomes. ASE operates from the assumption that all players in the school are indivisible, with varying degrees of influence on the total schooling system. Development of the individual person or school system occurs in reciprocal ways, with differing magnitudes of input and influence based on the constitution of the system and the nature of the school counseling intervention.

From an ASE perspective, intervention can occur at the individual level or at the systems level. However, a fully actualized version of the approach suggests that the corresponding intervention holds the greatest promise for ongoing and relevant development. The primary focus remains on the given student's experience; yet understood that each unique student is bound up in their own multiplicity of influences drawn from the surrounding school and other social systems. An ASE practitioner asserts that any individual or systemic vicissitude, even the most seemingly diminutive or distant, can reverberate throughout the system in profound or subtle ways.

ASE is a radical perspective on education, suggesting that the end aspiration is a type of proto-liberation that paradoxically remains tied to the activating systems. In principle, ASE is a social justice approach to education in that the school counselor must always petition the social forces that affect students, educators, and their families. At all times, the development of a particular student, educator, or stakeholder coheres in step with the dynamic changes in the school and social ecologies. However, ASE is a distinct type of social justice practice, inspired by Freire (1970), in that it retains an appreciation of the humanistic spirit; that is, the individual, when rightly positioned, can rail against oppressive circumstances. The student is simultaneously a manifest of the system and yet not fully identical to that system; as such, education and any related school counseling intervention can capitalize on the capacity of the student or other school agent to transcend prior states and conditions, in turn affecting self and environment as interacting determinants.

Pertinence of School Counseling Theories

The American School Counseling Association (A.S.C.A., n.d.) suggests that school counselors are trained to utilize "theories and evidence-based techniques that are effective in a school setting, including but not limited to rational emotive behavior therapy, reality therapy, cognitive-behavioral therapy, Adlerian, solution-focused brief counseling, person-centered counseling, and family systems" (p. 1). While laudable in intent, it is curious given that less than .01% of the recent counseling literature reflects interventions delivered by school counselors, nonetheless the questionable nature of the empirical designs and limited findings tied to theory or discernible practice behaviors (Griffith et al., 2019). To be fair, generic findings from the literature suggest that when school counselors perform direct services, the benefits abound for students and school systems alike (Whiston et al., 2011). While there are intuitive reasons to believe in the potential of school counselors and some nascent empirical evidence to support such claims, the pertinence of theory in these specific contexts remains dubious.

Each of the theories mentioned by A.S.C.A. (n.d.) are imported from community or clinical therapeutic contexts. Often psychological theories focus on the functioning and remediation of the single individual. While A.S.C.A. does provide space for emergent approaches, one must question the utility of any theory not necessarily explicitly intended for the K12 school context, nonetheless the specific roles and responsibilities of the professional who will embody that approach. In the case of school counseling, a theory must be able to inform practice in ways that are germane to students in classrooms; whole school communities; adult stakeholders as interactants with children in schools; academic, learning, personal, social, and career domains; and other factors that directly and indirectly affect the educational experience and beyond.

While psychological and other theoretical approaches certainly can be helpful guides for school counselors, it is unlikely that these theories can be thoroughgoing schemes for practice. As an alternative crafted specifically for the qualities implicit in school counseling, ASE offers practitioners and recipients a potentially more precise framework to inform practice, evaluate the intervention, and assess outcomes specific to K12 school systems.

Basic Position of ASE

The name Advocating Student-within-Environment, or ASE, was coined to highlight the primacy of advocacy. School counselors are affiliate to each person in a school and the encompassing school environment. Advocacy is the social justice imperative for all school counselors. Advocacy, as a noun, is a state of supporting a person or cause, especially when it has been compromised. *As a verb for ASE theory, advocating suggests the perpetual and developmental nature of advocacy. Advocating is a gerund.*

Too often, advocacy is performed with superficial intentions or activities (Lemberger & Lemberger-Truelove, 2016). From an ASE perspective, advocating for students requires constant scrutiny of one's intentions and the means to advocate for student or systems wellness. For example, one must penetrate the causes and consequences related to how a school administrator reprimands a tardy student. What circumstances, personal characteristics, cultural influences, or training influenced the administrators word choice and behaviors? How does the response affect the child as a learner in the immediate or long term, or how does the response to one child affect the total composition of the class of students and their perceptions of class customs and mores? Advocacy is a deep and reflective commitment to sustainable positive development.

Systems must be challenged to create and sustain student flourishing while embracing the inevitability of persistent change at both the individual student and total school or social systems levels. For example, scholars suggest that school counselors utilize ASE theory to confront the social determinants of mental health (S.D.M.H.) that compromise students or adults in schools (Johnson et al., in press). S.D.M.H. includes economic circumstances, physical environment, neighborhood cohesiveness, and healthy food options that influence people's mental functioning and outcomes. Improving the S.D.H.M. for students requires the school counselor to work directly with the student to capitalize on resources and confront challenges while advocating for more just student and community opportunities at the systems levels. These advocacy behaviors do not suggest that the school counselor pursue a fixed outcome, arbitrated by one person or even ethos; instead, there is a perennial community process of learning, questioning, and acting to dynamic systems in people and total school climates.

The epistemological claim of Student-within-Environment follows the prime objective of creating more just, equitable, and contributory school environments. This manner of phrasing highlights the embeddedness of each student in a school and other societal contexts. The student as a learner. The student as a classmate. The student as an expression of cultural influences. The student as an athlete, artist, and myriad other identities. The identities and activities commingle together and affect the contemporary experience and future aspirations. This stance highlights the reflexivity between the positionality of the student and the larger encompassing school environment; the hyphenated word *within* reminds the school counselor that any intervention must approach the student and school as mutual influencers.

There is a misperception that humans are absolutely compos mentis, that is, having complete control over one's mind and agency. Our intuitions suggest we are making contemporaneous decisions. But it is impossible to discern if we are making volitional decisions or merely observing the outcome of responses to a dense latticework of prior conditions of experience. Certainly, each person always contributes personally and socially, but the inevitable situatedness of the self in the environment suggests that learning, decision-making, and action are composite to prior biological, psychological, narrative, and social causes. Even the student in kindergarten, who appears to run from tire swing impulsively and indiscriminately to jungle gym and then skipping over to peers is influenced by a line of inconceivable prior forces that led to that moment, guided those behaviors, and resulted in one's felt experience. As a five-year-old (or 95-year-old), and every day before and after, we are at least in part an embodiment of various governing systems.

But the student is not completely emptied of the capacity to influence oneself or one's circumstance. The kindergartener, the prepubescent middle schooler, and the senior approaching graduation are each active agents that can have some determining influence on one's plight, even if one is always tied up in their guiding systems. In the source writings related to ASE theory (Lemberger, 2010; Lemberger & Hutchison, 2014), the concepts of contributory and detracting governors were introduced to describe social forces that co-occur with the student in schools. In the contemporary literature, one-half of the governing equation has adopted a related term, social determinants of mental health (Allen et al., 2014), an offshoot of an earlier term, the social determinants of health. Whereas the S.D.M.H. are an attempt to define and describe antecedent influences of psychological functioning, the term *governor* is retained in ASE theory to depict the collaborative nature of the Student-within-Environment. Additionally, governors highlight the non-normative and sophisticated manner in that prior influences can be helpful or harmful and evolve in function and influence over time; "contributory governors (assets) within the school environment, identify and conceptualize detracting governors (impediments), and intervene in concert toward the student generated desired outcome" (Lemberger & Hutchison, 2014, p. 32).

This distinction is important in a school counseling context, as school counseling must retain the essence of professional counseling, which is different from the other allied helping professions that tend to be concerned with a psychological self or fully socially consequential being. Professional counselors are distinguished by our identity, which is chiefly concerned with prevention, development, wellness, and social justice (Myers, 1992). School counselors are not positioned to remedy personal maladies, but rather our focus is chiefly on creating opportunities for the student to thrive in personally and socially germane ways over long durations of time.

Considering the types of counseling behaviors typical of school counselors, that is direct instruction in classrooms (typically psycho educational in nature), small groups of students in and outside of classrooms, individual counseling sessions, and consultation with teachers, it is reasonable that theory must cohere with the idea that counseling is additive as an interacting determinant in the student and school system. Stated more simply, school counseling is not simply inspiring insights; counseling binds to experience to govern new possibilities and likelihoods.

The highest aspiration of ASE can be found in the concept of sapience, "or wisdom as expressed through critical consciousness is an outcome status inbuilt with the cognitive, affective, and behavioral complexity for the student to anticipate and respond to oppressive environments, even after such environments evolve" (Lemberger & Hutchison, 2014, p. 37). In developmentally different ways dependent on the schooling level and cultural conditions for the student, sapience, as conceptually consistent with critical consciousness (Freire, 1970), is required so that the student has the agency to transcend or liberate from the oppressive or limiting social structures.

ASE poses an epistemological challenge to approaches primarily concerned with the student as a largely autonomous self or the student as a passive recipient of school and societal influences. But more than a conceptual framework, ASE informs school counseling praxis in specific ways. The basic assumption is that formal schooling structures are intended to activate and support students' inner capacities and aid their development. They might have more opportunities throughout life in and beyond the school environment. Therefore, school counselors aim to cultivate students' capacities while succoring people, phenomena, and qualities in the school environment so that student capacities might flourish. As stated otherwise, ASE is about creating personal and social conditions for opportunity.

Rather than focusing on circumstantial events or specific personal expressions, from an ASE perspective, the primary focus of intervention is on capacities that are generalizable to myriad outcomes. For example, cultivating students' executive functioning, which is the antecedent to goal-focused action, is relevant to learning, achievement, social skills, and multiple other life experiences (Jacob & Parkinson, 2015). As such, the practice focus for ASE differentiates itself from related approaches given the centrality of interactional causality in intervening with students-within-environments.

The theory of development implicit to ASE theory is patently consistent with the design of education, therefore, a unique fit for counseling services rendered in school environments. Like the assumptions of Bayesian analyses, the likelihood of something occurring in the future is predicated on the prior knowledge of a probabilistic event (Ghosh et al., 2007). Education draws from various cultural artifacts or information, whether from the natural or social sciences, to perpetuate advances into the future. In this manner, ASE suggests that school counseling includes the various processes to sharpen the capacities of the individual (e.g. a particular student, one or more educators, family members, or relevant community members) while simultaneously curating the most hospitable social conditions, and then linking these prior conditions for the student and dynamics in the school environment.

Whether academic content, social experiences, or career aspirations, school counselors must collaborate with students such that historical influences can culminate into more desirable and intentional ends. As a theory, ASE is concerned with the confluence of causal influencers and experiential governors. It is like a kaleidoscope where the capacities of the individual student are likened to one or a series of colors and filtered through the colors that represent the various aspects of the school environment. The interaction between the self and the environment reflects both originating colors in the kaleidoscope, but as the various colored crystals come together, they are a bit different. As a practice of counseling, the school counselor is like the fingers that grasp the kaleidoscope and work with the student to expose the various colored opportunities, especially as attractive to the student's perspective.

ASE school counseling focuses on student (and school system) outcomes but is not necessarily a primary driver in discerning how to support. Rather, the concern taps down on how the school counselor can engender capacities in the student that are iterative and flexible while also cultivating school conditions that propel continuous reflection and growth. As Vygotsky (1978) wisely offered:

> The search for a method becomes one of the most important problems of the entire enterprise of understanding the uniquely human forms of psychological activity. In this case, the method is simultaneously prerequisite and product, the tool and the result of the study.
>
> *(p. 65)*

For school counseling, this suggests that the practice is the outcome, as is the inverse. A school counselor provides the student and environment with the prior conditions to experience the desired outcomes and helps induce that experience to be general and flexible.

Orientation and Practice Foci for ASE School Counseling

At its core, ASE is a theory to support learning. School counselors support student learning, including academic learning, personal or social learning, or even learning pertaining to career development (A.S.C.A., 2019). School counselors also support adults and other community partners in learning how to interface with students as learners or as relational beings. Learning includes various profoundly complex personal and social processes (Darling-Hammond et al., 2020). School counselors can collaborate with students and representatives of the school environment to augment and amplify mutually beneficial learning that crosses academic, social, and vocational domains.

ASE theory contains specific orientations and practice foci intended to support students and aspects of the school environment. Collectively titled the "five Cs of ASE theory", these include curiosity, connectedness, co-regulation, compassion, and contribution. As orientations to experience, the five Cs represent the qualities aimed at sapience in students, educators, and even the school counselor. This orientation harkens to the suggestion proffered by Vygotsky (1978) that the method (of being or orientation) is the outcome. As practices, the five Cs of ASE provide the school counselor with a framework

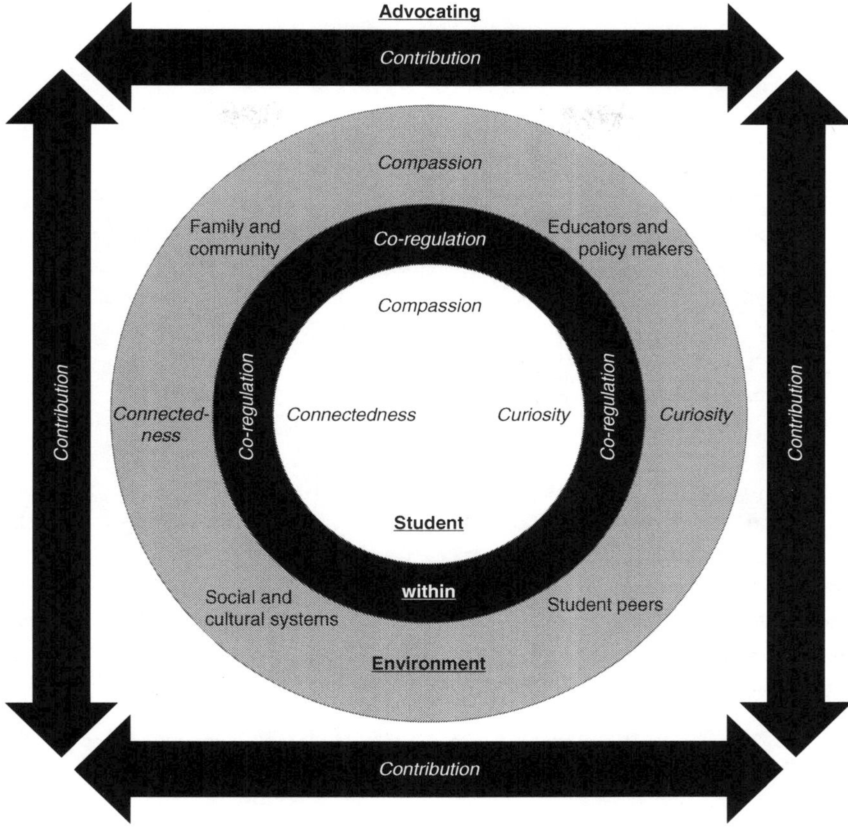

FIGURE 2.1 Advocating Student-within-Environment Theory Map.Note: From Lemberger-Truelove, Molina, Carbonneau, & Smith, (in press).

that can inspire theoretically unique counseling practices or overlays to guide general practices in an ASE motif.

Curiosity

The condition of curiosity is universally familiar to most people and yet a precise and shared definition is elusive or varied. Kidd and Hayden (2015) posited that curiosity is a "drive state for information" (p. 450). William James famously suggested that curiosity:

> is perhaps a rather poor term by which to designate the *impulse toward better cognition* in its full extent... In its higher, more intellectual form, the impulse

> toward completer knowledge takes the character of scientific or philosophic curiosity. ... Young children are possessed by curiosity about every new impression that assails them.
>
> *(James, 1899, p. 45–46)*

There is a teleological dimension to curiosity, wherefrom the curious seeker strives towards some conceptual or experiential resolve or end. Curiosity can also be sustainable through persistent inquiry and openness (Abdelghani et al., 2022). But curiosity also suggests emergence from a nescience state of being. To be curious is paradoxical in that one has some impression about a target and maintains an open and incomplete inquisitiveness about that target or its related aspects.

From an ASE perspective, curiosity is central as a personal quality and a counseling process. As a personal quality, school counselors who embody curiosity are more likely to establish a helpful rapport with the student or educator, and by extension, such rapport contributes to desirable counseling outcomes (Elliot et al., 2018). For student or educator recipients of counseling, a curious counselor is receptive to the personal and social qualities that contribute to one's experience and development. At the school environment level, curiosity is the humility necessary to apprehend the uniqueness of the particular student or educator. Considered together, curiosity as a state in schools includes qualities such as openness, reflexivity, tenacity, humility, inquisitiveness, flexibility, emotional dexterity, and many other attributes necessary in affiliating prior states with emergent states of being.

There are certainly developmental differences in how children and adults experience and express curiosity (Beiser, 1984). From an ASE perspective, one is not required to believe or even comprehend another person's state of curiosity but one is required to believe that that person experiences it. From there, the process of curiosity emerges from the various states of curiosity. A school counselor is meta-curious or curious about the curiosity of others. These efforts can amplify and validate the curiosity of the student or educator while also initiating the rapport necessary for effective counseling in a school environment.

Just as there are developmental differences in the experience and expression of curiosity, there can be cultural differences (Dyche & Zayas, 1995). While it is not necessarily the student's or educator's responsibility to satisfy the cultural curiosities of the school counselor, processes such as cultural broaching (see Day-Vines et al., 2021) can be a valuable way to learn how one's various identity structures affects experience in and outside of counseling.

Invoking curiosity in a school counseling session can be accomplished in various ways, not limited to the nature of the in-session activity or even the expression of curious language. Activities that encourage curiosity include prompts to challenge students to consider what influences decision-making processes. Additionally, minimally curious language might be something such as, "What did you accomplish?" whereas "How did you experience your accomplishments?" or "What contributed to your feelings of accomplishment?" are more inquisitive and generate greater curious reflection. In all three examples, you can receive specific information about the accomplishment, but only in the latter two does the prompt encourage elaboration beyond an isolated or normative outcome.

From an ASE perspective, curiosity is a necessary state and process that must be accomplished at the student and school environment levels. For curiosity to be personally relevant and environmentally sustainable, a persistent commitment to curiosity must be tended. Curiosity is a brilliant yet challenging orientation to experience; the great dream psychologist Carl Jung (1964) once offered a helpful prescription for curiosity when he described how he analyzes dreams:

> It is for this reason that I have always said to my pupils: "Learn as much as you can about symbolism; then forget it all when you are analyzing a dream." This advice is of such practical importance that I have made it a rule to remind myself that I can never understand somebody else's dream well enough to interpret it correctly. I have done this in order to check the flow of my own associations and reactions, which might otherwise prevail over my patient's uncertainties and hesitations.
>
> *(p. 42)*

There is a novelty in each moment and each opportunity for development. This brand of curiosity is its own process and outcome for the ASE-inspired school counselor.

Connectedness

To be curious about something or someone, there must be some affiliation to that thing or person; the conceptual location for that curiosity is the experience of connectedness. From an ASE perspective, connectedness is the experience of acceptance, safety, encouragement, and respect shared between students, school counselors, educators, or other school-related persons (Resnick et al., 1997). Given the systems nature of ASE, the concept of connectedness demonstrates the interrelatedness of experience with all school participants. Certainly, each person has a unique first-person perspective. That idiosyncrasy colors the kaleidoscopic experience in novel and emergent ways, yet the connections between people as the prior determinants of experience are ubiquitous.

Connectedness as a state of being can assist the school counselor in making tentative assessments about the student or school environment. Copacetic connections generally reflect a coherence between the student and the prompting environment. For academic content, connections represent the possible coherence of the content. Socially, when one is generally bonded to a certain peer group or cause. Alternatively, when one experiences disconnection, one can experience threats, uncertainty, and disengagement.

Just as ruptured or threatened connections can be problematic, overly entangled connections can potentially limit functioning. Returning to the kaleidoscope metaphor, if the student must conform to a certain way of being (i.e. a certain color in the prism), this potentially forecloses the profound diversity of experience feasible within each person, across time and potential experiences with others. This type of enmeshment is the antithesis of education, as it is a delimiting governor that stifles the student or the school environment.

A school counselor who utilizes connectedness in their work will toil to find and accentuate relatedness between the student and school environment. There is a delicate balance in connectedness practices, as one does not want to inadvertently promote coercion or conformity. This is especially important given the authority of one's role as a school counselor. Similarly, one must account for one's cultural capital in connectedness praxis, for the goal of ASE work is student sapience and critical consciousness, not merely assimilating into the school environment (which has assimilated from larger socio-cultural systems). Instead, connectedness is adopting an orientation that is both attentive to being embedded within a system while maintaining the wherewithal not to be fully consumed by that system.

For the particular student, connectedness in counseling should be validating and challenging. We validate that the lived experience is phenomenologically coherent and, yet, simply because that experience is valid, it does not preclude that there are other experiences or connections. In this way, connectedness is related to concepts such as empathy and yet is conceptually different. Like empathy, through connection, we bridge perspectives, and yet, it is different from empathy in that there is not the baggage of a single first-person experience.

This is an important distinction, especially for working with children and adolescents. For example, because connectedness talk does not essentialize the person or experience, the school counselor can differentiate a behavior from an absolute person or way of being. For example, a student can misunderstand a concept and retain the capacity to understand other concepts or later grasp the misconceived concept.

Co-regulation

In ASE theory, co-regulation is the fulcrum between the student and the school environment. McCaslin (2009) defined co-regulation as the interface of two or more self-aware, intentional individuals who draw from various cultural, social, and personal sources to inform and influence behavior. Experientially, the student cannot be reduced to an essential self but rather the student is an agent affected by various systems. How one regulates one's experiences and aspirations in those systems requires one to co-regulate. Imagine a rock being thrown into a river. The rock is predisposed by its gravity and form to pursue the riverbed, yet the current alters that trajectory based on the magnitude of the current. Students are certainly goal-directed, yet even the most volitionally able student responds to the learning and social opportunities, including opportunities that are either knowable or unknown.

As an orientation for experience, a self-regulated individual can monitor, predict, shift, and direct one's internal and external experiences (Schunk & Zimmerman, 1994), whereas operating out of a co-regulated orientation, one extends beyond one's inner psychological experiences and places total experience in a broader social and historical context. For the school counselor, a co-regulated perspective can help extend connectedness across peoples and contexts. For example, it is cliché to dismiss student behavior to tropes such as, "they are that way because of their parents." In contrast, a co-regulated perspective understands that across the generations, there are various personal and social causes and consequences. Those parents will not spontaneously develop parenting skills simply because they are procreated. Co-regulation as an orientation reminds the school counselor that there are myriad determinants of experience in all the various players in the school system.

As an orientation for students and members of the school environment, co-regulation is the emotional, cognitive, and behavioral capacity to respond in a way that is personally and socially relevant. Even at very young ages, children can often discern how certain conditions affect their experiences. From an ASE perspective, co-regulation is not necessarily an end in itself. Rather, the process of co-regulating oneself within a larger system will always deepen the connection between the student and school environment while contributing to mutual development.

This generative way of considering co-regulation can inspire school counseling approaches and behaviors. For example, consider the differences between the following two statements with similar intent: "What have you done to improve yourself?" is different than "How have you pursued your goals given the influences of (insert circumstance)?" In the former, the school counselor has inadvertently essentialized a single experience or interpretation; moreover, this form of question coerces the student to acknowledge improvement when maybe that does not cohere with the student's experience. In the case of the latter, with only a few more words, the student is encouraged to consider multiple possibilities, as each exists within their influencing context.

Just as co-regulation binds together the experiences and pursuit of the student and the aspects of the school environment, as a concept within ASE theory, it also binds together the five Cs. The curiosity required of the student must be co-regulated with curiosities found in the school environment. In the same way, connectedness requires feelings of safety, affiliation, and rapport to be co-regulated and distributed. Finally, co-regulation anticipates the final two Cs, which are primarily expressions of curiosity and connectedness.

Compassion

Being curious, connected, and co-regulated can exhaust the cognitive load on students and members of the school community. Compassion is the orientation and practice of personal and social acceptance with discernment. This form of acceptance does not suggest that agents in a school affirm and internalize deleterious experiences of social conditions; instead, compassion suggests that discerning prior causes and effects of experience in a benevolent and focused way can protect one's wellbeing and better position oneself for future personal and social development.

"*Com-*" as a prefix means together or with, as in Student-within-Environment. Passion is understood as the intense or enthused desire for or state of something. From an ASE perspective, compassion is being with the desire of the student or member of the school environment. This is a co-regulated process shared between the school counselor, student, and relevant parties in the school.

For the student, a compassionate orientation validates their various experiences as a social being. Although adults might romantically reminisce about childhood, each stage of one's youth can be littered with challenges of various sorts (Erikson, 1950). Compassion acknowledges the vigor necessary to pass through these stages while affirming that all personal or social pursuits are imprecise, context-specific, and emergent. The orientation of compassion is illustrated in the counselor statement suggested by Brigman and Webb (2010), "*Don't doubt your ability, try another strategy*."

Compassion suggests that all expressions are reasonable within context, yet it is shortsighted to essentialize any one or more expressions. A week before writing this chapter, my daughter (Matthew) asked me when she was walking to school, "Daddy, is it okay to be afraid of things?" To which I responded, "Certainly. Fear can be a great gift, even if it seems temporarily inconvenient and scary. It is your body letting you know that there is a potential threat out there and you should be attentive. What is not necessarily okay is to be stuck in our fear and only experience things in one way, especially long after the threat is mostly gone." Herein I tried to invoke compassion by validating her genuine experience of fear and yet also appreciate that she is complex and her circumstances will evolve over time.

A second anecdote to illustrate compassion comes from my experiences as a professor. I once had a colleague who struggled with mental well-being, culminating in misperceptions and literal hallucinations. Unfortunately, his status was so compromised that it impaired his work as a professor, and he stopped all professional activities. After a while, I was asked by representatives in the university about the colleague and some of the circumstances that afflicted him (e.g. workplace stress, harassment from colleagues). The perspective I offered was simply this, "I don't necessarily believe what my colleague believes, but I believe that my colleague believes these things." Compassion requires one to acknowledge that almost any perspective is experientially true, but there are also many interpretations, influences, and versions of truth. Compassion is being with the passion for the person to experience self-within-environment, while being with the passion required for the self to continue to pursue new vistas of experience.

The practice of compassion requires that the school counselor embody and express the first three Cs (curiosity, connectedness, and co-regulation) and couple those with the acceptance and discernment of compassion. This process can be accomplished by utilizing an adapted version of Rapoport's Rules (popularized by philosopher Daniel Dennett [2013]), see Table 2.1.

Compassion is a high order skill in ASE theory and should be pursued cautiously. Compassion can come off as supercilious. ASE is a social justice and personal liberation approach to school counseling; therefore, compassion is not some covert process to pacify the student or educator or exonerate unjust school environments. Instead, compassion is the orientation and practice of discerning the determinants of experience, conceiving of their various effects, and ascertaining composure such that one can continue to regulate the self and environment to new and benefiting ends.

TABLE 2.1 Rapoport's Rules and ASE

Rapoport's Rules	*ASE*
1. You should attempt to re-express your target's position so clearly, vividly, and fairly that your target says, "Thanks, I wish I'd thought of putting it that way."	
2. You should list any points of agreement (especially if they are not matters of general or widespread agreement).	
3. You should mention anything you have learned from your target.	
4. Only then are you permitted to say so much as a word of rebuttal or criticism.	Expand position to multiple alternative explanations (influences) and/or outcomes.

Contribution

The first four Cs of ASE generally co-occur in the counseling process, yet the final C is necessary to fully actualize ASE. Contribution is the co-regulated efforts to change social systems and personal commitments to social advocacy. Contribution operates as a proto-Archimedean point or ultimate ethic for the theory. Unlike many ethical positions, contribution is more than a concept; instead, it is a living value that must be committed to through action.

Given the incredible complexity of school and other social systems, it is logical that contribution follows the maturation of the four initial Cs. This said it is conceivable that the mere act of participating in the type of social advocacy to vivify contribution, experiences of curiosity, connectedness, co-regulation, and compassion might manifest. For example, a school counselor might work with a teacher to elucidate how district disciplinary policies over represent certain populations of students. In pursuing more restorative practices, the school counselor and teacher might have new understandings for students (curiosity), connect with these students' behaviors within systems, and co-regulate new classroom climates.

Contribution reflects Freire's (1970) belief in mutual liberation of the oppressed and oppressor; there is a total commitment to solidarity and prosperity at the personal and social levels. Consistent with the other four Cs in ASE theory, contribution is not a simple or always apparent course. Oftentimes, contribution must be scrutinized or run the risk of creating new hegemonies in the place of prior oppressive forces in the school system. For example, in efforts to create greater access to one group, educators must be attentive to implications for other oppressed students in the system.

> In practice, this recognition requires the humanistic practitioner to amplify the voices and agency of the oppressed, rather than simply serving as a proxy on their behalf. Certainly there are occasions when it is reasonable to use the social positionality of the practitioner or even oppressor to support the justice needs of the oppressed, but one's power is not an absolute and it should be allocated as soon as is possible. Social justice advocacy is not an end onto itself; rather, a goal of social justice praxis is to amplify the agency of the oppressed in such a manner that they are better able to self-advocate and confront injustices.
>
> *(Lemberger & Lemberger-Truelove, 2016, p. 576)*

ASE is not a theory that is sans ethical presuppositions. ASE is a dialogical approach, oscillating between the interests in the student and the social environment as interacting determinants of experience. Therefore, any just action in the school must be deemed ethical at the individual and systems level.

This is not to be confused with consensus building, as that ethical approach tends to tilt in the direction of the most powerful agent or stagnates through assimilation within the system.

This ethical stance in a school can be incredibly complex and stifling, yet it is not a reason for inaction. Participants in schools are always contributing. The dialogical nature of pursuing personally and socially just behaviors, therefore, suggests that curiosity, connectedness, co-regulation, and compassion must repeatedly filter any action on behalf of the student or school environment.

The Counseling Relationship

Penetrating through the middle of the five Cs of ASE theory is its adherence to the common factors of counseling literature (Wampold, 2015). This literature suggests that a particular theory only accounts for a small amount of client development. Instead, factors external to the counseling process largely dictate client outcomes; from an ASE perspective, this point endorses the role of the school counselor as a social justice advocate. Within the counseling relationship, common factors are certain qualities that contribute to desirable outcomes across theoretical orientations.

In a counterintuitive way, the common factors literature supports the uniqueness of ASE theory. One of the primary predictors of counselor influenced outcomes pertains to the cultural fitness of the intervention. As such, it is reasonable that the most appropriate approach to working with students, educators, and other stakeholders in schools is through the application of an approach tailored to the culture of schools, the developmental and functional needs of students, and the roles and responsibilities endemic to school counselors.

More than a tacit endorsement of ASE, the common factors literature explicitly highlights the importance of rapport as a healing ingredient (Wampold, 2015). The five Cs of ASE are the mechanism proscribed to establish mutual respect and to engender hopefulness in the client, which prove to be vital ingredients in counseling rapport.

Concluding Thoughts

School counselors operate in complex school systems. At their disposal includes various delivery systems to help support students and other parties, including classroom lessons and psycho educational activities, small group counseling, individual counseling, coordination and collaboration, and consultation. Filtered through an ASE framework, each of these counseling formats can potentially support students and elements of the school environment as interdependent governors of experience.

The ASE perspective can appear almost paradoxical. On the one hand, an ASE practitioner is required to act with (or within) a student's perspective. This suggests a deep respect for the current functioning of the client. If there are any maladies, those are honored as components of one's experience. On the other hand, to be with the student as a counselor suggests one must ameliorate the experiences of the student and the school environment.

There is a resolution. Unlike allied theoretical approaches that suggest a change in perspective or encourage the student to re-narrate one's constructed messages, the ASE approach is primarily concerned with creating the personal and social conditions as preventative positions pointing towards ongoing development. Stated more simply, school counseling reflects the acme of education, that is pulling from one's history and compelling the self to be an active participant in that unfolding history. As one's capacities are sharpened in the various counseling experiences and as social circumstances in the school are made more equitable and usable, the self within systems emerge in more intended and prosperous ends.

It still feels like a volitional choice directed by the student. The causal conditions of choice were established in the student as an indivisible system and the school as another aspect of myriad systems. There is a type of epistemological compatibilism in this resolve in that each student can affect one's destiny as it unfolds, but only insofar as those actions were enacted prior to their occurrence in the school. The student's acumen as a learner and their exposure to empowering contexts contributes to one's moral compass. How one engages in peer communication coupled with the peers in one's social groups affects what notes are or are not passed in geometry class.

The school counselor stands alongside each student and the total school environment. Like all other governors in the kaleidoscope that is the school environment, the school counselor's own orientation and practices contribute to future possibilities. The spirit of ASE can be best summarized in the following two quotes:

> To best prepare young children in poverty for later life challenges, professional counselors must make every attempt to improve social conditions; however, it is equally important that young children's internal capacities be strengthened either to accommodate improved social conditions or to maximize resilience in the face of persistent adversity.
>
> *(Lemberger-Truelove et al., 2018, p. 299)*

and

> students from disenfranchised communities do not accept inadequate or deleterious social conditions; instead, using... strategies, they accept their cognitive and affective reactions and respond with clearer intentionality.
>
> *(Lemberger-Truelove et al., 2018, p. 299)*

References

Abdelghani, R., Oudeyer, P. Y., Law, E., de Vulpillieres, C., & Sauzéon, H. (2022). Conversational agents for fostering curiosity-driven learning in children. *arXiv* (preprint). https://doi.org/10.48550/arXiv.2204.03546

Allen, J., Balfour, R., Bell, R., & Marmot, M. (2014). Social determinants of mental health. *International Review of Psychiatry, 26*(4), 392–407. https://doi.org/10.3109/09540261.2014.928270

American School Counselor Association. (2019). *ASCA National Model: A framework for school counseling programs* (4th ed.). Alexandria, VA: Author.

American School Counselor Association. (n.d.). *ASCA Standards for School Counselor Preparation Programs. www.schoolcounselor.org/getmedia/573d7c2c-1622-4d25-a5ac-ac74d2e614ca/ASCA-Standards-for-School-Counselor-Preparation-Programs.pdf*

Bandura A. (1986). *Social Foundations of Thought and Action: A Social Cognitive Theory*. Englewood Cliffs, NJ: Prentice-Hall.

Bandura, A. (1989). Human agency in Social Cognitive Theory. *American Psychologist, 44*(9), 1175–1184. https://doi.org/10.1037/0003-066X.44.9.1175

Baudrillard, J. (1983). *Simulations*. New York: Semiotext(e).

Beiser, H. R. (1984). On curiosity: A developmental approach. *Journal of the American Academy of Child Psychiatry, 23*(5), 517–526. https://doi.org/10.1016/S0002-7138(09)60341-1

Borders, L. D., & Drury, S. M. (1992). Comprehensive school counseling programs: A review for policymakers and practitioners. *Journal of Counseling & Development, 70*(4), 487–498. https://doi.org/10.1002/j.1556-6676.1992.tb01643.x

Burnham, J. J., & Jackson, C. M. (2000). School counselor roles: Discrepancies between actual practice and existing models. *Professional School Counseling, 4,* 41–49.

Brigman, G. & Webb, L. (2010). *Student Success Skills: Classroom manual* (3rd ed.). Boca Raton, FL: Atlantic Education Consultants.

Darling-Hammond, L., Flook, L., Cook-Harvey, C., Barron, B., & Osher., D. (2020) Implications for educational practice of the science of learning and development. *Applied Developmental Science (24)*2, 97–140. https://doi.org/10.1080/10888691.2018.1537791

Day-Vines, N. L., Cluxton-Keller, F., Agorsor, C., & Gubara, S. (2021). Strategies for broaching the subjects of race, ethnicity, and culture. *Journal of Counseling & Development, 99*(3), 348–357. https://doi.org/10.1002/jcad.12380

Dennett, D. C. (2013). *Intuition pumps and other tools for thinking*. WW Norton & Company.

Dewey, J. (1916). *Democracy and Education*. Teddington: Echo Library.

Dollarhide, C. T., Smith, A., & Lemberger, M. E. (2007). Critical incidents in the development of supportive principals: Facilitating school counselor–principal relationships. *Professional School Counseling, 10*(4), 360–369.

Dyche, L., & Zayas, L. H. (1995). The value of curiosity and naivete for the cross-cultural psychotherapist. *Family Process, 34*(4), 389–399. https://doi.org/10.1111/j.1545-5300.1995.00389.x

Elliott, R., Bohart, A. C., Watson, J. C., & Murphy, D. (2018). Therapist empathy and client outcome: An updated meta-analysis. *Psychotherapy, 55,* 399–410. http://dx.doi.org/10.1037/pst0000175

Erikson, E. H. (1950). *Childhood and society*. New York, NY: Norton.

Freire, P. (1970). *Pedagogy of the oppressed.* New York, NY: Herder and Herder.
Ghosh, J. K., Delampady, M., & Samanta, T. (2007). *An introduction to Bayesian analysis: Theory and methods.* USA: Springer.
Griffith, C., Mariani, M., McMahon, H. G., Zyromski, B., & Greenspan, S. (2019). School counseling intervention research: A 10-year content analysis of ASCA–and ACA-affiliated journals. *Professional School Counseling, 23*(1), 1–12. https://doi.org/10.1177/2156759X19878700
Jacob, R., & Parkinson, J. (2015). The potential for school-based interventions that target executive function to improve academic achievement: A review. *Review of Educational Research, 85*(4), 512–552. https://doi.org/10.3102/0034654314561338
James W. (1899). *Talks to teachers on psychology and to students on some of life's ideals.* New York: Holt.
Johnson, K. F., Kim, H., Molina, C. E., Thompson, K. A., Henry, S., & Zyromski, B. (in press). School counseling prevention programming to address social determinants of mental health. *Journal of Counseling & Development.*
Jung, C. G. (1964). *Man and his symbols.* New York: Laurel.
Kidd, C., & Hayden, B. Y. (2015). The psychology and neuroscience of curiosity. *Neuron, 88*(3), 449–460. https://doi.org/10.1016/j.neuron.2015.09.010
Lemberger, M. E. (2010). Advocating Student-within-Environment: A humanistic theory for school counseling. *The Journal of Humanistic Counseling, Education and Development, 49,* 131–146. https://doi.org/10.1002/j.2161-1939.2010.tb00093.x
Lemberger, M. E., & Hutchison, B. (2014). Advocating Student-within-Environment: A humanistic approach for therapists to animate social justice in the schools. *Journal of Humanistic Psychology, 54,* 8–44. https://doi.org/10.1177/0022167816652750
Lemberger, M. E., & Lemberger-Truelove, T. L. (2016). Bases for a more socially just humanistic praxis. *Journal of Humanistic Psychology, 56*(6), 571–580. https://doi.org/10.1177/0022167816652750
Lemberger-Truelove, M. E., & Bowers, H. (2019). An Advocating Student-within-Environment approach to school counseling. In C. T. Dollarhide & M. E. Lemberger-Truelove (Eds.), *Theories of school counseling for the 21st century* (pp. 266–294). Oxford.
Lemberger-Truelove, M. E., Carbonneau, K. J., Atencio, D. J., Zieher, A. K., & Palacios, A. F. (2018). Self-regulatory growth effects for young children participating in a combined social and emotional learning and mindfulness-based intervention. *Journal of Counseling and Development, 96*(3) 289–302. https://doi.org/10.1002/j.1556-6676.2014.00000.x
Lemberger-Truelove, M. E., Molina, C. E., Carbonneau, K. J., & Smith, M. (in press). Effects of school counselor consultation intervention on middle school teacher-student relationships, student curiosity, and teacher stress. *Professional School Counseling.*
Levy, I. & Lemberger-Truelove, M. E. (2021). Educator-counselor: A non-dual identity for professional school counselors. *Professional School Counseling, 24*(1b): 1–7. https://doi.org/10.1177/2156759X211007630
McCaslin, M. (2009). Co-regulation of student motivation and emergent identity. *Educational Psychologist, 44*(2), 137–146. https://doi.org/10.1080/00461520902832384
Myers, J. E. (1992). Wellness, prevention, development: The cornerstone of the profession. *Journal of Counseling & Development, 71*(2), 136–139. https://doi.org/10.1002/j.1556-6676.1992.tb02188.x

Resnick, M. D., Bearman, P. S., Blum, R. W., Bauman, K. E., Harris, K. M., Jones, J., et al. (1997). Protecting adolescents from harm: Findings from the National Longitudinal Study on Adolescent Health. *Journal of American Medical Association, 278*(10), 823–832. https://doi:10.1001/jama.278.10.823

Schunk, D. H., & Zimmerman, B. J. (1994). *Self-regulation of learning and performance: Issues and educational applications*. Lawrence Erlbaum Associates, Inc.

Vygotsky, L. S. (1978). *Mind in society: The development of higher psychological processes*. Cambridge, MA: Harvard University Press.

Wampold, B. E. (2015). How important are the common factors in psychotherapy? An update. *World Psychiatry, 14*(3), 270–277. https://doi.org/10.1002/wps.20238

Whiston, S. C., Tai, W. L., Rahardja, D., & Eder, K. (2011). School counseling outcome: A meta-analytic examination of interventions. *Journal of Counseling & Development, 89*(1), 37–55. https://doi.org/10.1002/j.1556-6678.2011.tb00059.x

3

UTILIZING ASE TO WORK WITHIN THE SCHOOL SYSTEM

Hannah Bowers Parker

Currently, counseling within schools is under enormous scrutiny, regardless if a school counselor or a school-based mental health counselor provides services. Herein lies the very rationale for this text: there needs to be an approach to working in the schools that systemically grounds all school system members that further aligns with the school's mission and vision. ASE provides that foundation as school counselors advocate for growth for their students and teachers, administrators, and family members. While ASE is a theory of practice, it is also a theory of being. By embracing the approach of ASE in all interactions, the school counselor can encourage a double feedback loop within the school, whereby growth is incurred reflexively through all relationships.

ASE is grounded in the tenet of systemic change. To make that achievable, the school counselor immerses oneself within students' perceptual reality, which colors their perspective of their social circumstance. Understanding that perspective and how to function as an advocate for students is heavily influenced by the structure of the school – who are the key players, how is power distributed, whom to reference for topic-specific resources, and how to intervene to build upon the capacities of school leaders to engage in activities that encourage co-regulation. This chapter frames ASE through a leadership mentality, focusing on skill sets to promote the development of internal capacities of school faculty and staff while also directly advocating for student needs. When considering a school's structure, many influencing factors reveal the systems in which an individual school is nested. This chapter focuses on a singular school as a structure, utilizing terminology applicable within a distinct K-12 environment.

DOI: 10.4324/9781003312871-3

Who's Who in the School, and What Do They Do?

Pulling from structural therapeutic techniques (Minuchin, 1974), physically organizing the power structure of each subsystem can be incredibly helpful in understanding the school environment and identifying areas that may need to be changed (see Figure 3.1). Each subsystem is differentiated by a boundary, which differs within every school. These boundaries are experienced physically and emotionally as one considers accessibility to each subsystem. Within ASE, the counselor must understand the undercurrent of power that impacts environmental functioning. Such power differentials and boundaries determine how each sub-system communicates to one another, either discouraging or encouraging communal relations between groups. This foundational understanding of the system makes counselors better equipped to join and accommodate.

For ASE, there is no ascribed curriculum whereby teachers or school counselors must read from a script. Instead, it is a foundational understanding of creating connection, communicating respect for individual experience, and

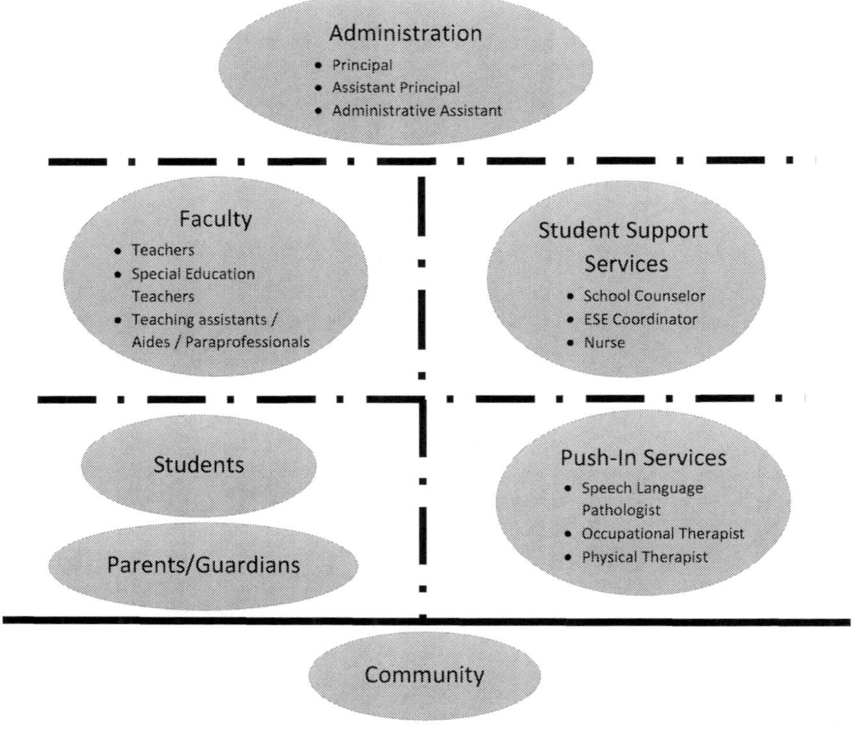

FIGURE 3.1 Structural Map of a School.

cultivating a sense of community through joining the already established system. Through dialectical relational skill sets, school counselors permeate the system to create change within each school subsystem, working within current power structures or striving to change power distribution through the alignment of shared goals.

Schools have been seen to thrive when there is shared power and responsibility across stakeholders (Webster & Litchka, 2020). To decrease turnover rates within the school system, recommended changes include considerations towards compensation, preparation, support, and school leadership (Carver-Thomas & Darling-Hammond, 2017). School environments can intentionally be addressed through transparency of such boundaries, allowing for an equal flow of information, honoring perspectives, and engaging in dialogue with others.

To navigate the school and access resources to better advocate for the student, all school stakeholders, whether it be faculty, administration, parents, and student, need to understand who assumes which job titles, what their roles and responsibilities are, and where they are physically located. Below is a list of common roles within a typical school structure organized by the administration, faculty, support staff, and external service providers. While not everyone a student may come into contact with is included (i.e. custodians, bus drivers, librarians), that does not diminish their role or contribution to the school. Instead, the individuals listed below are critical players in the decision-making process regarding student-based outcomes.

Administrators

Considering the structural map of the school in Figure 3.1, administrators typically have power within the school setting. They are responsible for establishing and maintaining day-to-day operations, which largely dictate the culture of a school. Administrators must be on board to permeate the system and enact change throughout. The following provides a description of each role as well as ways to create collaborative and supportive relationships to begin environmental changes.

Principal. With a presence in every elementary, middle, and high school, principals are generally responsible for overseeing all school operations, including setting academic goals and providing teachers with resources and support to obtain those goals best. Often, principals are required to have a master's degree, usually in educational leadership. They are provided with the foundation of various leadership theories and skill sets that will aid in their development to lead others within educational settings. Numerous studies have investigated the efficacy of different leadership approaches on school outcomes (Chin, 2007).

Within the public school setting, academic goals are largely influenced by standards set forth by the district. The principal oversees such implementation and ensures teachers have all materials needed to administer programming successfully. Principals are also responsible for overseeing the well-being of all members within their schools. For example, efforts to support teachers often include providing mentorship, opportunities for professional development, and overseeing remediation or potential retention. These efforts have a trickledown effect on improving students' lives; teachers feel supported in their roles in the classroom, and students are provided with a conducive learning environment.

Principals are encouraged to work collaboratively with school counselors for the betterment of students, sharing essential goals rooted in student success (Dahir et al., 2010). However, there has been a historical lack of understanding regarding the school counselor's role within the school system. For example, principals often assign non-counseling-related activities to the school counselor, leaving them with the burden of attending to overwhelming administrative tasks (Dollarhide & Lemberger, 2006). These tasks typically include scheduling, testing administration, or discipline (Lowery et al., 2018). Research on principals' perceptions of the school counselor's role shows that those perceptions are typically reflected within the actual school counseling role (Lewis et al., 2022). The power a principal yields within a school is to the magnitude that their vision is often encapsulated into practice. The more aligned these perceptions are with the A.S.C.A. National Model leads to a successful school counselor/principal collaborative relationship (Lewis et al., 2022).

Assistant Principal. Assistant Principals (A.P.s) interface with all school stakeholders, often engaging directly to mediate conversations between teachers, parents, students, and the community. They perform administrative tasks as well as assist in the development of the master class schedule and evaluate teacher performance. A.P.s support teachers, ensuring that the materials taught in the classroom align with curriculum standards set forth by the district and principal. A.P.s engage with students far more than the principal. They mediate the relationship between faculty, administration, family, and community.

Most larger schools have a position of an assistant principal (A.P.) to aid the principal in overseeing and facilitating day-to-day operations. However, these roles and responsibilities differ nationwide as schools and districts have different needs. Because there is so much variety in how this role is assumed, it may be challenging to provide formal training for A.P.s. Much of the day-to-day decisions made by the A.P. are related to their previous experiences, whether direct with the student, teacher, or parent. Alternatively, other A.P.s note how decisions may contradict their interpersonal styles, attempting to assimilate into the school system. These contradictions are often most noted in their role working on disciplinary infractions. From teacher instruction in the classroom to student behavior, assistant principals' roles revolve around ensuring compliance.

Regarding the role of disciplinarian, A.P.s often comply with teacher demands which center around removing the problematic student from the classroom. However, in engaging in this compliance on top of balancing the day-to-day responsibilities of school operation, A.P.s often neglect the diverse needs of each student, feeling forced to get the job done rather than take the time to explore the context behind each situation (Williams III et al., 2020). From an ASE perspective, the school counselors must support A.P.s, providing consultation on discipline and encouraging exploration of the underlying issues that may present, promoting the ability to advocate for the student within the environment. Simply engaging in disciplinary action without gaining contextual information regarding the student, joining them in their lived experience, often results in cultural blindness and disparities between how different groups of students are treated. Receiving support from the school counselor using ASE can promote equity across all students while improving connection and outcomes.

Administrative Assistants. While the title of this role changes from school to school (administrator, secretary), the general role functions remain the same – the administrative assistant is in charge of directing the flow of people and information in and out of the school. This person or multiple people are the first you engage with when entering or calling the school. They provide information, give direction, and make connections. Some oversee creating and distributing newsletters or emails regarding upcoming events. They communicate with parents, teachers, principals, and the community. The administrative assistants are essentially the school's gatekeepers, some ensuring outsiders follow safety procedures that enable them to enter the school. They track when students arrive on time and if they need to leave early. They are the ones parents speak to when their student is sick or has a doctor's appointment.

Depending on the school size, many administrative assistants may serve under various administration members. For example, a larger school's principal and assistant principal likely have an administrative assistant to help with tasks related to coordination, planning, and organization of the tasks that make up daily school activities. They may have crucial roles in implementing and reporting all fire or lockdown drills or organizing student bus transportation. Whenever there is a need from a student, teacher, or parent, the administrative assistant is the one who connects them or directly provides them with the information needed.

Administrative assistants can be crucial in aiding the school counselor in gauging the school's temperature. Their support can be essential in addressing ancillary duties that may detract from direct student intervention. With this position also comes a need for training and continued support by the school counselor. Administrators must understand the importance of confidentiality regarding students, whether protecting their private educational information to behavioral or discipline incidents. Understanding how information is shared and how such information significantly impacts the school's functioning is crucial.

Providing training and continued support of administrators, whether by training principals and A.P.s to oversee their staff, modeling appropriate communication skill sets, or providing professional development, school counselors can intervene with administrative assistants to change how information is shared throughout the school system and all related stakeholders.

Student Support Personnel

The following personnel work to coordinate efforts between all stakeholders to benefit all students. While the school counselor oversees all students' academic, social and emotional, and career development needs, student support personnel specialize in supporting specific populations from students struggling with mental health-related disorders, support for learning difficulties, and physical health concerns. While administrators oversee the school's general operations, student support personnel work directly with students to meet their needs.

School Counselor. This text is written from the perspective of supporting school counselors and school-based mental health professionals. A section on the school counselor is warranted as the need to understand the ideal of the position and how that role navigates the system is essential in being able to advocate for the role and those served. Traditionally, the school counselor is tasked with directly supporting student development in academics, career aspirations, and social and emotional skill sets (A.S.C.A., 2019). School counselors accomplish these activities by directly interfacing with students through individual counseling, small group counseling, classroom guidance, and consultation to implement comprehensive guidance curriculums.

To ensure the support given to the student is effective, school counselors are also charged with engaging in data-driven decision-making whereby they use student information to guide the programming offered within a multi-tiered system of support. For example, a needs assessment may indicate that students struggle significantly with test anxiety school-wide. The school counselor then focuses a component of their comprehensive guidance curriculum on stress reduction, mindfulness-based activities, or student success skills (Brigman & Webb, 2010). School counselors engage with all students through tier one intervention and classroom guidance lessons. Should they notice students continue to struggle after engagement in that format, school counselors may form small groups with those who continue to struggle, intervening at the tier two level. Should the small group not suffice for some, school counselors utilize tier three intervention by engaging in individual counseling sessions. At that time, the school counselor would have ample data to make an informed referral should the student need outside support.

While most of the work focuses on direct contact with students, the school counselor serves as someone any school member can turn to for support, including working with teachers, parents, and administration. School counselors mediate parent-teacher conferences and meetings, utilizing counseling skill sets to encourage all members to feel heard and validated in their unique perspectives. The school counselor approaches these relationships to better the student outcomes. Should a teacher come to the school counselor regarding stress from a specific class, the school counselor's efforts to support that teacher directly benefit the students within that class.

While the description above is ideal, the school counselor is often assigned ancillary duties, including testing coordination, student schedules, and other clerical duties. This, coupled with limited classroom access due to teachers' stressors to meet mandated standards, decreases the school counselor's ability to access all students. The school climate also dramatically impacts the school counselor's ability to implement ideal programming, whether there is support from faculty and administration or the communal needs of the school is nested in. Numerous factors impact school counselor efficacy in the school.

School-Based Mental Health Counselor. Mental health needs amongst school-aged children continue to increase, especially in the aftermath of the COVID-19 pandemic. While these needs may continue to rise, access to mental health care can be limiting for children, dependent on parents to arrange and provide transportation to appointments after school hours. Given the demand and high caseload experienced by school counselors, meeting students' mental health care needs is not feasible. Therefore, schools will often contract or hire mental health counselors to serve in the school. School-based mental health counselors are trained in clinical mental health and usually specialize in working with children and adolescents.

School counselors and school-based mental health counselors are encouraged to work together in a collaborative relationship. As school counselors ascribe to implementing a comprehensive guidance curriculum, it is unrealistic to meet the mental health needs of all students. Often, those who have worked through all three tiers of intervention are ready for an outside referral for further support (Christian & Brown, 2018). Rather than having that referral be to a community counseling agency, school counselors can work closely with the school-based mental health counselor to ensure the transfer of services, consult on background information, and make a seamless transition. Furthermore, these services offered at the school allow all students to receive adequate mental health-based services, removing common barriers such as access and affordability.

School counselors and school-based mental health counselors are fully equipped to utilize ASE throughout their practices. While both professionals are considered mental health experts, each has a unique experience that can be beneficial in consulting and collaborating. Considering that clinical mental health counselors may not have extensive experience in the school setting, the school counselor can take the opportunity during onboarding to provide background on

ASE and how to work within the system. A common background and similar language can ease the transition, allowing for an opportunity to share insights into navigating the system. Both recognize the shared goal of meeting students' social, emotional, and mental health needs. Establishing that collaborative relationship will allow for success.

Exceptional Student Education Coordinator. Between 2020 and 2021, 15% of all public school students received special education services under the Individuals with Disabilities Education Act (I.D.E.A.). The exceptional student education (E.S.E.) coordinator oversees all E.S.E. students and ensures the services each student receives best meet their educational needs. In order to do so, E.S.E. coordinators work with students, parents, counselors, and other stakeholders to prepare individual education plans (I.E.P.) for each student and ensure accommodations are put into place. The E.S.E. coordinator continuously monitors student progress to ensure those accommodations that are put into place are effective and allow the student to meet their identified goals. E.S.E. coordinators must comply with national laws consistent with the individuals with disabilities act.

E.S.E. coordinators work closely with all student support personnel to ensure students receive equitable opportunities as their general education peers. Such supports include ensuring access to external supports and resources. School counselors working from the ASE perspective understand that students with individual education plans have unique experiences and needs, often struggling socially, emotionally, and academically. Collaborating on the I.E.P. process allows consultation efforts to be applied with all supporting the student, including the parent, teacher, school counselor, and all other external support. Utilizing ASE in this process promotes the opportunity to allow each stakeholder to share their experiences and model a dialogue connection. Everyone at the table can feel heard in a process often overwhelming for parents and teachers.

Nurse. The school nurse is a registered nurse who helps students with the treatment and prevention of medical issues and ailments and coordinates routine health assessments. The school nurse is a resource for all things physically related to students. They aid in medication dissemination should medications need to be taken during the school day and fix up scraped knees from the playground. The nurse provides health education to students and coordinates vision, hearing, and speech assessments.

While a school nurse's role may be self-explanatory, they are often an underutilized resource within the school system. The school counselor can consult with the school nurse on situations whereby a student's physical health may impede their ability to perform. The school nurse can also assist in identifying students struggling with underlying mental health struggles as children experience emotional distress through somatic complaints (headaches, stomach aches, exhaustion, etc.). Student support personnel can work together to ensure students receive access to all supports within the system, increasing access to social and emotional support and mental health services.

Faculty

Faculty are the heart of a school. Faculty work with students all day, often knowing what is going on in their lives inside and outside school. It is through the faculty-student interaction that learning occurs. Within that interaction comes the opportunity for co-regulation. Within ASE, co-regulation is a foundational factor referring to the interaction of two self-aware individuals. Becoming self-aware requires intentional reflection on one's self as well as reflection on those around you. School counselors can aid faculty and students to enhance their self-awareness, students through the comprehensive guidance curriculum, and faculty through professional development and consultation. Through support, faculty can genuinely change the environment and encourage the development of optimal student outcomes.

In practice, the ASE consultation model has been seen to increase teachers' awareness and attention to the present and decrease stress within the classroom (Molina et al., 2022). As teachers increase their self-awareness, they can better engage in a co-regulatory relationship with their students, changing the nature of the environment. Acting with co-regulation within the classroom environment allows teachers to see beyond the student's behavior, identifying that such actions extend beyond the student's capacity and speaks to a myriad of factors. Teachers reflect on their own experiences within each moment and how their experiences impact their students. Similarly, as students engage in their own ASE curriculum, they also experience increased self-awareness, promoting the ability to engage in the co-regulation process. The impact ASE has on teacher satisfaction is profound, especially considering the high rate of teacher burnout, decreased perceptions of self-worth, and depressive symptoms (Méndez et al., 2020). School counselors using ASE as a model for consultation and professional development allows for repeated exposure to ASE, providing that foundation through professional development and continuous reinforcement through modeling and encouragement within the consultation.

General Education Teachers. As defined by the U.S. Bureau of Labor Statistics, a teacher's role is to instruct students in various basic subjects that prepare them for future schooling (2022). The homeroom teacher is your student's main point of contact in an elementary school setting. They are engaged in their daily learning activities and exposed to their social growth and developmental milestones. At the high school level, a student has exposure to numerous teachers, all of whom have different experiences and perspectives on the student. Teachers work with all other members of the school system, especially parents and other support personnel, to best meet their students' needs. Teachers work beyond the time they are in the classroom, using evenings and weekends to prepare lessons or grade papers. They utilize classroom management skills and ensure lessons align with a developmentally appropriate curriculum. As with many other school professionals, teachers are often tasked with ancillary duties within an ever-changing educational environment. Given such, many teachers are plagued with burnout and this leave the classrooms for more favorable work environments with increased accessibility has given advancements in technology. This is more true for teachers with fewer than 11 years of experience in teaching (Kim & Seo, 2018), teachers with a specialty in S.T.E.M., or special education teachers (Nguyen, 2020). Overall, teacher satisfaction, commitment to their jobs, and feelings of self-efficacy are all impacted by the environment set forth by leadership in school administration (Cansoy et al., 2020; Kim & Seo, 2018).

Special Education Teacher. Special education teachers work with students who struggle with unique learning abilities, emotional and behavioral disorders, and physical disabilities (U.S. Bureau of Labor Statistics, 2022). While general education teachers use a standard curriculum, special education teachers must modify instruction to best meet the needs of their students, often in one on one or small group settings. In working with students whose needs constantly change, special education teachers must continuously monitor their student's progress to make informed decisions about their individualized education plans and communicate any changes with parents, other teachers, and outside service providers. Considering the intense stressors of working with a high-needs population, there is a shortage of special education teachers and a high rate of burnout (Carver-Thomas & Darling-Hammond, 2017; McLeskey et al., 2004).

Teacher Aides. Also titled a paraprofessional or instructional assistant, a teacher aide is in place for students with special learning circumstances to provide academic, social, and behavioral support (Howard & Ford, 2007). The structure of schools has shifted significantly over time, especially with consideration to meeting the needs of special education students. Rather than pulling out those with special learning needs and placing them into exclusion classrooms, schools now practice from an inclusive setting, ensuring all students have access to the same structures and supports regardless of their unique learning needs. This shift in learning structures leads to a need for more hands in classrooms where students may need increased support that exceeds the classroom teacher's capacity. For example, students that struggle with emotional or behavioral disorders (see Chapter 6) benefit significantly from having someone they trust to help them manage difficult situations. Instructionally, teacher aides support students through direct instruction, such as reviewing specific concepts discussed in class, and indirect instruction, whereby they monitor students' completion of work (Howard & Ford, 2007). Teacher aides may have a more robust and detailed perspective of a student that differs from the classroom teacher, given the time and intensity by which they connect to their students.

External Supports

The following include support services that may float between multiple schools. These personnel may not be included in the day-to-day interactions; however, it is vital to know that such services are accessible to any student who may need them. Faculty and student support staff must communicate with these individuals to track progress and meet student needs. Since these external service providers float between many schools, they may not have the opportunity to engage in professional development opportunities to receive direct training on ASE. Regardless, these providers are essential in providing necessary services that promote growth in human capacity, further promoting the student's ability to self-advocate. All student support personnel needs to be aware of these services so they can be utilized to best meet the needs of all students.

School Psychologist. The primary duty of a school psychologist comes into the realm of testing and evaluation for students in need of special services. Such assessments may be conducted by pulling a student from their classroom to complete valid and reliable assessments or observe student behavior in various learning environments. School counselors then communicate their findings to the school during an individual education planning meeting. In asking for feedback on roles and responsibilities, school psychologists reported their primary role as conducting student assessments but wished they could engage in more counseling-related activities (Agresta, 2004). Newer school psychologists find their consultation efforts did not align with problem-solving consultation models, preventing effective collaboration to support students through a multi-tiered system of support (Newman, 2018). Feedback on each effort included a need for collaboration between all members of the school system, working towards the betterment of the students in need. Supported students lead to supported teachers, improving classroom environments and transcending into school environment improvements.

Social Worker. In the school setting, social workers are mental health professionals who provide direct and indirect support services to students regarding their social, emotional, and life circumstances (School Social Work Association of America, 2022). More specifically, social workers conduct mental health assessments, respond to crises in emergencies, and connect students and their families to community resources such as emergency housing, food programs, or healthcare (U.S. Bureau of Labor Statistics, 2022). School social workers report feeling overwhelmed by caseloads and culturally diverse school environments, making it challenging to implement empirically supported practices (Horton & Prudencio, 2022). Recommendations for best practices include increased training for social workers to take a more collaborative role within the schools, understanding the dynamics of the various groups, and how to work together to make systemic change.

Speech and Language Pathologist. Another professional that provides services outside school environments, a speech-language pathologist (S.L.P.), plays a crucial role in the school setting. S.L.P.s work with students through prevention, assessment, intervention, and individual education planning input within the school setting (American Speech-Language-Hearing Association, 2022). While S.L.P.s are equipped to conduct student assessments, they often rely on outcomes from standardized testing to identify students needing service (Flucher-Rood et al., 2018). S.L.P.s are another professional at the table to collaborate with faculty, student support services, and administration to meet students' needs.

Physical Therapist. While physical therapy might be a practice seen more often in hospitals, private practice, or rehabilitation centers, they are also viewed as a crucial member of school-based teams. School-based physical therapists provide appropriate services for students with disabilities to prepare them for future education, employment, and independent living (American Physical Therapy Association, 2022). Should students struggle with adapting to activities within a typical school day (i.e. using the playground, climbing stairs, walking over various terrains), a physical therapist may assess the student, identifying areas to intervene. Assessment results are communicated to the school in adapting a student's individual education plan, accounting for possible physical therapy services to aid the student in fully engaging in the school environment (Kaminker et al., 2004).

Occupational Therapist. Like the role of physical therapists, occupational therapists based in the school provide services to students in need to ensure they can take part in everyday school-based activities. School-based activities related to fine motor development span from handwriting and scissor abilities to functionally using utensils or opening lunch containers. Occupational therapists engage in student observation, assessment, and continual evaluation. They develop recommendations and treatment plans which are then implemented into the student's individual education plan. Furthermore, they educate students, parents, and teachers about the needs of the students, providing recommendations for accommodations or educating on exercises and stretches that may be helpful outside of therapy sessions. Occupational therapists regularly consult with school teams to meet the needs of students and encourage positive student outcomes (Villeneuve, 2009).

Using ASE to Change the School Environment

Effecting change throughout the school environment begins with providing a foundation of ASE throughout the school system. Such can be accomplished through professional development workshops, then reinforced within consultation. The workshops provide a mindfulness curriculum in addition to social and emotional learning dialogue prompts (Molina et al., 2022), which is reinforced through consultation grounded in embracing curiosity, compassion, connectedness, and co-regulation through each interaction and modeled through dialogical connection within consultation. An embodiment of these tenets leads to full capacity of contribution.

Given that the principal usually yields the most power within the school system, the school counselor must utilize ASE to form collaborative relationships rooted in advocacy and shared goals related to student outcomes. School counselors can use their comprehensive guidance curriculum, which is informed by data and grounded in ASE, to demonstrate a plan for each school year. By being grounded in ASE, the comprehensive curriculum presents the theory of change, identifying how each intervention tier relates to the student's experience in the here and now. Tier one intervention, seen through classroom guidance lessons, is focused on building students' internal capacities to promote the betterment of life outcomes. As discussed in Chapter five, these internal capacities are linked to positive student outcomes such as increased attendance, academic achievement, and decreased discipline referrals. Those students who struggle with the tier one intervention are then encouraged to participate in tier two intervention, small group counseling, focused on continuing to build those internal capacities but allowing for more space to explore the student experience. Tier three intervention refers to short-term individual counseling. The school counselor embraces the five C's of ASE in each tier. Presenting a semester plan, as informed by school-based data, grounded in ASE, with identified outcomes related to student success, provides a tool to gain principal support and buy-in. When these plans are created collaboratively, the principal's contribution increases commitment.

In training others, counselors encourage school stakeholders to embrace curiosity. Curiosity relates to the counselor's empathetic ability, the willingness to be open with students and stakeholders, and comprehend unique circumstances related to the environment. In training others to be leaders within the school, counselors encourage leaders to engage in curiosity, listen empathetically to what others in the environment have to say, and fully understand that, regardless of truth, what is communicated is the truth of that individual's experience. Leaders can be taught to utilize language that encourages dialogue of other experiences. For example, a principal may ask a teacher, "What did you do differently that led to successful outcomes this week?" While dialogue can change, the key component is that leaders utilizing the ASE modality care about the response, leading to compassion.

Considering curiosity specifically from the context of the school system, the school counselor needs to understand what drives each system member's behavior. For example, A.P.s often report feeling that discipline-based decisions are consistent with the system as opposed to their training or prior professional experiences. Supporting A.P.s in understanding the school system's environmental context and their own experiences and training is essential for change. An A.P. can have every intention of bettering the environment for students, but getting swept up in an often overwhelming role can lead them towards assimilation rather than advocating for change and taking action to see that change occur. Without these supports, the system cannot evolve, remaining homeostatic as people of power enter the system and assimilate to the current standard.

While in practice, compassion, leaders validate the various experiences communicated to them by those within their environment. However, in that validation does not come blind acceptance. A leader can understand each side of a "he said, she said" argument that leads two students to the assistant principal's (A.P.) office. Each student had an experience whereby they believed they were justified in their responses. While validating that experience is essential, so is mediating the information. Considering Rapoport's rules (see Chapter 2, Table 2.1), a conversation may look like this:

Student 1: *They started it! They said mean comments, and his arm came flying towards me!*

Student 2: I did not. They started it! They wouldn't stop talking! And they hit me first!

A.P.: It sounds like you both have different perspectives on how this fight started and who should be responsible. Rather than focusing on who is responsible, we need to understand what led each of you to respond with violence.

Student 1: Because they attacked me!

A.P.: When we feel attacked, it is natural to respond with strong feelings. Sometimes we can feel attacked just by words. This leads us to feel sad and angry. Before you both started physically fighting, what was happening in the classroom that led to such strong emotions?

As seen within this vignette, the A.P. communicates curiosity and compassion, even in a situation that typically results in punitive measures. If both parties feel supported and validated, they are more likely to view their roles in the situation and identify personal goals centered around their strengths. Leaders must also be mindful of co-regulation and aware of their social and emotional capacities to regulate. For example, counselors and leaders utilizing an ASE leadership modality can also increase their social and emotional learning skill sets to better co-regulate within their environment. That is, they can internally practice and strengthen capacities of emotional intelligence, which includes identifying thoughts and emotions, understanding these emotions, and managing them within us and others (Mayer et al., 2000). This reflexivity encourages leaders to consider their practices, evaluate their efficacy, and make necessary changes.

Should most situations be approached with this spirit, members of the school environment would inherently feel more connected to one another. Connectedness allows leaders to assess the school environment adequately. Students thrive when in an environment in which they feel safe and secure. Alternatively, when disconnected, students are often disengaged, fearful of not feeling rooted in their environment, and often display maladaptive behaviors such as not doing homework or acting out. Connectedness allows the counselor or school leader to know what areas within the environment warrant intervention. For example, disconnection between students and teachers may result in students acting out behaviorally within the classroom and teachers' increased dissatisfaction. Seeing this disconnect, counselors and principals can intervene to mediate the relationship between these two highly connected groups, advocating for student needs within the environment while attending to the needs of teachers and supporting their ability to provide quality experiences for their students.

Finally, the culmination of these consultation efforts results in contribution. The base of any leadership endeavor is foundationally supported by the desire to improve the school environment through curiosity, compassion, co-regulation, and connectedness. Contribution is not motivated by inherent wants and needs. Instead, it is informed by the needs of the students, leading from a socially just capacity.

Conclusion

Counselors are encouraged to work with other members of the school environment to aid in the creation of safe and stable social conditions by which effective learning can take place (Lemberger-Truelove & Bowers, 2019). Counselors can provide professional development workshops and consultation efforts to key stakeholders outlined in this chapter to aid in their personal actualization of internal capacities, fostering the development of co-regulation, which is the crux for environmental change within ASE. When working for the betterment of students, all stakeholders need to be on the same page. All school system members must be allowed to practice skill sets that highlight their strengths. The environmental impact of ASE promotes the delicate balance of responding to the complex needs of the environment as well capacities of all members within that environment (Bowers & Lemberger, 2016). This chapter explored the various subsystems within the school environment, identifying how ASE can encourage environmental change. While there is an inherent focus on co-regulation, the following chapters will dive further into the concept of internal capacities, which speaks to the areas of growth for all stakeholders.

References

Agresta, J. (2004). Professional role perceptions of school social workers, psychologists, and counselors. *Children & Schools*, *26*(3), 151–163.

American Physical Therapy Association. (2022). School based physical therapy. www.apta.org/your-practice/practice-models-and-settings/school-based-physical-therapy. Retrieved September 11, 2020.

American School Counselor Association (ASCA) (2019). *ASCA standards for school counselor preparation programs*. www.schoolcounselor.org/getmedia/573d7c2c-1622-4d25-a5ac-ac74d2e614ca/ASCA-Standards-for-School-Counselor-Preparation-Programs.pdf

American Speech-Language-Hearing Association. (2022). Roles and Responsibilities of Speech-Language Pathologists in Schools. www.asha.org/policy/pi2010-00317/#:~:text=SLPs%20become%20key%20players%20in,are%20integrated%20within%20a%20school. Retrieved September 11, 2022.

Bowers, H., & Lemberger, M. E. (2016). A person-centered humanistic approach to performing evidence-based school counseling research. Person-Centered & Experiential Psychotherapies, 15(1), 55–66. https://doi:10.1080/14779757.2016.1139502

Brigman, G. & Webb, L. (2010). *Student Success Skills: Classroom manual* (3rd ed.). Boca Raton, FL: Atlantic Education Consultants.

Bureau of Labor Statistics. (2022). Occupational Outlook Handbook, Kindergarten and Elementary School Teachers, at www.bls.gov/ooh/education-training-and-library/kindergarten-and-elementary-school-teachers.htm (visited September 10, 2022).

Cansoy, R., Parlar, H., & Polatcan, M. (2020). Collective teacher efficacy as a mediator in the relationship between instructional leadership and teacher commitment. *International journal of leadership in education*, 1–19.

Carver-Thomas, D., & Darling-Hammond, L. (2017). Teacher turnover: Why it matters and what we can do about it. *Learning Policy Institute*.

Chin, J. M. C. (2007). Meta-analysis of transformational school leadership effects on school outcomes in Taiwan and the USA. *Asia Pacific Education Review*, *8*(2), 166–177.

Christian, D. D., & Brown, C. L. (2018). Recommendations for the role and responsibilities of school-based mental health counselors. *Journal of School-Based Counseling Policy and Evaluation*, *1*(1), 26–39.

Dahir C. A., Burnham J. J., Stone C. B., Cobb N. (2010). Principals as partners: Counselors as collaborators. NASSP Bulletin, 94(4), 286–305. https://doi.org/10.1177/0192636511399899

Dollarhide, C. T., & Lemberger, M. E. (2006). "No Child Left Behind": implications for school counselors. *Professional School Counseling*, 295–304.

Fulcher-Rood, K., Castilla-Earls, A. P., & Higginbotham, J. (2018). School-based speech-language pathologists' perspectives on diagnostic decision making. *American Journal of Speech-Language Pathology*, *27*(2), 796–812.

Horton, K. B., & Prudencio, A. (2022). School Social Worker Performance Evaluation: Illustrations of Domains and Components from the National Evaluation Framework for School Social Work Practice. *Children & Schools*.

Howard, R., & Ford, J. (2007). The roles and responsibilities of teacher aides supporting students with special needs in secondary school settings. *Australasian Journal of Special Education*, *31*(1), 25–43.

Kaminker, M. K., Chiarello, L. A., O'Neil, M. E., & Dichter, C. G. (2004). Decision making for physical therapy service delivery in schools: A nationwide survey of pediatric physical therapists. *Physical Therapy*, *84*(10), 919–933.

Kim, K. R., & Seo, E. H. (2018). The relationship between teacher efficacy and students' academic achievement: A meta-analysis. *Social Behavior and Personality: an international journal*, *46*(4), 529–540.

Lemberger-Truelove, M. E., & Bowers, H. (2019). An Advocating Student-within-Environment approach to school counseling. In C. T. Dollarhide & M. E. Lemberger-Truelove (Eds.), *Theories of school counseling for the 21st century* (pp. 266–294). Oxford.

Lewis, T., Jones, K. D., Militello, M., & Meisenhelder, R. (2022). A clear and consistent focus on students: Principals' perceptions of the role of school counselors. *Journal of School Leadership*, *32*(1), 3–26.

Lowery, K., Quick, M., Boyland, L., Geesa, R. L., & Mayes, R. D. (2018). It wasn't mentioned and should have been: Principals' preparation to support comprehensive school counseling. *Journal of Organizational and Educational Leadership, 3*(2), 1–30.

Mayer, J. D., & Cobb, C. D. (2000). Educational policy on emotional intelligence: Does it make sense? *Educational Psychology Review, 12*, 163–183.

McLeskey, J., Tyler, N. C., & Saunders Flippin, S. (2004). The supply of and demand for special education teachers: A review of research regarding the chronic shortage of special education teachers. *The Journal of Special Education*, *38*(1), 5–21.

Méndez, I., Martínez-Ramón, J. P., Ruiz-Esteban, C., & García-Fernández, J. M. (2020). Latent profiles of burnout, self-esteem and depressive symptomatology among teachers. *International Journal of Environmental Research and Public Health*, *17*(18), 6760.

Minuchin, S. (1974). *Families and Family Therapy*. London: Tavistock

Molina, C. E., Lemberger-Truelove, M. E., & Zieher, A. K. (2022). School counselor consultation effects on teachers' mindfulness, stress, and relationships. *Professional School Counseling*, *26*(1a), 2156759X221086749.

Newman, D. S., Hazel, C. E., Barrett, C. A., Chaudhuri, S. D., & Fetterman, H. (2018). Early-career school psychologists' perceptions of consultative service delivery: The more things change, the more they stay the same. *Journal of Educational and Psychological Consultation*, *28*(2), 105–136.

Nguyen, T. D., Pham, L. D., Crouch, M., & Springer, M. G. (2020). The correlates of teacher turnover: An updated and expanded meta-analysis of the literature. *Educational Research Review*, p. *31*, 100355.

School Social Work Association of America. (2022). Role of school social worker. www.sswaa.org/school-social-work. Retrieved September 11, 2022.

Villeneuve, M. (2009). A critical examination of school-based occupational therapy collaborative consultation. *Canadian Journal of Occupational Therapy*, *76*(1_suppl), 206–218.

Webster, K., & Litchka, P. (2020). Planning for Effective School Leadership: Teachers' Perceptions of the Leadership Skills and Ethical Behaviors of School Principals. *Educational Planning*, *27*(1), 31–47.

Williams, J. A. III, Lewis, C., Starker Glass, T., Butler, B. R., & Hoon Lim, J. (2020). The discipline gatekeeper: Assistant principals' experiences with managing school discipline in urban middle schools. Urban Education. Advance online publication. https://doi.org/10.1177/0042085920908913

4

THE PRACTICE OF ADVOCATING STUDENT-WITHIN-ENVIRONMENT

Matthew E. Lemberger-Truelove

Although each person is always a student, there is a special signature to the experience of being a student in a formal school environment. The broad intention of a school is to provide various conditions for each student to develop in personally and socially useful ways. Unfortunately, not all schooling conditions are supportive and, instead, students are often confronted by deleterious conditions. Both helpful and injurious experiences in schools result in learning. In turn, learning opportunities are internalized and shared back into the school and societal environments.

For school counselors, the inevitability and complexity of learning require intervention foci that are both compliant and additive. Interventions are compliant when they are germane to the cultural, environmental, and circumstantial condition of the student. Almost paradoxically, interventions must consistently apprehend these relevancies while also stretching the student in novel ways. Lev Vygotsky alluded to this when he posited the "*zone of proximal development*" more than a century ago; that is, learning occurs in that space between the prior unmediated capacities of the learner and the introduction to experiences that encourage new vistas of development (Zaretiski, 2009).

Advocating Student-within-Environment (ASE) is a school counseling-specific theory intended to describe students as learners, schools as systems, and how school counselors can best support the development of all participants in educational systems as interacting determinants of experience (Lemberger, 2010; Lemberger & Hutchison, 2014; Lemberger-Truelove & Bowers, 2019). Utilizing manualized counseling protocols, advocacy activities pointed at various social systems, and spontaneous counseling dialogue and behaviors, ASE-informed

DOI: 10.4324/9781003312871-4

school counselors intervene both with students and adult stakeholders in corresponding ways such that individual capacities ripen into co-regulatory experiences and outcomes.

As mentioned in previous chapters, ASE is not necessarily a collection of counseling techniques; rather, it is a theoretical overlay that can be applied to almost any classic or emergent school counseling practice. Specifically, ASE is a steadfast concern with how personal and social capacities can be cultivated in ways that result in improved outcomes for students and others in the school environment as interacting determinants of experience. This conceptual focus suggests that school counseling interventions must be relevant to the student and school context alike, which can be challenging given that these entities might not always exist in concert with the other.

It is assumed that interventions inspired by ASE can have multiple outcomes for the student and the school system given the focus pertains to amplifying the prior conditions of experience, as opposed to the pursuit of fixed or even specific goals. Certainly, specific outcomes can be accomplished using ASE, but given the labyrinthine nature of schools and the complexity of the person within various systems of influence, it is more prudent for school counseling to aim at general and flexible capacities rather than distinct results. This position is liberating in various ways, as it suggests that it is the student's capacity to develop and that such development can continue to evolve in helpful ways beyond the intervention. In this way, the ASE school counselor is not the sole arbitrator of the intervention or the outcome but another additive determinant of experience with the student and school environment.

The Structures of ASE Interventions

More than two decades before this current chapter was written, I (Matthew) found myself as a school counseling practicum student in a high school. I was assigned to work with a freshman who was experiencing a variety of academic struggles. Many of the ideas found in ASE today were percolating in my mind, and yet I wasn't always the most consistent practitioner in implementing the acme of ASE with students. Nonetheless, this early professional experience was a watershed moment and became an important influence on the structure of ASE related interventions.

The student described constant anxiety as he neared a state-mandated academic test. At the time in Florida, passing each section of these high-stakes tests was necessary to move on to the next academic grade. My intention was to introduce relevant and accessible strategies for learning. We practiced several strategies, but he was particularly drawn to mnemonics (i.e. prompts that aid in information retention and memory retrieval). I knew that working memory is critical to learning and an executive functioning skill associated with various desirable personal and learning outcomes for children and adolescents (Otero et al., 2014).

He left an individual meeting one afternoon particularly excited about a mnemonic strategy we practiced. I recall vividly how he expressed his excitement to use it in his next class. To my dismay, he didn't return to see me the next week as he had customarily done for more than a month prior. I then saw him as he was finishing his lunch and I asked him how he had been and briefly asked about his progress with the mnemonics. His response was chilling. He said, "You know. It didn't work. I sat in class waiting to use it. The teacher just never did anything in class where I could use it. I decided not to come back to counseling with you. School is already hard enough for me. Why should I learn new things with you if they don't help me? Other kids don't need to learn these things. They just get it. I don't get it if I try new things or if I do the same old thing, so why try something new?"

I found myself genuinely impressed with his logic. I was also disappointed that this was his experience. As he walked away to his next class, my thoughts then pivoted to his teacher, "What must she be thinking? She let him out of class and there were no observable differences. Maybe the only observable difference was that her distressed student is further dispirited."

It then hit me. There were probably no less than ten or more times that the teacher said or did something in class when the student could have used a mnemonic or one of the other skills we worked on in our times together. Further, the teacher could have made these opportunities more explicit had she known how to specifically prompt and reinforce one of the student's strategies. At this moment, it was clear that the student and teacher were co-determinants of experience and related outcomes. It was clear to me the importance of reflexive interventions.

Reflexive interventions occur when the school counselor connects the capacities of the student with the conditions of the school environment. The acme reflexive intervention occurs when the school counselor connects with the student in such a way that the intervention helps cultivate one or more capacities in the student, and those capacities are further connected to the behaviors and conditions in the school. For example, a school counselor can work with a student on the executive function of emotional regulation (Zelazo & Cunningham, 2007). While protecting the privacy of the specific student, the school counselor can then work with that student's classroom teacher to fortify emotional regulation. In this manner, the intervention operates with the student and teacher (as a representative of the school environment) as a co-determining system, as different than a deficit to be remedied in either the student or teacher discretely.

Although school counselors who adopt the ASE approach are encouraged to deliver reflexive interventions targeted at both students and people in their various systems (often teachers or other influential adults), it is feasible to work directly with one entity and assume that such efforts will affect other players in the system. For example, one of my early experiences as a first-year professional school counselor occurred between a student who came to see me wanting to change math teachers. After a few minutes of conversation, it was evident that her concern with this teacher reflected relational dynamics with older female authorities (especially those who resembled her grandmother, who was her caregiver). While her veteran teacher was unwilling to consult with me, the student and I worked on approaches to regulate her reactivity to the teacher and remain engaged in the instruction. The focus of the work was the Student-within-Environment, which in turn affected her performance in the class and subsequently affected her relationship with her grandmother.

The reality for many school counselors is that they are outpaced by the critical needs in schools, with student caseloads that often exceed recommendations and empirical evidence (ASCA, 2019; Woods & Domina, 2014) and outstanding student learning and mental health needs (DeKruyf et al., 2013). The demanding nature of reflexive interventions might seem infeasible, yet, the generative manner that such approaches can affect total systems might merit investment and sacrifice.

Additionally, school counselors might incur resistance, especially from school personnel who are also overwhelmed with responsibilities and who are often given messages that they are singularly responsible for the plight of a student or the overall conditions of education. For example, one type of reflexive intervention endorsed by ASE theory is when a school counselor performs one or more classroom guidance activities (i.e. psycho educational and counseling approaches targeting entire classes of students and their teacher[s]) where the teacher actively engages in the in-class experience and often further participates in consultation with the school counselor before or after the in-class activities. The intention is varied, including generating investment in the teacher and priming skills to be exposed to students and to the teacher (that can be used by that teacher in subsequent classroom experiences). There have been several ASE empirical studies that substantiate the value of these reflexive interventions (e.g. Bowers et al., 2020; Lemberger et al., 2018(b); Molina et al., 2022), yet the duration and commitment can be daunting. Alternatively, persisting without substantive change can be even more daunting; as such, the school counselor can advocate the potential for change that is mutually gratifying to students and educators over longer periods of time and with myriad desirable outcomes. In fact, qualitative studies of ASE interventions have yielded surprising and unintended outcomes for teachers, where the benefits were not only felt in their classrooms and with students but also in their personal lives beyond the school environment (Molina et al., under review).

Anticipated Student and School Environment Outcomes

Foremost, ASE is a social justice approach to school counseling in the tradition of the various liberation psychologies (Chávez et al., 2016). In this manner, social change occurs through empowering various individuals within systems. The individual (student) is not understood as an automaton but rather as a co-determinant of personal and social experiences.

It appears like we're making contemporaneous decisions, but mental and physical actions are bound up in prior personal and social determinants. Our intuitions suggest a type of teleology where purposeful effort drives experience (rather than prior material causes), whereas ASE theory is more in line with teleonomy (Pittendrigh, 1958), which retains a goal-oriented denouement but concedes that natural and social forces mediate and shape outcomes for people and events. This posture suggests that the student emerges out of prior influences, yet the student still does have some volitional influence over one's experience within the environment.

When a student experiences new insight (learning) or new social conditions, it appears like personal development manifests as a consequence of personal insight. This is a dualistic way of thinking about student development that does not fully cohere with ASE. Instead, insight is experiential within a social context and thus embodied with varying magnitude of influence. The experience of development occurs as an embodied observation, which in turn affects contemporary experience and the trajectory of future learning. Development for the student (and school environment) is the observation of the experienced self (student) and reflexive observations of change in the school environment. School counseling, therefore, is the creation of the personal and social experiences that contribute to this appearance of development, which in turn affects the actual experience of the student and other people in the school environment.

School counseling intervention is thus a persistent process of priming. When working with the individual student, the school counselor does not pursue specific desirable schooling outcomes. Pursuing fixed goal completion is an alluring approach to school counseling practice, but it is infeasible, unsustainable, and ultimately disarming to the student. A specific outcome, like finding a specific solution to disagreements amongst peers, suggests that the past will replicate the future with perfect precision. Instead, it is more prudent to draw from past experiences and collaborate with the student so that the student can anticipate and respond with flexibility and adroitness. Correspondingly, the school counselor is in a persistent process of priming the relevant features found in the school environment. Are there conditions in the family or classroom context that contribute to peer conflict? Priming the student and school environment contributes to simpatico outcomes, even given the profound complexity of systems and the evolution that occurs across time in schools.

In some of the original ASE writings (Lemberger, 2010), the term student sapience was used to describe a deep wisdom in the design and operation of experience (Trowbridge, 2011). In the tradition of philosophers such as Baruch Spinoza (1677) and Metzinger (2004), sapience does not operate as a mental phenomenon outside of one's body or circumstance in the world; rather, it is an integrated and experiential way of being. This is to say, a student does not have to understand the total composition of experience or all consequences, but only that some intentional contribution to self and the environment affects outcomes.

This distinction is important for the psychological and social development of students. A school counselor does not necessarily anticipate that a kindergartener will be fully aware of the influences of poverty on their plight as a student, but a classroom activity on how to balance healthy sleep habits in challenging environments might help avert some biological delimiters and contribute to better schooling outcomes (Hayes & Bainton, 2020). The technical insights about sleep biology are less important than the experiential perspective.

In practice, the outcome of student sapience reflects the emerging term allostasis, that is, how the student accomplishes efficient regulation of needs and capacities prior to incidents when those needs and capacities are required for survival or thriving (Sterling, 2012). Regulation of the self is not to be confused with accomplishing some hypothetical homeostatic state, rather, it is a perpetual predictive pursuant of outcomes (Schulkin et al., 1994). School counselors connect with students in a manner that encourages the cultivation of capacities that are usable in various ways. There is some evidence in support of these claims in the empirical literature in support of ASE. For example, Lemberger and colleagues trained school counselors to deliver psycho educational content to entire classrooms of students and teachers and found that the intervention that focused on social and cognitive skills contributed to social and emotional learning outcomes in addition to improvements in academic achievement tests (Lemberger-Truelove et al., 2018). The content of the psycho educational activities was not explicitly academic in nature, and yet changes in personal and social development cohered with math and reading achievement.

Outcomes at the student level are primary, although the student is never understood as the single or even primary cause of experience or the school environment. The student in the center of change ensures that advocacy on behalf of the student is always relevant to the emerging capacities and values of the student, not the school system or even well-intended school counselor as arbitrators. Just as students are understood as co-determinants of change, agents in schools are expected to ameliorate outcomes that must cohere with the immediate experience of the student.

In practice, accompanying any anticipated outcomes in students, the school counselor must advocate for changes at the school level. Outcomes can vary based on the recipient or circumstance. For example, in some cases, merely providing empirical insights into how ethnic discrimination affects academic outcomes and disciplinary practices can result in radical new perspectives. More invasive interventions might require the school counselor to work extensively with educators or policymakers to challenge implicit biases pertaining to groups of students.

The highest aspiration of ASE is to manifest co-regulated contribution that is shared amongst as many relevant players in the school environment, including but not limited to the student. Contribution (as one of the five Cs of ASE theory) is an outcome and a practice where the schooling process includes tangible activities of personal and social liberation. For example, students who were formerly participants in a grief group might later serve as support agents for students in subsequent years. Teachers who engage in consultation with school counselors might be recruited to advocate for gender and identity equality policies at the district level.

ASE Counseling and Advocacy Relationships

Across all forms of counseling, scholars have found that a quality relationship shared between counselor and client is predictive of desirable outcomes (Wampold & Budge, 2012). Many clinicians misconstrue these findings in some pollyannish manner. Instead, adherents to the ASE approach conceptualize healing relationships in a very specific manner. When interacting with any agent in a school, the school counselor approaches each new moment with a radical curiosity that is mediated by a sense of connectedness and compassion and aimed at personal and social contribution. See Table 4.1.

At the core, there is an uncompromising belief in the potential of the student (and school environment) for growth (Yeager & Dweck, 2020). This recognition that changes and development are inevitable is not confused with asserting or

TABLE 4.1 Advocating Student-within-Environment Relational Map

Student	*within*	*Environment*	*Educators & policy makers, guardians & family members, social & cultural systems*
Curiosity Connectedness Compassion	Co-regulation (endogenous) Contribution (allostasis)	Curiosity Connectedness Compassion	

pushing a top-down outcome for the student (or school); instead, this is a steadfast commitment by the school counselor to share in the unique circumstance of the student and their environment.

The exemplar ASE informed relationship is endogenous. Endogenous is defined as "within" or "increasing by internal growth," which reflects the word "within" in Advocating Student-within-Environment. The counselor strives to experience *within* the student's perspective and context. The K12 student, as a child and adolescent, is emerging from the various influences of one's biology, one's experience, and one's positionality in the various environments that one inhabits. Similarly, the counselor operates *within* the various social contexts that constitute or influences the school environment. With both the student and features of the school environment, the *within* posture is not stagnant; rather, it is assumed that development emerges when the school counselor engages the student (or school) with curiosity, connectedness, and compassion, that is, in turn, co-regulated in the school environment and might lead to mutual contribution.

There is a double-sidedness to an endogenous orientation as a school counselor. *Within* suggests a sincere commitment to the student or school as each is and yet further suggests that within both the student and school are more capacities and possibilities than are often known or expressed. For example, the practice of cultural broaching (Day-Vines et al., 2021), which is when the counselor engages in a direct and respectful conversation about the client's various intersecting identity positions, from an ASE perspective is both prizing the student's cultural influences and yet pushing for the most facilitative version of those cultural forces. In this manner, each interchange prizes the determinants of experience, present perceptions and predilections, and future possibilities.

Vygotsky (1978) wisely offered, "the method is simultaneously prerequisite and product, the tool and the result of the study" (p.65). The endogenous (within) relationship is what the school counselor presents but also the anticipated outcomes for the student and school environment. The school counselor utilizes curiosity which will stoke curiosity in the student, which will, in turn, serve the student and school environment in ways that extend beyond the initial counseling relationship. In similar ways, the school counselor will embody connectedness and compassion, and the mere experience will prime these generative capacities in students. How these various capacities expressed will be unique to each student, as the counselor holds no preconceived notion or expectation of their manifestation.

The counseling literature has matured over the decades, with an advancing concern with issues of diversity, equity, and inclusion. These are important for the various mental health professions including school counseling and foundational for ASE theory. This said, the preponderance of the diversity, equity, and inclusion literature often discusses counselor values and less often articulates the praxis necessary to produce such laudable ends. ASE takes a hard stand on how a school counselor can pursue justice in and beyond school systems. Sustainable change comes from within co-regulating individuals and systems. The school counselor is both within the school system and yet something different as a student advocate. Therefore, the school counselor can identify the mechanisms to change the system while recruiting the student to be a self-advocate of change that is, therefore, more likely to be relevant and persistent.

From an ASE perspective, the school counselor always intervenes with relevance to the student and the school environment as co-determinants of desired outcomes. What dictates the intervention focus are the assessed needs and the anticipated magnitude of effect. There are occasions when the structural issues in the school are so profound that it is most reasonable to initiate intervention at the school level. The school counselor remains steadfast to the needs and capacities of the student, and yet the greatest change for that student most likely will result from support provided at the school system level. For example, if a teacher is experiencing debilitating stress that is affecting classroom pedagogy, the school counselor certainly works with the teacher but does so insofar as the efforts towards stress reduction contributes to classroom climate and student support. Alternatively, the school counselor might choose to intervene directly with one or a group of students based on personal or social struggles. In focusing on the individual student's need, the ASE-informed school counselor intervenes with environmental resources and the context in mind.

Regardless of the intervention focus, the development of the Student-within-Environment is the Archimedean point for the school counselor. Social systems greatly influence the experience of the student, and yet the persistence of relevant systemic change is catalyzed in the individual student. In the spirit of liberation approaches to social justice, the ASE-informed school counselor conceives of the K12 student as newly emerging and therefore has the greatest time and influence on the future permutations of the social environments.

Personal liberation and social justice are baked into ASE. There is an oscillation between practice activities directed at the student or at the various constituent aspects of the school environment, with the ideal interventions simultaneously engaging as many individual participants as possible in the school environment. This position does not suggest that students are solely responsible for confronting discriminatory, oppressive, or generally unhelpful forces in schools but it does propound that student engagement is necessary for any systems change to be relevant, sustainable, and adaptive as threatening personal and social forces evolve over time and across circumstances.

ASE Informed School Counseling Behaviors

As stated, ASE is not a mere assemblage of techniques that a school counselor uses to work with students or members of a school environment. Instead, ASE is an orientation that is concerned with cultivating student capacities and creating just and complementary schooling environments. In this way, the theory is concerned with amplifying diversity, prizing a diversity of student experiences, and valuing a rich ecological diversity in a school that might provide ample opportunities for student development.

While ASE cannot be whittled down into techniques, it can inform specific school counseling behaviors. It has been used in manualized psycho educational interventions delivered to whole classrooms or small groups of students (e.g. Lemberger & Clemens, 2012; Webb et al., 2019) and teachers (Molina et al., 2022). Furthermore, it can be used in various formats such as small and large group work, individual and planning activities in schools, and consultation, collaboration, and advocacy in schools. ASE practice integrates into various delivery frameworks including experiential activities, verbal counseling, and psycho educational activities. Although there are various applications, the practice of ASE is truly a theory intended to be a conceptual orientation that dictates spontaneous helping behaviors throughout the school environment.

The five Cs (curiosity, connectedness, co-regulation, compassion, and contribution) of ASE are merely mnemonic devices intended for a school counselor's practice behaviors. These devices are not the full extent of intervention behaviors; instead, almost any appropriate school counseling behavior that is concerned with cultivating student capacities while advocating for more contributory environments is compatible with ASE theory. As such, ASE theory can be actualized using transtheoretical counseling skills or even nascent techniques more closely originated to ASE theory.

Curiosity

Curiosity is a "drive state for information" (Kidd & Hayden, p. 450); as a practice, curiosity is the non-evaluative expression of inquisitiveness about one's circumstance and experience. In this way, the outcome of curiosity is not the acquisition of an unchanging or ideal end; rather, curiosity is a persistent openness to ongoing development.

As an intervention focus, curiosity is foundational in establishing rapport with the student (or other recipients of school counseling services). More than merely capturing information about the student, the school counselor is eliciting and attending to the experiences of the student. Assumingly, when a student experiences curiosity from a school counselor, it introduces a new dimension of experience that is both germane to one's past determinants of experience and also pertinent to nascent experience. Curiosity expands the character of experience.

For example, consider the standard open-ended question often used by counseling practitioners. Open-ended questions are intended to elicit information from the client, generally requiring more than a simple response and generating client reflection. From an ASE perspective, open-ended questions elucidate how one is capable of responding with intention to one's influences (as self-within-environment).

"What did you have for breakfast this morning?" This example question is certainly open-ended, as it requires the respondent to answer with more than one or a few words. But this is not an example of a fully curious question, for it inadvertently compels the child to restrict their answer to what one eats. In so doing, the counselor is not curious about the student or the environment, as the student's family might be experiencing economic stressors and, therefore, not typically have access to breakfast. Not only is this question not curious, but it can also potentially rupture the trust of the student or incline the student to misrepresent experiences.

Alternatively, asking the student, "What are your typical morning rituals before school?" is more fully curious as the onus is on the student to detail information and priorities. The structure of this more curious question is specific enough for the counselor to generate relevant information and yet unfurled enough that the student's experience is centered.

A school counselor can generate curiosity in more directive ways. For example, in the Student Success Skills program that has been associated with ASE theory (Webb et al., 2019), there are many mantras that school counselors exercise with students that illustrate the practice of curiosity. One example mantra is, "Don't doubt your ability, try a different strategy." Although this phrase is a directive initiated by the school counselor, it embodies curiosity in that it encourages the student to consider one's various capacities. Further, it suggests that behaviors do not fully define one's total constitution, but rather there are other manifestations that are possible. Curiosity is concomitantly about one's prior determinants of experience and various permutations of new experience.

Connectedness

Connectedness is the experience of acceptance, safety, encouragement, and respect shared between the student and other member of the school environment (Resnick et al., 1997). Whereas one can be curious about an experience, connectedness pertains to the relational quality of that experience. Curiosity can be exempt from value while connectedness acknowledges the interrelatedness of experience and how necessary contributory relationships are for students and members of the school community.

Student: I don't like sitting in class with them... (pause) those kids and that teacher... (pause) they're all pretty stupid, and they treat me like I am stupid.

School Counselor: It is frustrating to have to be in place and with people where there is not a feeling of mutual respect.

In this short couplet, the school counselor utilized the classical counseling skill called reflection of feeling. A generic reflection of feeling only requires the school counselor to identify the student's most salient feeling and anchor it in some causal condition – you feel this, because. An ASE reflection of feeling pertaining to connectedness validates the student's experience while placing it in the context of the school environment. Here the student's frustration is experientially personal and yet provoked by what has occurred in the classroom.

One of my (Matthew) more memorable experiences as a school counselor was working with a sixth-grade boy named Michael. He was universally feared throughout the school by peers, teachers, and administrators. In fact, during my first week at this school, the principal was contemplating expulsion from the district as a consequence of persistent fighting. I asked the principal for one week to intervene as I knew a longer request would be met with resistance.

I watched Michael in his classroom, on the playground at recess, and at lunch. In each setting, he was either sleeping or in some extreme conflict with others. It didn't help that he was one largest sixth graders I have seen, almost eye-to-eye with me at six foot, three inches. On the playground, other kids cowered away in mortal dread. His relationships with teachers were equally adversarial, and each warned me that no matter how much kindness I extended, he would resist.

I didn't want to take total credence in the reports and the brief episodes I witnessed during my brief observations, yet after a few introductory statements, it was clear that he was unimpressed and there was no inherent connection between him and me. What came to mind was, "He might be large like an adult, but there is a kid housed in that impressive stature." Given the little bit of time I had with him before expulsion, his outstanding history, and the critical importance of supporting this young person, I tried something risky to inspire connectedness.

School counselor: I have been told that you have this amazing ability for new adults to try and talk with you, and you can sit there and be completely unaffected and unimpressed. As a school counselor, I always want students to do their best at what they are the best at doing. So, I am going to ask you a few questions, and I want you to continue to do what you do best, that is, sit there and not feel required to respond. Just like you have a talent for sitting there and not responding, I have a hidden talent too. Without you answering, I have a pretty good hunch to the answers of the questions I will ask you. So I ask, you sit, and then I answer. Cool?

Student: (nothing; except doing what he did best to adults).

School Counselor: Great!!! This seems to be working. Okay, I can imagine that it can be pretty lonely on the playground with no one wanting to play with you. I also imagine that those feelings of loneliness turn to anger pretty quickly, which could explain some of the fights.

Student: (smiling) How did you do that?

This story has many more details when I tell it to my graduate students, and I generally suggest to them not to try this approach. I don't typically recommend assuming you know your K12 student's experiences, but in this case, I had a real deadline with high stakes consequences for his life. What occurred after was that I told Michael that what I did was a kind of magic that we all possess. The magic was empathy. For the next few weeks, he and I worked on anticipating the reactions of others and responding with empathy. Certainly, there were occasions when he was being mistreated, but creating connections in these cases made him more able to control his internal experience and instigate change in those around him.

This story illustrates the conceptual relatedness between ASE and social and emotional learning (S.E.L.) (Elias et al., 1997), which are competencies necessary to recognize and manage emotions, pursue goals, appreciate the perspectives of others, and interface constructively with others. From an ASE perspective, feelings of connectedness through S.E.L. is not a prescription for student compliance, rather it

> refers to students' experiential discernment and the inclination to suspend pernicious identification or evaluation of these experiences. Stated otherwise, students from disenfranchised communities do not accept inadequate or deleterious social conditions; instead, using social-emotional and mindfulness strategies, they accept their cognitive and affective reactions and respond with clearer intentionality.
>
> *(Lemberger-Truelove, et al., 2018(a), p. 299)*

Co-regulation

As a school counseling practice, co-regulation is the interface of two or more self-aware, intentional individuals who draw from various cultural, social, and personal sources to inform and influence behavior (McCaslin, 2009). For example, a self-regulated individual can monitor, predict, shift, and direct one's internal and external experiences, whereas operating out of co-regulation one extends beyond one's inner experiences and places total experience in a broader social and historical context. "What have you done to improve yourself?" is different than "How have you pursued your goals given the influences of (insert circumstance)?"

Recently I was working with a group of teachers at an elementary school. As we concluded a consultation session on teachers' stress responses in the classroom, we saw a teacher's aide disseminating snacks to the students. One young boy was sitting at his desk banging a cup vigorously on his desk, yelling,

"I want my milk, I want my milk…!" The teacher looked over at me, and we had the following interchange:

Teacher: So, Dr. Expert, what would you do with this little darling?

Me: (walking over to the student) I can hear from your song that you're really enthused to get your milk. But I wonder, how can the teacher pour the milk into your cup if you are banging it upside down on the table?

Student: My milk would be all over the floor (as he turned his cup right side up).

In this episode, it would be easy to be recruited into the student's discontentment and over-eagerness. It would also be easy to disregard the student's intentions or the habits of the classroom. Co-regulation engages the attentional and inhibitory control necessary for volition while not disregarding other students or desirable classroom procedures.

Returning to another S.S.S. mantra, school counselors are encouraged to expose students to the phrase, "Little by little, bit by bit, I am improving every day." Students are encouraged to notice and celebrate small yet important changes that contribute to larger aspirations. This can be a co-regulatory lesson for students if the school counselor prompts the students to consider environmental factors that contribute to or inhibit ongoing and intentional growth.

Compassion

For an ASE-inspired school counselor, compassion is the composed concern with either persistent or circumstantial feelings of suffering. The etymology of compassion is com (to be with) and passion (strong emotional connection). Compassion is a precursor to empathy, focused on ameliorating suffering or one's emotional reactivity. From an ASE perspective, compassion is a mechanism to break or slow down emotion-laden reactivity and introduce more co-regulated responsiveness.

In Chapter 1, the concept of co-determinants of experience was explicated. There are various social forces that contribute to contemporaneous experiences for students and other individuals in schools. For ASE theory, these are called governors. Governors do not fully dictate experience, but they are the ingredients that profoundly influence both opportunity and response. Compassion is a counterforce to the various personal and social governors of experience.

There are various strategies that the school counselor can use to vivify compassion when working with students or school personnel. A few examples include but are not limited to the following framing (Rothman & Salovey, 1997), priming (Bargh & Chartrand, 2014), and mindfulness (Bishop et al., 2004). In the case of mindfulness, there are various ASE intervention studies with students (Lemberger-Truelove et al., 2021) and teachers (Molina et al., 2022) to illustrate its utility. Rather than becoming passive and compliant, ASE mindfulness can help elicit one's reactions to governed experiences and respond with greater compassion to these responses.

In a similar way, school counselors can encourage compassion in teachers working with students. By reframing student expressions as governed responses to the determinants of experience, there can be greater connectedness and co-regulated intentionality in the classroom. Further, a teacher can extend compassion inward, especially when the tribulations of teaching are most grueling.

The spirit of compassion in the ASE approach is encapsulated in the following prompt provided to classroom teachers in a recent consultation intervention study (Lemberger-Truelove et al., in press):

> The purpose is neither to invalidate an experience or even provide new, more appealing alternatives. In the context of your experiences, any reaction is reasonable. Instead, we simply want to interrogate your inner experience and some of its influences, which might lead to you coming to accept the experience as one response (*acceptance)*. In this process of interrogation, other perspectives on experience might manifest (*discernment*). Again, the purpose is not to invalidate or replace, but curiosity in these alternatives might allow you to simultaneously appreciate the conditions of the initial experience while with nascent alternatives emerging, you can respond out of awareness of more options rather than reacting to the impression that there is only one experiential option feasible (*compassion for self and others*).

Contribution

The most aspirational intervention strategy in ASE theory is contribution, which is the curious, connected, co-regulated, and compassionate commitment to action. For the student, contribution includes how one responds to the determinants of experience in and beyond the school environment. For the adults in the school environment, contribution includes the explicit behaviors to advocate for student development.

Contribution also demands that the student and other members of the school community act in solidarity for the purposes of social change. This does not suggest compliance or assimilation, as ASE requires constant personal introspection and social revision; rather, there is a shared and general agreement to participate in tangible behaviors to improve the school climate.

The ASE informed school counselor must ardently ensure that contribution is not exploitative or trivial. The action of contribution must be mediated by the other elements of the five Cs. For example, a school counselor can partner with a teacher to eradicate ethnic and gender identity discrimination in the school. In so doing, the school counselor must consider one's own privileges and ally with that teacher and the various students the advocacy will affect.

Contribution demonstrates the liberation focus of ASE theory. The process is the outcome; engaging in liberating experiences ushers in liberation at the individual level while embracing the inevitable situatedness within various systems. A change in the student affects the school environment, just as changes in the school affect the student.

ASE and the Use of Time

Adherents of ASE theory prioritize direct counseling and education services that are intended to support students and the various adults in their lives. While these value-added services are privileged, many school counselors are mired by other indirect and administrative duties that can distance interventions from the desired targets. It is often helpful for the school counselor to think pragmatically about these other professional tasks. In differing ways, these activities affect the school environment, and therefore they have some potential influence on the experiences of students. As such, rather than unthinkingly resist and resent these opportunities, in the spirit of ASE, a school counselor should approach each task with the skill and perspective to amplify student opportunity and advocate for more contributory school environments.

This recommendation is neither an endorsement of inappropriate school counseling duties nor permission for school counselors to passively adopt an identity or practices that are removed from counseling and education. Instead, the suggestion is to re-imagine each moment in a school as a potential contribution to the determinants of experience students and the people in their lives. For example, while it is unequivocally inappropriate for a school administrator to use a school counselor as a standardized testing coordinator or proctor, I (Matthew) vividly recall a student who benefited from me occupying such a role. A student who I advised and who also participated in one of my small counseling groups was riddled with anxiety as the state mandated test approached. Upon seeing me walk into her classroom to disseminate the test materials, she smiled at me and said, "Just seeing you gave me confidence to make it through this test." Prior to this moment, I used such vituperation when I was told that I had to suspend my meetings with students and hand out test papers; but in that instance, I realized that that student received as much or more educational and emotional value from our shared smile as she did in any advising session or group meeting.

The use of a school counselor's time is so valuable. Deciding how to prioritize one's contribution to students and the total school environment can be layered and often dispiriting. Foremost, it is important to recognize that all cannot be accomplished at once and every action in a school affects the total school system, in varying ways and in differing magnitudes of influence. In this manner, what matters most is *how* one approaches each moment. From an ASE perspective, providing direct services to students matters, consulting with teachers and parents matters, maintaining data and self-reflective practices matters, and so on. What binds these different school counseling activities and usages of time together is the disposition of ASE; that is, the ASE school counselor is led by intention to cultivate student capacities and improve schooling opportunities in all possible moments, regardless of the setting or activity.

The ASE informed school counselor considers the likely magnitude of influence. No school counseling activity is zero-sum, yet the school counselor must be scrupulous how one's use of time yields the deepest and most sustainable germination. For example, a school counselor does not engage students in small group activities simply because the A.S.C.A. National Model suggests a certain percentage of time performing such a task. A school counselor does not deliver a psycho-educational activity as a reflection of one's passion for a certain topic. Rather, a school counselor invests time and commits to intervention because the related activities project more desirous outcomes.

Earlier in this chapter the phrase "Little by little, bit by bit, I am improving every day" was introduced as a mechanism to encourage students to recognize persistent growth and accomplishment. In the spirit of reflexive interventions, an ASE-inspired school counselor inverts this sagacious phrase and applies it to one's comprehensive school counseling program. With intention to amplify capacities of students and members of the school environment, over time and across various aspects of educational systems, school counselors incrementally contribute to people and systems better positioned to evolve and thrive.

References

American School Counselor Association. (2019). *ASCA National Model: A framework for school counseling programs* (4th ed.). Author.

Bargh, J. A., & Chartrand, T. L. (2014). Studying the mind in the middle: A practical guide to priming and automaticity research. In H. Reis & C. Judd (Eds.), *Research methods in social psychology*. Cambridge University Press.

Bishop, S. R., Lau, M., Shapiro, S., Carlson, L., Anderson, N. D., Carmody, J.,.... Devins, G. (2004). Mindfulness: A proposed operational definition. *Clinical Psychology: Science and Practice*, 11, 230–241. https://doi:10.1093/clipsy/bph077

Bowers, H., Lemberger-Truelove, M. E., Whitford, D. K. (2020). Kindergarteners are ready to learn: Executive functioning and social-emotional effects for a pilot school counseling intervention applying Advocating Student-within-Environment theory. *Journal of Humanistic Counseling 59*(1), 3–19. https://doi.org/10.1002/johc.12126

Chávez, T. A., Fernandez, I. T., Hipolito-Delgado, C. P., & Rivera, E. T. (2016). Unifying liberation psychology and humanistic values to promote social justice in counseling. *Journal of Humanistic Counseling, 55*(3), 166–182. https://doi.org/10.1002/johc.12032

Day-Vines, N. L., Cluxton-Keller, F., Agorsor, C., & Gubara, S. (2021). Strategies for broaching the subjects of race, ethnicity, and culture. *Journal of Counseling & Development, 99*(3), 348–357. https://doi.org/10.1002/jcad.12380

DeKruyf, L., Auger, R. W., & Trice-Black, S. (2013). The role of school counselors in meeting students' mental health needs: Examining issues of professional identity. *Professional School Counseling, 16*(5), 271–282. https://doi:10.1177/2156759X0001600502

Elias, M. J., Zins, J. E., Weissberg, R. P., Frey, K. S., Greenberg, M. T., Haynes, N. M., et al. (1997). *Promoting social and emotional learning: Guidelines for educators.* Association for Supervision and Curriculum Development.

Hayes, B., & Bainton, J. (2020). The impact of reduced sleep on school related outcomes for typically developing children aged 11–19: A systematic review. *School Psychology International, 41*(6), 569–594. https://doi.org/10.1177/014303432096113

Kidd, C., & Hayden, B. Y. (2015). The psychology and neuroscience of curiosity. *Neuron, 88*(3), 449–460. https://doi.org/10.1016/j.neuron.2015.09.010

Lemberger, M. E. (2010). Advocating Student-within-Environment: A humanistic theory for school counseling. *The Journal of Humanistic Counseling, Education and Development, 49,* 131–146. https://doi.org/10.1002/j.2161-1939.2010.tb00093.x

Lemberger, M. E., Carbonneau, K., Selig, J. P., & Bowers, H. (2018). The role of social-emotional mediators on middle school students' academic growth as fostered by an evidence-based intervention. *Journal of Counseling and Development, 96*(1), 27–40. https://doi.org/10.1002/jcad.12175

Lemberger, M. E., & Clemens, E. V. (2012). Connectedness and self–regulation as constructs of the Student Success Skills program in inner-city African American elementary students. *Journal of Counseling & Development, 90*(4), 450–458. https://doi:10.1002/j.1556- 6676.2012.00056.x

Lemberger, M. E., & Hutchison, B. (2014). Advocating Student-within-Environment: A humanistic approach for therapists to animate social justice in the schools. *Journal of Humanistic Psychology, 54,* 28-44. https://doi.org/10.1177/0022167816652750

Lemberger-Truelove, M. E., & Bowers, H. (2019). An Advocating Student-within-Environment approach to school counseling. In C. T. Dollarhide & M. E. Lemberger-Truelove (Eds.), *Theories of school counseling for the 21st century* (pp. 266–294). Oxford.

Lemberger-Truelove, M. E., Carbonneau, K. J., Atencio, D. J., Zieher, A. K., & Palacios, A. F. (2018). Self-regulatory growth effects for young children participating in a combined social and emotional learning and mindfulness-based intervention. *Journal of Counseling and Development, 96*(3) 289–302. https://doi:10.1002/j.1556-6676.2014.00000.x

Lemberger-Truelove, M. E., Ceballos, P. L., Molina, C. E., & Carbonneau, K. J. (2021). Growth in middle school students' curiosity, executive functioning, and academic achievement: A theory-informed SEL and MBI school counseling intervention. *Professional School Counselor, 24*(1b): 1–8. https://doi:10.1177/2156759X211007654

Lemberger-Truelove, M. E., Molina, C. E., Carbonneau, K. J., & Smith, M. (in press). Effects of school counselor consultation intervention on middle school teacher-student relationships, student curiosity, and teacher stress. *Professional School Counseling.*

McCaslin, M. (2009). Co-regulation of student motivation and emergent identity. *Educational Psychologist, 44*(2), 137–146. https://doi.org/10.1080/00461520902832384

Metzinger, T. (2004). *Being no one: The self-model theory of subjectivity.* MIT Press.

Molina, C. E., Ceballos, P. L., Lemberger-Truelove, M. E., Carbonneau, K. J., & Branch, M. L. (Under review). Phenomenological study of teachers' mindfulness and social and emotional learning experience after a school counselor led consultation intervention.

Molina, C. E., Lemberger-Truelove, M. E., & Zieher, A. K. (2022). School counselor consultation effects on teachers' mindfulness, stress, and relationships. *Professional School Counseling, 26*(1a), 1–9. https://doi.org/10.1177/2156759X221086749

Otero, T. M., Barker, L. A., & Naglieri, J. A. (2014). Executive function treatment and intervention in schools. *Applied Neuropsychology: Child, 3*(3), 205–214. https://doi.org/10.1080/21622965.2014.897903

Pittendrigh, C. S. (1958). Adaptation, natural selection and behaviour. In A. Roes & G. G. Simpson (Eds.), *Behaviour and evolution* (Vol. 1, pp. 390–416). Yale University Press.

Resnick, M. D., Bearman, P. S., Blum, R. W., Bauman, K. E., Harris, K. M., Jones, J., et al. (1997). Protecting adolescents from harm: Findings from the National Longitudinal Study on Adolescent Health. *Journal of American Medical Association, 278*(10), 823–832. https://doi:10.1001/jama.278.10.823

Rothman, A. J., & Salovey, P. (1997). Shaping perceptions to motivate healthy behavior: the role of message framing. *Psychological Bulletin, 121*(1), 3.

Schulkin, J., McEwen, B. S., & Gold, P. W. (1994). Allostasis, amygdala, and anticipatory angst. *Neuroscience & Biobehavioral Reviews, 18*(3), 385–396.

Spinoza, B. de (1677 [1994]) *The Ethics and Other Works* (trans. E. Curley). Princeton University Press.

Sterling, P. (2012). Allostasis: a model of predictive regulation. *Physiology & Behavior, 106*(1), 5–15. https://doi.org/10.1016/j.physbeh.2011.06.004

Trowbridge, R. (2011). Waiting for Sophia: 30 years of conceptualizing wisdom in empirical psychology. *Research in Human Development, 8*(2), 149–164. http://dx.doi.org/10.1080/15427609.2011.568872

Vygotsky, L. S. (1978). *Mind in society: The development of higher psychological processes*. Cambridge, MA: Harvard University Press.

Wampold, B. E., & Budge, S. L. (2012). The 2011 Leona Tyler Award Address: The relationship–and its relationship to the common and specific factors of psychotherapy. *The Counseling Psychologist, 40*(4), 601–623. https://doi:10.1177/0011000011432709

Webb, L., Brigman, G., Carey, J., Villares, E., Harrington, K., Wells, C., Sayer, A., & Chance, E. (2019). Results of a randomized controlled trial of Student Success Skills. *Journal of Counseling & Development, 97*(4), 398–408. https://doi.org/10.1002/jcad.12288

Woods, C. S., & Domina, T. (2014). The school counselor caseload and the high school-to–college pipeline. *Teachers College Record, 116*(10), 1–30. https://doi.org/10.1177/016146811411601006

Yeager, D. S., & Dweck, C. S. (2020). What can be learned from growth mindset controversies?. *American Psychologist, 75*(9), 1269. 1269–1284. https://doi.org/10.1037/amp0000794

Zaretiski, W. K. (2009). The zone of proximal development: What Vygotsky did not have time to write. *Journal of Russian and East European Psychology, 47*(6), 70–93. https://doi.org/10.2753/RPO1061-0405470604

Zelazo, P. D., & Cunningham, W. (2007). Executive function: Mechanisms underlying emotion regulation. In J. Gross (Ed.), *Handbook of emotion regulation* (pp. 135–158). Guilford Press.

5

DEVELOPING STUDENT LEARNERS IN SCHOOL SYSTEMS

Matthew E. Lemberger-Truelove and Hannah Bowers Parker

Adherents of the Advocating Student-within-Environment (ASE) theory for school counseling adopt a distinct lens for systems work. Practitioners of ASE are equal parts concerned with bolstering the internal capacities of each student as they are improving school systems and other social forces that influence schools. School systems range from incredibly facilitative and supportive to downright dehumanizing and baleful; regardless of the condition of the school, an ASE school counselor collaborates with agents in and out of schools so that each might flourish in more intentional, meaningful, and contributory ways.

Brisance refers to destructive fragmentation that occurs when an explosion happens inside a contained structure. A blast's strength contributes to the amount of damage done, but equally or more important is the position of the explosion. The most profound explosions are generally embedded within the structure, as opposed to on its surface husk. ASE theory operates from similar assumptions. The most prudent and efficient approach to disrupt any harmful or limiting qualities of a school is to empower the inhabitants within that school, especially as we engage and accentuate students' inherent capacities as developing learners. This said, for ASE practitioners, neither disruption nor destruction is the end aspiration; instead, ASE advocacy is akin to the Japanese art of Kintsugi, where the sharpened edges from broken pieces are mended together with gold lacquer resulting in a more seasoned and more beautiful and capable crucible.

At the individual student level, the student is a recipient of various influences coming from a great number of systems. While these forces are indivisible from the student, the student is unique as the assemblage of personal and cultural experiences occurs over a lifetime. Similarly, the school is affected by each individual student, educator, or other person that directly or indirectly participates

DOI: 10.4324/9781003312871-5

in the school. The student and the school environment are bound together, reciprocally determining what occurs, with differing magnitudes of influence. Therefore, the practice of counseling must be both culturally responsive to the student's circumstance and personally engaging to maximize their unique position in the world.

Even though ASE is an ecological and systems scheme for school counseling, the theory of change cannot be aligned with any type of radical determinism. Prior personal and social influences partially determine student outcomes, but the idiosyncratic manner that these influences collide with personal experience suggests that prior governors of experience do not fully explain students' contemporary experiences or volitional control. Alternatively, as a systems approach to school counseling, the diametric position is equally untenable; simply focusing on building up the students' internal cognitive, affective, or behavioral resources with brash disregard for their context is as naive as it is potentially harmful.

Information from the student's past and circumstance is clearly helpful content in working with the child, but we cannot time travel and ameliorate what has occurred. Even the contemporaneous here-and-now experience unfolds as the student experiences it, pushed by prior biological, psychological, and social determinants of experience. Instead, the brisance required to alter the trajectory of the student – what gives the student and those who care for the student the impression of volitional control of one's environment – is priming the self and modifying the social environment so that the student can best actualize their capacities and predilections, as different than being automaton adhering to the influences in and beyond the school system. In this way, school counselors personify our priority on prevention, development, wellness, and social justice, as a school counselor is concerned chiefly with cultivating internal student and external social conditions that are prepared in flexible and meaningful ways for a dynamic future.

Professional counseling emerged from educational and vocational guidance at the turn of the 20th century, generally in response to environmental and systemic needs such as urbanization and new work circumstances (Herr, 1999). Educators, including classroom teachers, administrators, and occasionally counselors, facilitated activities intended to support youths' vocational and civic development (Gysbers, 2010). In 1952, the American School Counselor Association (A.S.C.A.) was established, providing structure to school counselor selection and training. By the 1960s, school counseling expanded from vocational settings into more traditional K-12 education by providing personal and social counseling services while honoring holistic development (Lambie, 2004). However, the middle of the twentieth century saw a decline in school counselors due to a lack of efficacy outcomes and budget constraints; school counseling positions were often eliminated. Feeling unseen within the schools, school counselors took on administrative tasks such as record keeping, scheduling and placement, and collaboration with parents. The passing of the Education for All Handicapped Children Act in 1975, now known as the Individuals with Disabilities in Education Act (I.D.E.A.), called for advocates for all students, including those with disabilities (I.D.E.A., 2023), paving a more permanent role for school counselors within the school system as they collaborated with special education services (Lambie, 2004). In the final two decades of the twentieth century, school counseling shifted again, with an investment in implementing comprehensive programs that spanned the entire schooling lifespan. Many states adopted models that specified roles that support students in their career development, social and emotional growth, and academic achievement.

Given that the history of school counseling is influenced by and responsive to educational contexts and mental health culture, the profession toils to establish a consistent and coherent identity. Some believe that school counseling is primarily situated in education, whereas others identify it predominately with counseling, and most view it as some hybrid of the two where the school counselor adopts one role in certain contexts and the other identity in other contexts (Betters-Bubon et al., 2021). ASE adherents adopt a third alternative identity, where the school counselor is always an educator and counselor in an indivisible manner. Levy and Lemberger-Truelove (2021) suggest that this non-dual educator-counselor identity means that "school counselors are situated as educators who are oriented by counseling," and this "has the potential to mitigate much of the role ambiguity that has persisted in the profession for decades" (p. 2).

The non-dual educator-counselor identity shapes all school counseling beliefs and behaviors. For example, suppose a student introduces mental health concerns. In that case, the type of counseling delivered by the school counselor will have a different complexion than if a child client initiated these concerns in a clinical mental health treatment setting. Responding to the student's psychological suffering influences classroom and peer student experiences, and therefore, counseling behaviors are colored by the educational context, learning and school performance considerations, and other school specific factors. In a similar way, when a school counselor enters a classroom to deliver a psycho educational instructional activity, their orientation as a counselor will alter what and how the content is delivered, as different than a teacher or other school professional who instructs in a classroom setting.

This non-dual educator-counselor identity has profound implications for ASE theory. It suggests that school counselors are assuredly tied to the context of the school and yet provide a unique brand of intervention to education. In this manner, school counseling always contributes to the anticipated outcome of student learning and development. This suggests that intervention is intended to be internalized by the student so that that student can later express and contribute that learning to various settings in and beyond the school itself.

Learning and development as the focus of ASE counseling suggest that the school counselor is concerned with providing the student with varied opportunities, yet, one is not fully tied to any specific student outcome. For example, a school counselor can work with a student to integrate mnemonics when studying for a language arts test, but that student might decide to use, adapt, or even disregard these cognitive tools. This posture requires the ASE school counselor to adopt a radical trust in the student to be one's greatest advocate and embodiment of learning and development. Certainly, the student is encouraged to invest one's learning and development back into the most relevant and meaningful systems. However, it requires profound humility in the school counselor to accept that student contribution can take on many forms and even evolve over time and circumstance.

The focus on learning and development in ASE theory provides a locus for intervention at the student and systems levels. Learning and development suggest expansion and progression, the intentional cultivation of opportunity. When more students feel connected and empowered in a classroom, it increases access to information and opportunity. For example, if a student learns an arithmetic procedure, they can later apply it to a subsequent learning prompt. Alternatively, a student might develop a new manner of experiencing and communicating one's feelings, which might result in new friendships or leadership opportunities. Similarly, the focus on learning and development has social consequences, as there are collective benefits to individual learning and development. For example, suppose a particular student activates more attentional capacity. In that case, the likelihood of classroom disruption is minimized, and more students are potentially engaged in their shared space and energy as classmates. Such outcomes from learning and development are not simply to uphold or pursue the hegemonic desires of educators and the systems affiliated with the school; learning and development can also result in the refinement of attributes necessary to identify and intentionally challenge limiting school contexts.

Students and school systems that are already largely copacetic also potentially benefit from a focus on learning and development. The process of learning and development requires inquiry into the determinants of experience and investing in intentional decisions as to when to sustain helpful conditions and when to invest in new and more functional opportunities. Learning, therefore, is an expansion of ideas, connections, and opportunities, but it is also a co-regulated process to ensure that learning and development does not inadvertently privilege or perpetuate unmitigated self-interest or -advantage. This harkens back to the foundational aspiration of ASE theory, that is that school counselors, students, and other members of school environments commit to sapience, which is a deep personal and social wisdom that is dynamic, flexible, and sedulous to our shared world. See Figure 5.1.

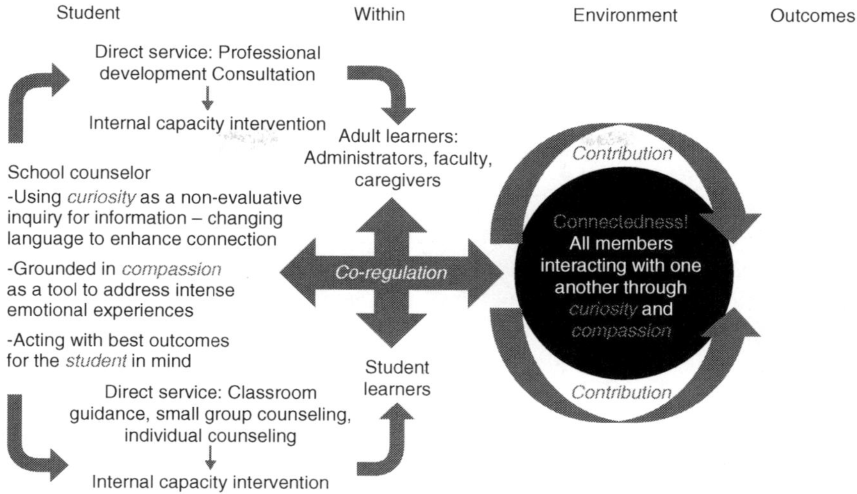

FIGURE 5.1 Advocating Student-within-Environment Theory Flow.

Internal Student Development Contributing to Systems Change

The concept of student necessitates antecedent concepts such as adaption, development, and learning. Too often, in a schooling context, the primary focus tends to be whittled down to academic performance, whereas learning and student development are associated with a certain mixture of content knowledge, cognitive and social development, and social support (Peng & Kievit, 2020). To stoke these capacities, school counselors support various forms of learning, including cognitive and learning skills, self- and co-regulatory skills, and social and emotional learning skills. These various forms of learning are critical for students to adapt and respond to school systems, which in turn better prepare oneself beyond the school context.

Cognitive and Learning Skills

School counselors practicing from an ASE viewpoint are concerned with student cognitive development and learning. Cognitive development and learning include student proficiency in academic content, but not as a fixed meaning or normative end. In other words, the school counselor does have a part to play in supporting student academic performance, but not necessarily specific to re-teaching classroom content. In this way, ASE points the school counselor to assist educators with how the student learns rather than what specific academic content is learned.

Of course, there are exceptional occasions when the school counselor might want to provide supplemental learning content. For example, if a school or instructor does not provide equal access to the successes of all cultural groups, it is incumbent on the ASE school counselor to integrate diverse identities and cultural histories into the schooling experience. Even on these occasions, the primary focus of the school counselor is pointed at how students' perspectives are expanded and generalized to the greater social good rather than privileging one group or history.

Practically speaking, the school counselor can help students (and educators) with developmentally appropriate learning strategies and other skills necessary to be successful in their immediate classroom environment or in other life settings. This focus is consistent with the epistemological position of ASE theory in that the school counselor is priming capacities that are germane to the systems students exist, yet the intention of intervention is not simply on recapitulating the prior context and, instead, empowering students to be more intentional in how they assimilate learning content or evolve content for more personally and socially meaningful outcomes.

There are many important learning skills that can help children succeed in school and in life. ASE school counselors can utilize these skills for the basis of entire classroom or small group instruction units or lessons, and they can also be used more spontaneously when working individually with a student. For example, a school counselor might help students by demonstrating how mnemonics is a powerful learning tool when attempting to memorize facts. The mnemonic "**ACT with COMP**etence" is an example of a learning skills that encompasses other learning skills valued by ASE school counselors:

***A*ttentional** skills are when the school counselor provides exercises intended to help students and educators focus and concentrate, which includes sustaining and shifting attentional focus. For example, in a small group counseling setting, a school counselor might encourage the students to identify circumstances when attention tends to get distracted and provide cues to return attentional focus to the center. This approach is consistent with the ASE theme of capitalizing on prior determinants of personal and social experience. A school counselor might say to students, "Can you think back to the instance you lost attention in class? What was occurring?" After the student identifies the conditions of experience (who, what, when, or how), the school counselor might follow up by encouraging the student to consider ways to apprehend the loss of attention, "Losing attention happens to all of us, but now that it is sometimes more predictable by identifying what occurs when it can occur, I wonder if you can come up with something that is personally helpful to you that will bring your attention back to center and under your control?"

***C*ommunication** in and outside of the classroom is essential, although it can be quite challenging for students or educators to accomplish. Ruptures in communication can have profound and lasting effects in learning settings. For example, a student struggling in class might throw their pencil in disgust. Effective communication is reciprocal. A school counselor might work with a teacher to reconceptualize the intention of the action. Certainly, the act of throwing the pencil reflects contemporaneous frustration in the student, but there might be a more foundational message that reflects the student's experience (e.g. lack of sleep or comfort at home, learning struggles). Elucidating the various messages can expand empathy and understanding, resulting in more useful teaching behaviors. In parallel, the school counselor can assist the student in articulating their emotions in more intentional and receptive ways. This approach to improving communication between the teacher and student illustrates the reciprocal determinism implicit to ASE theory; while it might initially appear onerous and inconvenient to invest so much time and energy in this single student behavior, improving the communication can have profound and lasting implications on the teacher-student relationship and thus prove more efficient and effective.

Time management is the ability to manage time, including initiating goal-focused behaviors, sustaining tasks, shifting attention and action when necessary, and identifying and accomplishing end goals. A classical strategy to amplify time management is working with students and educators to create a priority planner. The most effective planners include larger goals that require protracted investment and generally reflect more grandiose personal and social values. Larger goals can be very important as they encourage the participant to consider the perceived value of a goal and the amount of time and energy required to accomplish said goal. This said, it can occasionally be overwhelming to pursue such goals, especially given the various obligations and distractors in peoples' lives. Therefore, a potentially valuable classroom instruction activity delivered by school counselors is working with students and educators to prioritize their commitments, create smaller and more attainable sub-goals leading to overarching goals, and strategies to manage time especially after one has become temporarily distracted or disrupted.

with (also known as collaboration skills) are pivotal to ASE theory. Given schools are by nature social arenas, the ability to work effectively with others is critical to learning and social interactions. Theory of mind (T.o.M.) has roots in philosophy and is understood as the awareness that other people possess mental states (e.g. desires, emotions, beliefs) that may be similar or dissimilar to oneself (Wellman, 2017). T.o.M. is compatible with ASE theory, particularly the centrality of *within* or the manner that all participants in schools are with each other as co-determinants of experience within the school system. An example skill that a school counselor can use to engender T.o.M., or with-ness, is to encourage perspective-taking. This is different than suggesting students merely compare themselves to others. Perspective-taking requires that students empathize deeply. For example, "What types of experiences do you believe Nazir had had when (insert event) occurred?" is qualitatively different than "Can you imagine what it is like for Nazir?" The former requires the student to consider Nazir's particular internal experiences, whereas the latter might induce comparison or impertinent judgment.

***C*ritical thinking** is the ability to recognize, analyze, and evaluate information. This is a process that requires the participant to discern what is important from the superfluous, employ inductive and deductive logic, and activate creativity and spontaneity. One of the foundational tenets of ASE theory is curiosity, which is a requisite ingredient to critical thinking. To stoke curiosity, a school counselor must first demonstrate their own radically curious orientation, especially in relation to the students. "What is this like for you?" should be a precursor to the school counselor's internal dialogue. With curiosity as a base, the school counselor can stoke critical thinking in various ways, not limited to fun and engaging classroom guidance lessons that include critical thinking skills baked into the curriculum. These skills might include identifying the features of a challenging predicament, brainstorming varied solutions (and their consequences), recognizing patterns and exceptions, and making connections between events or ideas. Follow-up queries such as "What evidence supports your claim/position?" or "What biases or beliefs influenced your claim?" could be asked. Critical thinking skills illustrate the ASE priority to engender cognitive, affective, and behavioral flexibility, each essential for personal development and desired social change.

It is important to note that critical thinking skills are not the same as thinking as a critic. An ASE-informed school counselor models the following credo: to question or doubt with optimism is skepticism, whereas to doubt with pessimism and indignation is cynicism. One should certainly remain skeptical that the current social conditions and personal functioning are persistently ideal or befitting for everyone and in all ways. Alternatively, cynicism is a state of essential stuckness and inadequacy. School counselors do not want to typify or promote pollyannish naivety, but critical thinking should be pointed to the persistent development of oneself (as student, counselor, educator) and social progress.

***O*rganization** skills challenge participants to prioritize information, materials, and tasks. The ability to organize and prioritize tasks and materials is important for learning and productivity. For example, a school counselor can work with individuals or groups of students in the creation of a color-coded visual aide to organize due dates for assignments. Organization skills generally requires youth to break up lofty aspirations into smaller, more manageable parts. Incremental progress towards larger goals tends to be more accomplishable and sustainable once completed.

***M*emory** is often erroneously believed to be an inherent and stable capacity. Alternatively, it is a skill that can be refined and sharpened with intentional exposure and effort. The ability to retain and recall information is important for learning and problem-solving. School counselors might create psycho educational sessions with the following ingredients to accentuate memory: 1) Association is when the school counselor prompts a student to affiliate a familiar story, artifact (e.g. story, picture), or experience with novel content; 2) Chunking is the process of breaking information down into smaller relatable parts; 3) Rehearsal includes the effort to practice information, especially in a relevant context to the desired retrieval; 4) Spaced practice suggests that deep integration and retention of information will more likely occur when the content is approached multiple times and using the height of one's attention and other mental faculties; and 5) Visualization occurs when a student creates vivid mental images or symbols.

Problem-solving is the intentional effort to analyze and resolve challenges. The cascade of events and agendas that transpire every moment in a school often make decision-making a rapid and challenging process for students. Generally speaking, the most effective problem-solving strategy is for the student to come prepared for myriad challenges before they manifest in untenable ways. Too often, adults shut down or diminish children's problem-solving efforts; therefore, a potentially powerful school counseling practice might be to work with students and teachers in classrooms to plan, implement, and evaluate typical challenges in the classroom. Employing other skills such as effective communication and critical thinking can deepen the shared value in problem-solving efforts.

Self- and Co-regulatory Skills

If learning is the expansion of personal and social opportunities, self- and co-regulatory skills are how expansion fits within the broader systems children operate. These regulatory processes are associated with people's executive functioning, which includes each of the subordinate mental processes required to pursue goal-focused outcomes (Baumeister, Schmeichel, & Vohs, 2007). Executive functions include operations such as one's working memory, inhibition, interference control, cognitive flexibility, reasoning, problem solving, shifting of attention, and planning (Diamond, 2014). The priming and support of children's executive functioning is associated with a number of psychological and learning outcomes desired in school contexts (Takacs & Kassai, (2019). The ASE-informed school counselor can bolster student and educator regulatory skills by providing interventions that activate and reinforce executive functioning, especially in accommodating school systems.

Predictable, safe, and inviting environments are a requisite ingredient when cultivating regulatory skills. When students feel more connected and valued in a system, they are generally more willing to invest effort and make attempts to expand and integrate their experiences with self and others. To create a safe school environment, the school counselor encourages; more than mere praise, which can often be experienced as shallow and evaluative, the school counselor must model curiosity and compassion in a consistent and compelling manner. A linguistic devise that might aid the school counselor is to think of the construction of the word encourage; deconstructed, it suggests that the school counselor shares in-the-courage of the student or educator. The school counselor understands that all prior determinants of experience contributed to the current experience and behavior, and any learning or development requires courage to both be and become.

Much of the school environment is the antithesis of this becoming orientation, as illustrated by how stagnant kids are expected to be sitting in rows and isles for hours upon hours each day out of the week. Each student is the embodiment of a non-dual mind and body, tethered indivisibly from one's physical context. The empirical literature clearly suggests that executive functions and other important mental and physical regulatory skills require activity and movement (Barenberg, Berse, & Dutke, 2011). Activities that engage a student's placeness and physicality in appropriate ways to the classroom context can have far-reaching mental and learning benefits.

Similarly, mindfulness activities, which includes the regulation of attention in a non-judgmental manner, are consonant with ASE school counseling interventions and contribute to important regulatory experiences (Lemberger-Truelove et al., in press; Molina, Lemberger-Truelove, & Zieher, 2022). Multiple studies have shown the potential benefits of mindfulness in schools, including effects on student and teacher learning performance and in-school behaviors (Zenner, Herrnleben-Kurz, & Walach, 2014). Although such outcomes are laudable and potentially contributory to student development and systems change, the historical intention and value of mindfulness (and how it is adopted specifically with ASE) is less concerned with anesthetizing maladies or inducing wanton tranquility; instead, mindfulness is a process of internal state interrogation, eliciting the various determinants of experience, and responding in more intentional and contributory ways. This sentiment is best depicted in the following quote from a recent study describing an ASE-informed school intervention:

> mindfulness refers to students' experiential discernment and the inclination to suspend pernicious identification or evaluation of these experiences. Stated otherwise, students from disenfranchised communities do not accept inadequate or deleterious social conditions; instead, using social-emotional and mindfulness strategies, they accept their cognitive and affective reactions and respond with clearer intentionality.
>
> *(Lemberger-Truelove, et al., 2018, p. 299)*

Mindfulness often challenges individuals to experience self and others at a very granular level, attending to details, relationships, and distinctions. Beyond formal mindfulness practices, self- and co-regulated executive functions can be fostered by teaching people to dissect and restore prompts or experiences into smaller more manageable parts. For example, the evidence-based school counseling intervention Student Success Skills (S.S.S.) encourages students to adopt the following phrase – "little by little, bit by bit, I am improving every day." In this articulated mental device, the school counselor is subtly challenging the students to identify and prize the constituent parts of any larger goal pursuit.

Interventions such as S.S.S. and other school-based interventions can ameliorate regulatory skills and vitalize executive functioning. The key to making these practices compatible with ASE. theory is that they engender the focus on Student-within-Environment. Developing the student to be compliant to the school or societal ethos often merely perpetuates student disenfranchisement and listlessness. The mission of education should empower and rally so that the current generation of learners can contribute to better personal experience and the social systems we share.

Social and Emotional Learning Skills

Social and Emotional Learning (S.E.L.) skills assist people in how they manage affective experiences, build mutually contributory relationships, and commit to conscientious decisions (Weissberg et al., 2015). School interventions grounded in S.E.L. are associated with higher levels of academic achievement, lower amounts of disciplinary concerns, and heightened psychological and social experiences (Domitrovich et al., 2017). The pertinence of S.E.L. for school counselors is evident, as the American School Counseling Association (A.S.C.A.) created the A.S.C.A. Student Standards: Mindsets and Behaviors for Student Success (2021), which were largely influenced by S.E.L. scholarship and also, many educational systems and school counseling programs, in particular, are informed by the Collaborative for Academic, Social, and Emotional Learning (C.A.S.E.L.), an organization comprised of researchers and educators who focus on the continued advancement of S.E.L.. C.A.S.E.L. has proffered the five competency areas relevant from childhood throughout adulthood that make up social and emotional learning, including self-awareness, self-management, social awareness, relationship skills, and responsible decision-making (C.A.S.E.L., 2022). Each of these competencies can be integrated into ASE praxis and used to fortify internal learning and develop the capacities of students and educators.

Recently, there are scholars who caution against the vacuous or superficial proliferation of S.E.L. and related psychological interventions in schools (Stearns, 2019). Yeager and Walton, (2011) reviewed the literature related to brief interventions intended to support students or teach social or psychological development. Many of the randomized controlled trials reported only modest effect sizes with uncertain to dubious durability. Other thinkers such as Stearns (2019) posed more epistemological and ethical concerns, particularly the cultural fitness of interventions that might unintentionally subvert or distract from pernicious inequalities and harmful practices in schools. School counselors must heed these precautionary positions, therefore neither overpromising the specific outcomes from interventions nor using interventions to pacify or assimilate learners or the people in their various systems.

From an ASE perspective, S.E.L. interventions are not something done "onto" a student or educator, rather the "within" posture is always championed. For learners, the preponderance of experience is predicated and largely dictated by prior determinants. Using S.E.L. draws together cognitive and learning skills and self- and co-regulatory skills such that each student and each other individual in the school can express and negotiate intentional experience and decision-making. In this way, S.E.L. and other ASE-related intervention foci are intended to empower such that systems will develop in personally and socially contributory ways.

Conclusion

The primary charge for a school counselor influenced by ASE theory is to cultivate each individual learner so that there is a collective of able, valued, and connected members of the school environment. Other theories of practice are certainly attentive to the influence of various social systems on individuals. However, given the school counselor's positionality in the naturalistic school context, ASE theory offers a unique approach to systems work. By tapping into the learner's cognitive and learning skills, co- and self-regulatory skills, and S.E.L. skills, it changes the complexion of experience for students and other members of the school community.

References

American School Counselor Association (2021). *ASCA Student Standards; Mindsets and Behaviors for Student Success*. Alexandria, VA: Author

Barenberg, J., Berse, T., & Dutke, S. (2011). Executive functions in learning processes: Do they benefit from physical activity? *Educational Research Review*, *6*(3), 208–222.

Baumeister, R. F., Schmeichel, B. J., & Vohs, K. D. (2007). Self–regulation and the executive function: The self as controlling agent. In A. W. Kruglanski & E. T. Higgins (Eds.), Social psychology: Handbook of basic principles (2nd ed.). New York: Guilford Press.

Betters-Bubon, J., Goodman-Scott, E., & Bamgbose, O. (2021). School counselor educators' reactions to changes in the profession: Implications for policy, evaluation, and preparation. *Journal of School-Based Counseling Policy and Evaluation*, *3*(2), 40–50.

Collaborative for Academic, Social, and Emotional Learning. (2022). *What is the CASEL Framework? A framework creates a foundation for applying evidence-based SEL strategies to your community*. Retrieved from https://casel.org/fundamentals-of-sel/what-is-the-casel-framework/

Diamond, A. (2014). Want to optimize executive functions and academic outcomes? Simple, just nourish the human spirit. In *Minnesota Symposia on Child Psychology: Developing cognitive control processes: Mechanisms, implications, and interventions* (Vol. 37, pp. 203–230). Hoboken, NJ: John Wiley & Sons, Inc.

Domitrovich, C. E., Durlak, J. A., Staley, K. C., & Weissberg, R. P. (2017). Social-emotional competence: An essential factor for promoting positive adjustment and reducing risk in school children. *Child Development*, *88*(2), 408–416. https://doi.org/10.1111/cdev.12739

Gysbers, N. C. (2010). *Remembering the past, shaping the future: A history of school counseling*. American School Counselor Association.

Herr, E. L. (1999). *Counseling in a dynamic society: Contexts and practices for the 21st century*. American Counseling Association: Alexandria, VA.

Individuals with Disabilities in Education Act. (2023). *A History of the Individuals With Disabilities Education Act*. Retrieved Feb 27, 2023 from https://sites.ed.gov/idea/IDEA-History

Lambie, G. W., & Williamson, L. L. (2004). The challenge to change from guidance counseling to professional school counseling: A historical proposition. *Professional School Counseling*, 124–131.

Lemberger-Truelove, M. E., Carbonneau, K. J., Atencio, D. J., Zieher, A. K., & Palacios, A. F. (2018). Self-regulatory growth effects for young children participating in a combined social and emotional learning and mindfulness-based intervention. *Journal of Counseling and Development, 96*(3) 289–302. https://doi.org/10.1002/jcad.12203

Lemberger-Truelove, M. E., Molina, C. E., Carbonneau, K. J., & Smith, M. (in press). Effects of school counselor consultation intervention on middle school teacher-student relationships, student curiosity, and teacher stress. *Professional School Counseling.*

Levy, I. P., & Lemberger-Truelove, M. E. (2021). Educator-counselor: A nondual identity for school counselors. *Professional School Counseling*, *24*(1b), 1–7. https://doi.org/10.1177/2156759X211007630

Molina, C. E., Lemberger-Truelove, M. E., & Zieher, A. K. (2022). School counselor consultation effects on teachers' mindfulness, stress, and relationships. *Professional School Counseling*, *26*(1a), 2156759X221086749.

Peng, P. & Kievit, R. A. (2020). The development of academic achievement and cognitive abilities: A bidirectional perspective. *Child Development Perspectives*, *14*(1), 15–20. https://doi.org/10.1111/cdep.12352

Stearns, C. (2019). *Critiquing social and emotional learning: Psychodynamic and cultural perspectives*. Rowman & Littlefield.

Takacs, Z. K., & Kassai, R. (2019). The efficacy of different interventions to foster children's executive function skills: A series of meta-analyses. *Psychological Bulletin, 145*(7), 653–697. https://doi.org/10.1037/bul0000195

Weissberg, R. P., Durlak, J. A., Domitrovich, C. E., & Gullotta, T. P. (2015). Social and emotional learning: Past, present, and future. In J. A. Durlak, C. E. Domitrovich, R. P. Weissberg, & T. P. Gullotta (Eds.), *Handbook of social and emotional learning: Research and practice* (pp. 3–19). New York, NY: Guilford.

Wellman, H. M. (2017). The development of theory of mind: Historical reflections. *Child Development Perspectives*, *11*(3), 207–214. https://doi.org/10.1111/cdep.12236

Yeager, D. S., & Walton, G. M. (2011). Social-psychological interventions in education: They're not magic. *Review of Educational Research*, *81*(2), 267–301.

Zenner, C., Herrnleben-Kurz, S., & Walach, H. (2014). Mindfulness-based interventions in schools: A systematic review and meta-analysis. *Frontiers in Psychology*, *5*, 1–20. https://doi.org/10.3389/fpsyg.2014.00603

6

ADVOCATING FOR THE NEURODIVERSE STUDENT

Hannah Bowers Parker

Parents have been assessing their child's development from the moment they entered the world. Doctors evaluate the child to ensure they breathe correctly and that blood flows to the correct areas. Doctors test babies to ensure they can see and hear. Physically, these developmental milestones continue to be assessed as children develop, usually through check-ups that occur every three months until their first or second year of age. Neurodevelopmental disorders typically become apparent early in life, often before traditional schooling begins (American Psychiatric Association; A.P.A., 2013).

Within the school setting, whether in kindergarten or preschool, students are assessed through similar methods employed by pediatricians. Consider the ages and stages questionnaire (A.S.Q.; Bricker et al., 1999), whereby children are assessed by the parent every two months from four months until six years in the areas of communication, gross motor, fine motor, problem-solving, personal-social, and overall physical health. Screening methods such as these have positively identified areas of concern, resulting in physician referral for further testing (Roane et al., 2012).

Navigating a new world of neurodiversity is difficult for parents of young children. With a diagnosis of this nature comes a multitude of feelings. Parents may experience grief that the idea of the life they expected their child to lead would not be a reality. Usually, these expectations are deeply in parents' own experiences, passed down through familial generations of parenting practices. Counselors must attend to the parents as much as the student when working with neurodevelopmental disorders. Parents can enhance their ability to navigate life circumstances through enhanced internal capacities. However, they, too, need psycho educational support to become an advocate for their child.

DOI: 10.4324/9781003312871-6

Such is also true for special education teachers. Special education teachers are in high demand as there are many positions and not enough teachers willing to fill them. Special education is a highly stressful position as each student has a range of unique needs. A counselor based in the school is best to intervene with teachers to provide them with social and emotional support to decrease environmental stressors. Furthermore, counselors can psycho educate the special education teacher in their advocacy role; that is, the teacher advocates for the betterment of the student's learning and advocates for themselves for favorable work environments.

The foundational goal of maximizing students' internal capacities is unique to the ASE theory. These internal capacities are made of the intersection between cognitive determinants and social skills, directly impacting a child's ability to achieve fully. However, internal capacities differ in diverse populations. This chapter identifies what happens when our children are not considered "normal." An overview of defining terms such as neurodiversity is presented. Critiquing how such terminology impacts the field of education provides the counselor with a critical lens that can be used when advocating for the student within the school setting.

ASE and Neurodiversity

As with all disorders categorized within the DSM 5-TR (American Psychiatric Association; A.P.A., 2022), an inherent deficit is used to identify and categorize individuals. Such a process is dehumanizing as we consider parts of a whole, identifying these parts as problematic and abnormal. This practice is particularly concerning for neurodiverse individuals. Neurodiversity in and of itself refers to diversity in neurological functioning. In essence, "Neurodiversity describes the idea that people experience and interact with the world around them in many ways; there is no one 'right' way of thinking, learning, and behaving and differences are not viewed as deficits" (Baumer & Frueh, 2021). While schools make it their mission and vision to attend to all students – striving to meet all differences and abilities in positive learning environments – many school infrastructures make it impossible to accommodate students with autism, attention deficit and hyperactivity disorder, dyslexia, dyscalculia, dyspraxia, and Tourette's syndrome (Smagorinsky, 2020).

When mass education was first introduced as a concept in the United States, the goal was to bring together groups of people that made up the melting pot of American society. The objective was assimilation and colonization – what constituted the perfect students was essentially a reflection of the ideal for American citizens, united under one national identity (Smagorinsky, 2020). Placing these concepts in schools today is antiquated, given the immense diversity within the school systems. Forcing students to engage in expected classroom behaviors, academic goals set by the school, or even language is ostracizing and unachievable for many. The current structure of schools rewards those that fit into established norms typically filled by neurotypical, able-bodied individuals (Smagorinsky, 2020). Neurodiverse students do not meet this established norm, often displaying behaviors deemed disruptive in the school setting, positioning students as a problem that needs to be dealt with instead of identifying and capitalizing on their uniqueness and strengths brought to the environment. Furthermore, evidence-based practices utilized within the school setting are geared towards inhibiting these "problem behaviors" through applied behavioral analysis, not to value and support diversity but to extinguish any differences students may have from one another (Smagorinsky, 2020). Traditional educational settings aim for everyone to be one and the same – if you do not fit the norm, you are encouraged to change or leave.

Changing K-12 culture nationally is lofty for the practicing school counselor. Though ASE, it is possible to change the singular school environment to create an atmosphere allowing students to maximize their internal capacities' development. To do so, counselors must know how to support neurodiverse individuals. Such advocacy acts include finding support in others or providing psycho education to parents, teachers, and administrators. Furthermore, best practices can be reviewed to support students individually to enhance their internal capacities, such as social and emotional learning skill sets, executive functions, and perceptions of connectedness.

While diagnostic criteria, as stated in the DSM 5-TR (A.P.A., 2022), are presented, it must be noted that the deficit approach used within diagnosis is the antithesis of ASE. However, diagnostic terminology must be utilized within the schools to allow for advocacy capabilities, uniting the school system in a common language for the betterment of the students. These terms do not define a student who they are; instead, it allows the counselor to identify strengths and provide further support services. In a way, diagnosis also equals access from the ASE perspective.

Intellectual Disabilities

Intellectual developmental disorder (I.D.D.) presents when children struggle to develop and display general mental capabilities such as problem-solving, planning, abstract thinking, academic learning, or learning from experience (A.P.A., 2013). What leads to disorder diagnosis lies in how adaptive a child is in completing tasks of daily living and to what degree they are independently functional, social aptitude, and academic functioning (A.P.A., 2013). As parents complete assessments for their pediatrician regarding their children's developmental milestones, awareness is raised on whether developmental delays occur. Through this identification, pediatricians can make informed referrals for early intervention services, which in most cases, can be a miracle for children (Guralnick, 2017).

Counselors utilizing the ASE perspective consider the need of the student and identify all involved players. This includes parents, guardians, teachers, and administrators. Parents and guardians often serve as lifelong resources for children with intellectual disabilities (Talapatra, Miller, & Schumacher-Martinez, 2019). Through advocacy efforts led by parents, students with intellectual disabilities have access to schools and general education classrooms and curricula as students without disabilities (I.D.E.A., 2023). When considering students with I.D.D. included in the general education classroom, an ASE counselor must advocate for the training and use evidence-based practices that align with the environmental implementation. For example, many programs grounded in universal design for learning (U.D.L.), curricular modifications, or private accommodations have been effective in more structured learning environments specifically for students receiving special education services (Kuntz & Carter, 2019). However, these interventions have not been tested in general education classroom settings. The effects of teacher implementation or how normative students may respond is unknown and could impact outcomes for students with I.D.D. (Kuntz & Carter, 2019).

The ASE counselor must move between subgroups with the school system at ease, calling for a process of joining and accommodating. To be effective in the school environment, the ASE counselor must understand the language and terminology and maintain a general understanding of evidence-based educational practices within the classroom. This does not require returning to school for another degree, but staying informed about best practices can aid conversations with special education teachers, teacher aids, administrators, and parents. Just as the ASE counselor uses curiosity to understand student experience fully, the system does the same.

Communication Disorders

Communication disorders include specific deficits in children's development in language, speech, and social communication (A.P.A., 2013). These disorders are typically categorized as either expressive language disorders, mixed receptive-expressive language disorders, stuttering, and phonological disorders (Sices et al., 2007; Zebron et al., 2015). Symptoms of communication disorders present differently for each child. For example, children may have difficulty following directions or paying attention in conversation, understanding what is being communicated by others, struggling with pronouncing words, expressing themselves, or being understood (Gerber et al., 2012).

School-age children with communication disorders struggle to build social skills, executive functions, and other internal capacities that aid in their ability to advocate for themselves (Gregg, 2017). Consider the transition from preschool to elementary school. During this time, schoolchildren usually improve their ability to self-regulate and express their wants and needs more clearly. A child struggling with a communication disorder may be unable to effectively communicate their needs, leading to frustration and feeling unheard and invalidated within their system. These behaviors can then translate to peer relationships. Sometimes these frustrating feelings may translate to a behavioral outburst or social withdrawal. Because of such, utilizing an ASE advocating calls for advocacy efforts with teachers, families, and service providers to provide comprehensive support for students (Gregg, 2017).

Autism Spectrum Disorder

While communication disorders generally focus on a child's ability to express oneself through different language-related struggles, autism spectrum disorder (A.S.D.), related to the aspect of social communication and social interactions across multiple contexts that present as deficits in social reciprocity, ability to communicate in social situations, and skill sets related to building and maintaining relationships (A.P.A., 2013). In addition to these expressive communication skills related to social abilities, A.S.D. diagnosis includes restricted, repetitive behaviors, interests, and activities (A.P.A., 2013). The way A.S.D. presents in children varies significantly. Moreover, symptomology can change over time based on developmental and environmental influences. Students diagnosed with A.S.D. struggle most with executive functioning skills, social-emotional control, and fine motor skills (Saggers et al., 2016). Research on school outcomes suggests that those students with A.S.D. are not supported and often struggle to engage fully and achieve in school environments (White et al., 2009).

Counselors practicing from an ASE foundation must maintain a central belief that all students can achieve (Lemberger-Truelove & Bowers, 2019). This foundation encourages counselors to advocate for students with A.S.D. systemically through collaboration with family, faculty, and administration. Considering the characteristics of effective programs for students with A.S.D., collaborative efforts must focus on psycho education, educating faculty and administration on general information about neurodevelopmental disorders while embracing each individual student's unique characteristics. Family can be an essential resource for learning about the student, specifically their needs in managing behavior, engaging in transitions, or understanding systemic supports (Roberts & Webster, 2022). For interventions that directly work with students, counselors practicing from ASE are encouraged to meet the student where they are by identifying areas of interest as points of connection. These topics serve as the medium to strengthen social communication skills. As these social communication skills are enhanced, the counselor can better aid the student in vocalizing sensory needs and learning to identify and communicate their needs effectively to better advocate for themselves.

Attention-Deficit/Hyperactivity Disorder

When children struggle with attention-deficit/hyperactivity disorder (A.D.H.D.), it often presents through educational problems, difficulty establishing and maintaining peer relationships, accidental injuries, and substance use in adolescents (Bélanger et al., 2018). While categorized as a neurodevelopmental disorder by the Diagnostic and Statistical Manual V-TR (DSM V-TR), the source occurs from multiple etiologies, including genetic, neurological, and environmental factors. A.D.H.D. is the most common neurodevelopmental disorder, impacting 5% to 7% of children worldwide (Rushton et al., 2020). Students with A.D.H.D. often struggle to engage in on-task classroom behaviors and utilize other internal capacities such as attention, working memory, planning, and organization (Rushton et al., 2020). These struggles often lead to poor academic outcomes in reading and math, lower engagement, and increased reports of peer victimization (Zendarski et al., 2020).

Research on A.D.H.D. has found that student severity significantly impacts student-teacher relationships and the relationship between student's emotional engagement and their school among elementary and middle school students (Rushton et al., 2020). From an ASE perspective, counselors must support teachers in advocating for change within the environment. When teachers were assessed on their knowledge regarding A.D.H.D. symptoms, the accuracy of responses was as low as 47.8% (Poznanski et al., 2021). Research also shows that teachers with more knowledge about A.D.H.D. and related symptoms have greater positive perceptions of A.D.H.D. and are more willing to work with the child within the classroom environment (Poznanski et al., 2021). Furthermore, school-based interventions for students with ADHD are most effective when teachers have a positive relationship with the student (Moore et al., 2019). While expressed symptomology will differ in presentation and severity for each student, teachers must have compassion and curiosity for those students struggling with A.D.H.D., which can be further supported by counselors practicing ASE theory.

Counselors must also understand that schools have specific student goals, typically related to academic achievement and the behaviors that impact achievement most. For students with A.D.H.D., these goals may focus more on symptom reduction when it comes to off-task behaviors. The ASE counselor understands the school's goals but also recognizes that these goals may not align with the family's beliefs. Through inquiry by which the counselor does not impart judgment about pushing a school agenda, conversation can occur about the student's family's goals and individual goals the student may have for

TABLE 6.1 Environmental Considerations for Students with A.S.D. and A.D.H.D.

Environmental Considerations for Students with A.S.D. and A.D.H.D.	
Small changes to the environment can go a long way. Baumer and Frueh (2021) recommend the following considerations toward sensory needs:	
Sound sensitivity	• Communicate expected loud noises like fire drills • Offer noise cancelling headphones • Offer quiet break space
Tactical	• Anything to the touch that may serve as a distraction or discomfort for the student • May include uniforms or apparel, the texture of the desk or chair
Movement	• Students may engage in self-soothing techniques that involve movement • Allowing access to fidget toys, movement breaks, flexible seating
Communication	• Direct and clear communication style is essential • Use of graphic organizers or pictures as cues • Verbal and written instruction must be concise • Tasks should be broken down into small steps • Avoid sarcasm, euphemisms, and implied messages • Give advance notice if plans are going to change

themselves. ASE prioritizes the practice of student lead goal setting. Students and families who identified their goals related to A.D.H.D. symptomologies were more successful than those forced into goals aligned with the school (Fiks et al., 2012). See Table 6.1 for a summary of environmental considerations for students with A.S.D. and A.D.H.D..

Specific Learning Disability

Specific learning disorders (S.L.D.) is a broad definition that encompasses students who struggle to achieve in reading, writing, and mathematics at the same level as their peers (Maki & Adams, 2019). S.L.D.s often present at various points during a student's academic career, typically during early elementary school, and may include dyslexia, dyspraxia, and dysgraphia at varying degrees (mild, moderate, and severe). Addressing S.L.D.s in the school is challenging as the identification and diagnosis process differs across schools and districts. Before the Individuals with Disabilities Education Improvement Act (I.D.E.A., 2023), S.L.D.s were only diagnosed based on academic ability. That is, students had to fail specific academic tasks over a period before support could be put into place to help them achieve. This practice caused students to develop an "I cannot" identity.

Currently, many districts identify students struggling early on and utilize a response to intervention (R.t.I.). R.t.I. refers to using evidence-based early intervention services coupled with multiple assessment measurements to identify, support, and track struggling students (Alahmari, 2019). After students engage in R.t.I., results inform the following steps, whether it be a referral for a formal evaluation or data to include within an individual education plan (I.E.P.). However, there is much criticism of R.t.I. as it can cause delays in the comprehensive evaluation of students with suspected disabilities (Alahmari, 2019).

Much of the school's approach to identifying and treating S.L.D.s is reductionistic, leaving the student feeling as though they are their diagnosis and unable to achieve. Because of the time-consuming process of R.t.I., some students may go years before being provided services that effectively treat their learning difficulties, which is reflected in classroom participation, peer perception of the student, and potential frustrations related to academics at home. For example, students who struggle with reading may be reluctant to engage in reading activities, but rather than saying, "I do not like to read," they act out instead to avoid it. These avoidant behaviors may distract the class, leaving peers angry at the distraction within their environment or at home. Parents may feel frustration and anger towards their child as they refuse to engage in homework activities.

An ASE counselor must approach these students with curiosity to fully understand their lived experiences of these students when concerning academics while being mindful of the language used and engaging in conversation in a way that the student best understands. A student with an auditory processing disorder may need a different approach than a normative developing student. Redefining a student's cognitive schema about themselves can be difficult, especially when the schema is heavily reinforced in the student's sense of self.

ASE in Practice with Neurodiverse Students

Educators and parents need to focus on the enjoyment of learning-based activities rather than performance to encourage a love of learning, which is critical during this time. However, such a perspective contradicts the intense culture of school-based performance evaluations that indicate teacher and student success in the classroom. The pressures permeate the school system, making it more challenging to create an environment focused on celebrating learning and instead turn it into toxicity and stress. These toxic environments impede the student's critical development, leaving them with lasting impressions that learning is not fun. Instead, they create labels for students that they will carry with them for the rest of their lives.

Working from the foundational perspective that all children can succeed (Lemberger & Hutchison, 2014), counselors can identify how to intervene to support neurodiverse students. In intervening at any level, ASE counselors are encouraged to maintain curiosity, both in seeking understanding from the perspective of the student and their lived experience within the school environment, as well as from the teacher in how the student engages, impacting the classroom environment and the teacher's internal capacities to function. Furthermore, counselors must go beyond and engage with family members on their experience with the student at home, understanding successes, difficulties, and goals. Hearing a totality of experiences allows the counselor to have compassion toward all involved while identifying effective means to intervene.

Special education teachers are in higher demand than ever, with high turnover and lower professionals entering the field. Such shortage in special education speaks to the intensity of the job, whereby special education teachers report feeling unsupported by the administration, leaving them feeling as though their job was detrimental to their quality of life (Hester, Bridges, & Rollins, 2020). To improve teacher burnout, ASE counselors are encouraged to support teachers through consultation that will support their well-being and model such practices to their students. This process of co-regulation has been shown to support teachers' reported stress levels (Molina et al., 2022). Neurodiverse students often struggle with self-regulation, engaging in behaviors out of their control that is disruptive to the environment, leaving teachers often feelings dysregulated within an environment by which they already report feeling unsupported (Hester et al., 2020). Working directly with teachers on self-care is an effort by which ASE counselors change the environment, leaving teachers feeling more supported and less likely to burn out. At the same time, modeling appreciates self-care behaviors that can transcend into the classroom and improve outcomes for students receiving special education services.

Based on the standard protocol in schools, following the multitiered system of support for neurodiverse students is recommended as an effort to join the environment to be better able to make a change. Tier one interventions speak to advocacy within the school environment. Such efforts occur through collaboration and are school-wide with support to faculty and administrators. Professional development on neurodiversity addresses the curiosity of ASE theory. Encouraging faculty and staff to increase their understanding can validate teachers' struggles within the classroom while providing an opportunity for increased compassion towards neurodiverse students and evidence-based strategies that can support the classroom environment for optimal learning.

Systemically narrowing down to the classroom level, targeted interventions can occur at the small group or classroom level, specifically on strengthening skill sets that increase student capacity. These practices speak to connectedness within ASE theory. For example, counselors can utilize an evidence-based classroom guidance curriculum like the Exceptional Student Success Skills program (E.S.S.S.; Bowers et al., 2020) to increase social and emotional learning skills within a classroom setting. Grounded in the ASE theory and universal design of learning for special education, the E.S.S.S. program was designed to meet the educational needs of students with exceptional learning circumstances. Based on outcomes from classroom guidance efforts, counselors can identify students needing further support through small group counseling. Small groups can consist of lunch bunches, aiding students with similar struggles and interests to come together to build social skills in a safe environment when they may experience ostracizing behaviors from their peers. Small groups allow students to utilize their internal capacity skill sets to make authentic connections with one another.

Should students continue to struggle after tier-two interventions, an individual approach is recommended. Shifting the focus to the individual student requires both advocacies through consultation with the teacher and one-on-one work with the student. These consultation efforts with the teacher focus on one student instead of general consultation that addresses teacher needs or professional development towards general psycho education on a specific neurodiverse topic.

Conclusions

All children experience major life events, some normal and expected, some extraordinarily positive, and others adverse. When writing this text, all children have experienced the lasting impacts of a global pandemic, completely disrupting routine life at home and in schools. These extenuating situations, some of which will be discussed in more detail in later chapters, further strain our non-normative or neurodiverse children. Considering the ASE perspective, the goal is to change conditions within the environment, allowing students to maximize their internal capacities' development. With neurodiverse populations, this is done through advocating for their skill obtainment, often shifting preconceived negative self-concepts that have been imposed by the school system, as well as advocating for change in environmental conditions, which is done through consultive support of faculty and administration, whether through the development of wellness activities or professional development to increase awareness of best practices with neurodiverse students. Neurodiversity is an ever-evolving field, and counselors are encouraged to maintain awareness of how schools continue to engage and support students.

References

Alahmari, A. (2019). A Review and Synthesis of the Response to Intervention (RtI) Literature: Teachers' Implementations and Perceptions. *International Journal of Special Education, 33*(4), 894–909.

American Psychiatric Association. (2013). Diagnostic and statistical manual of mental disorders (5th ed.). https://doi.org/10.1176/appi.books.9780890425596.

American Psychiatric Association. (2022). Diagnostic and statistical manual of mental disorders, Text Revision (DSM-5-TR™). American Psychiatric Association publishing. Washington, DC, USA.

Baumer, N., & Frueh, J. (2021). What is neurodiversity? *Harvard Health Publishing, Harvard Medical School.* www.health.harvard.edu/blog/what-is-neurodiversity-202111232645. Accessed September 18, 2022.

Bélanger, S. A., Andrews, D., Gray, C., & Korczak, D. (2018). ADHD in children and youth: Part 1—Etiology, diagnosis, and comorbidity. *Paediatrics & child health, 23*(7), 447–453.

Bowers, H., Lemberger-Truelove, M. E., Whitford, D. K. (2020). Kindergarteners are ready to learn: Executive functioning and social-emotional effects for a pilot school counseling intervention applying Student-within-Environment theory. *Journal of Humanistic Counseling 59*(1), 3–19. https://doi.org/10.1002/johc.12126

Bricker, D., Squires, J., Mounts, L., Potter, L., Nickel, R., Twombly, E., & Farrell, J. (1999). Ages and stages questionnaire. *Baltimore, MD: Paul H. Brookes.*

Fiks, A. G., Mayne, S., Hughes, C. C., DeBartolo, E., Behrens, C., Guevara, J. P., et al. (2012). Development of an instrument to measure parents' preferences and goals for the treatment of attention deficit–hyperactivity disorder. *Academic Pediatrics, 12*(5), 445–455. https://doi.org/10.1016/j.acap.2012.04.009.

Gerber, S., Brice, A., Capone, N., Fujiki, M., & Timler, G. (2012). Language use in social interactions of school-age children with language impairments: An evidence-based systematic review of treatment.

Gregg, K. (2017). Communication disorders and challenging behaviors: Supporting children's functional communication goals in the classroom. Early Childhood Education Journal, 45, 445–452.

Guralnick, M. J. (2017). Early intervention for children with intellectual disabilities: An update. Journal of Applied Research in Intellectual Disabilities, 30(2), 211–229.

Hester, O. R., Bridges, S. A., & Rollins, L. H. (2020). 'Overworked and underappreciated': special education teachers describe stress and attrition. *Teacher Development, 24*(3), 348–365.

Individuals with Disabilities in Education Act. (2023). *A History of the Individuals With Disabilities Education Act.* Retrieved Feb 27, 2023 from https://sites.ed.gov/idea/IDEA-History

Kuntz, E. M., & Carter, E. W. (2019). Review of interventions supporting secondary students with intellectual disability in general education classes. *Research and Practice for Persons with Severe Disabilities, 44*(2), 103–121.

Lemberger-Truelove, M. E., & Bowers, H. (2019). An advocating student-within-environment approach to school counseling. *Theories of school counseling for the 21st century*, pp. 266–294.

Lemberger, M. E., & Hutchison, B. (2014). Advocating student-within-environment: A humanistic approach for therapists to animate social justice in the schools. *Journal of humanistic psychology, 54*(1), 28–44.

Maki, K. E., & Adams, S. R. (2019). A current landscape of specific learning disability identification: Training, practices, and implications. *Psychology in the Schools, 56*(1), 18–31.

Molina, C. E., Lemberger-Truelove, M. E., & Zieher, A. K. (2022). School counselor consultation effects on teachers' mindfulness, stress, and relationships. *Professional School Counseling, 26*(1a), 1–9. https://doi.org/10.1177/2156759X221086749

Moore, D. A., Richardson, M., Gwernan-Jones, R., Thompson-Coon, J., Stein, K., Rogers, M., ... & Ford, T. J. (2019). Non-pharmacological interventions for ADHD in school settings: An overarching synthesis of systematic reviews. *Journal of attention disorders*, *23*(3), 220–233.

Poznanski, B., Hart, K. C., & Graziano, P. A. (2021). What do preschool teachers know about attention-deficit/hyperactivity disorder (ADHD) and does it impact ratings of child impairment?. *School Mental Health*, *13*(1), 114–128.

Roane, B. M., Valleley, R. J., & Allen, K. D. (2012). Impact of Ages and Stages Questionnaire scores on pediatrician referral patterns. *Infants & Young Children*, *25*(2), 149–157.

Roberts, J., & Webster, A. (2022). Including students with autism in schools: a whole school approach to improve outcomes for students with autism. *International Journal of Inclusive Education*, *26*(7), 701–718.

Rushton, S., Giallo, R., & Efron, D. (2020). ADHD and emotional engagement with school in the primary years: Investigating the role of student–teacher relationships. *British Journal of Educational Psychology*, pp. *90*, 193–209.

Saggers, B., Klug, D., Harper-Hill, K., Ashburner, J., Costley, D., Clark, T., ... & Carrington, S. (2016). *Australian autism educational needs analysis-What are the needs of schools, parents and students on the autism spectrum? (Full Report)*. Cooperative Research Centre for Living with Autism (Autism CRC).

Sices, L., Taylor, H. G., Freebairn, L., Hansen, A., & Lewis, B. (2007). Relationship between speech-sound disorders and early literacy skills in preschool-age children: Impact of comorbid language impairment. *Journal of developmental and behavioral pediatrics: JDBP*, *28*(6), 438.

Smagorinsky, P. (2020). Neurodiversity and the deep structure of schools. *Ought: The Journal of Autistic Culture*, *2*(1), 4.

Talapatra, D., Miller, G. E., & Schumacher-Martinez, R. (2019). Improving family-school collaboration in transition services for students with intellectual disabilities: A framework for school psychologists. *Journal of Educational and Psychological Consultation*, *29*(3), 314–336.

White, S. W., Oswald, D., Ollendick, T., & Scahill, L. (2009). Anxiety in children and adolescents with autism spectrum disorders. *Clinical psychology review*, *29*(3), 216–229.

Zebron, S., Mhute, I., & Musingafi, M. C. C. (2015). Classroom Challenges: Working with Pupils with Communication Disorders. *Journal of Education and Practice*, *6*(9), 18–22.

Zendarski, N., Haebich, K., Bhide, S., Quek, J., Nicholson, J. M., Jacobs, K. E., ... & Sciberras, E. (2020). Student–teacher relationship quality in children with and without ADHD: A cross-sectional community based study. Early Childhood Research Quarterly, 51, 275–284.

7

AN ASE APPROACH TO SCHOOL-BASED MENTAL HEALTH

Hannah Bowers Parker

Thus far, we have explored ways a school counselor embracing ASE navigates the school system to advocate for students within the school environment. As we continue to focus on individual student needs, first identifying internal capacities, then paring down into neurocognitive disorders, we continue to support students struggling with mental health disorders. Tackling all individual student needs within the school takes a village. Utilizing all available supports and services is essential, further highlighting the importance of ASE and understanding the school environment to work towards meeting the needs of all students.

Considering students' mental well-being without the COVID-19 pandemic and related outcomes is impossible. Mental health concerns among children and adolescents are widespread and have been under scrutiny over the past two decades. According to the Centers for Disease Control and Prevention (C.D.C.), more than 37% of all high school students reported having poor mental health following the COVID-19 pandemic (C.D.C., 2022). Students are in a situation where they are under cumulative risk, being exposed to numerous co-occurring risk factors that then increase the likelihood of mental health struggles (Wade et al., 2020).

Environmental impacts cannot be ignored when considering school-aged children's mental health. Over the past two years alone, school-age children have lived through a pandemic, economic crisis, and social unrest. Outcomes from the COVID-19 pandemic are still emerging. When looking only at the mandated stay-home orders issued, school-aged children were found to be more at risk for symptoms of depression, anxiety, and obsessive-compulsive disorder as related to their parents losing work (McKune et al., 2021). Furthermore, high school students' poor mental health was found to be directly impacted by their

DOI: 10.4324/9781003312871-7

level of education, negative coping skill sets, or suffering from the impact of trauma (Liang et al., 2020).

Schools are a common gathering place for students with diverse backgrounds and experiences nested within a shared community. While 87% of schools around the world were closed during the pandemic (Tang et al., 2021), students lost a massive point of connection within their daily lives. Placing students in isolation leads to significant increases in reported anxiety and depression through symptoms such as fear, helplessness, worry, insomnia, and sadness (Meherali et al., 2021). In attempts to make connections to others, adolescents were found to spend five to ten hours per day online, a behavior significantly correlated with symptoms of depression (Duan et al., 2020). During past epidemics (i.e. Ebola, S.A.R.S.), widespread mental health services such as psycho education and intervention helped those impacted identify and manage related stressors (Hsieh et al., 2021). Services offered to children and adolescents at their school were successful. Such interventions included expressive art therapy, yoga, play therapy, psycho educational groups on child-specific trauma and related coping skills, and how to build safe places for children to express themselves (Decosimo et al., 2019). Students who participated in this mental health programming experienced a significant decrease in symptoms of psychological distress.

Conversations on diagnosis in the mental health field are not new. The word disorder typically refers to a lack of order, implying that there is a standard on what is considered "normal." The medical model utilized within the field of medicine is based on the goal of treatment and prevention of disorders (Bortolotti, 2020). Without mental disorders, practitioners would not need to treat mental health-related disorders (i.e. psychiatrists, psychologists, and mental health counselors). Much like a mechanic to a car, diagnosing identifies something wrong with a person, pulling apart one aspect based on experienced symptomology. Such actions are counterintuitive to the practice of ASE as it is often reductionistic to people, dehumanizing an individual down to symptoms and then assigning a label often coupled with shame and negativity. Instead, the ASE approach to mental health captures the ideals that "life is riddled with challenges that disrupt living" (Lemberger-Truelove & Bowers, 2019, p. 278). Our duty as counselors is to understand those challenges as experienced by the student.

The ASE approach was conceptualized as a tool to aid students within complex social and school environments. A meta-analysis of 43 controlled trials with 49,941 elementary school children found that over 50% of students who received mental health services within the school setting identified as coming from an economically disadvantaged ethnic and racial minority background (Arora et al., 2019). Given the current status of schools and the mental health crisis that impacts children and adolescents, ASE is an ideal approach when working with students in extraneous environments. When considering mental health in children, a wide variety of diagnoses are applicable in the DSM 5-TR (A.P.A., 2022). ASE-grounded evidence-based approaches will be provided to support educators in supporting students with mental health struggles.

ASE Approach to Common Mental Health Concerns in Schools

As individuals, we engage in many systems by which we assume various roles with various influences. For example, I am both a professional and a mother – my role and influence change based on whether I am at home or school. The way I engage with the roles, and the experiences I have with others in those engagements, largely influence the environment of each setting. As outside influences permeate that environment, my previous habitual state of functioning in challenged, causing me to shift and create a new way of engaging within those environments. However, when each environment is heavily impacted by external stressors such as a pandemic, natural disaster, or extenuating factors such as chronic illness or loss of a loved one, my ability to utilize internal capacities is profoundly challenged, making it hard to engage with others.

ASE foundationally functions from two facets: 1. To prepare school-aged children to maximize resiliency in the face of adversity, and 2. Improve social conditions whereby school-aged children can ripen their social capacities (Lemberger-Truelove et al., 2018). As students experience extenuating stressors within their environments, it is the role of the counselor to intervene at various system levels to advocate for a nurturing environment in which the student can grow and thrive. Utilizing a common language for student support is essential. While understanding the implications of diagnosis, it is crucial to value access. For example, a student who receives a mental health diagnosis may receive multifaceted support and services within their school system, granting access to supports that may not have been received should a diagnosis not have been made. While assigning a diagnosis to a student is foundationally counterintuitive to the ASE theory, the practice also concerns environmental advocacy. For this purpose, we will review mental health diagnose seen within school settings, how these symptomologies may be commonly communicated, and provide suggested supports for students struggling with related symptoms.

Depressive Disorders

In looking at surveys of school support staff across the country, there are marked concerns regarding student social, emotional, and mental health as well as student depression and student attempted suicide (Kaufman et al., 2015). In 2016, only 3.2% of children aged 3–17 years struggled with symptoms of depression (Ghandour, 2019). Considering the context of today's world, over the

2020–2021 school year, roughly 44% of school-aged children reported feeling sad or hopeless (C.D.C., 2022).

From an ASE perspective, symptoms of depression are not singular in defining a student's experience. Instead, it is a culmination of experiences from various environments and is impacted by socio-cultural and familial structures and generational patterns. For example, research on childhood depression and thoughts of suicide is correlated with families whereby parents have committed suicide or struggle with depression (Koshollek, 2020). Environmental factors have a considerable impact on symptoms of depression. While much of the diagnostic criteria revolves around the observed or expressed cognition, feeling, and behavior, an ASE practitioner must also consider external stimuli and experiences.

A recent addition to the DSM 5-TR, *disruptive mood dysregulation disorder* (D.M.D.D.), was initially constructed as a disorder that combines aspects of bipolar disorder with conduct disorder specifically for children. While relevant for children at least six years and older, D.M.D.D. is predominantly characterized by chronic and persistent irritability, expressed through frequent temper tantrums or outbursts, and must occur before age ten (APA, 2022). Typically, such outbursts are in response to frustration, are deemed developmentally inappropriate, and occur at least three or more times a week. For example, a 5th-grade student may drop to the ground and start rolling around, like a toddler, while yelling and kicking. This response is not developmentally appropriate for a 5th grader. Once an outburst has occurred, the student is dysregulated for the rest of the day.

Much critique has occurred with the DMDD diagnosis, given that many symptomologies overlap with Oppositional Defiant Disorder, Conduct Disorder, and Attention-Deficit/Hyperactivity Disorder (Bruno, 2019). Such confusion supports the premise of ASE in that humans are complex in their being. Simply assigning a list of symptomologies does not create defining terms to capture lived experiences accurately. Given the lack of empirical research on treatment outcomes and overall diagnostic validity, the symptomology overlap can aid the counselor in identifying evidence-based modalities that may be effective for students (i.e. pulling from effective interventions for O.D.D. or A.D.H.D.). Given the expressed behaviors, students struggling with D.M.D.D. symptoms clearly experience a disconnect from their environment. Influential risk factors have been identified threefold from familial impacts (substance abuse, psychiatric problems, maternal depression before and after birth), stressful life events (early life trauma, recent family divorce/loss/relocation), as well as nutrition status (deficiency in iron, vitamin B12, and folate). As a counselor, it would be essential to join the student in their expressed understanding of their environment and their perceived place, whether at home or school.

While statistics show high rates of depression among school-aged children, the onset of *major depressive disorder* (M.D.D.) does not typically occur until puberty and later peaks for adults in their 20s (A.P.A., 2022). This suggested onset is consistent with research on the pandemic, which reports adolescents in high school as having significantly higher levels of depression than children in elementary and middle school (Meherali et al., 2021). Early identification and treatment are essential for those struggling with M.D.D. as the service could be potentially lifesaving.

One of the key symptoms of M.D.D. is a depressed mood, which for children and adolescents, may present as irritable nearly every day for over two weeks. For a child and adolescent student, this may look more isolating, the student choosing to sit alone for lunch or not engaging with their peers during recess, walking the halls slowly between classes by themselves. With M.D.D., there is also a lack of pleasure in things commonly found to provide enjoyment. A student who previously loved playing basketball now sits out during the games or refuses to go to practice. Additional symptoms include insomnia or hypersomnia, psychomotor agitation, fatigue and loss of energy, feelings of worthlessness or inappropriate guilt, decreased concentration, and recurrent thoughts of death (A.P.A., 2022). For children three to eight years of age, there are often more somatic complaints, such as frequent headaches, stomach aches, or complaints of pain throughout the body (Mullen, 2018).

Throughout younger years, children struggle considerably to verbalize feelings (Mullen, 2018), making it difficult for a counselor in the school setting to assess mood. From an ASE perspective, the counselor must make considerable effort to determine mood based on other modes of evaluation, especially for children ages three to eight. For example, considering feedback from other members of the environment is essential, but it should also not be a defining construct for the student. Gaining feedback from parents and teachers can be informative and provide a comprehensive picture of what the environment looks like for the student. However, it does not capture the student's actual expressed experience. Curiosity aids the school counselor in being open and receptive to receiving the student's lived experience. Should the student struggle with verbalization of feelings, tools, and techniques could be used by the counselor to validate expressed experiences that may be more concrete and include verbiage to begin conversation leading to self-actualization regarding feeling identification such as art expressions or use of play modalities to displace intense emotions.

Student: I don't know how I am feeling. I just am what I am. Everyone keeps asking me what's wrong, and I want to yell at them that I don't know. Stop asking me!

Counselor: *You don't know what you are feeling right now. I can see how that can be frustrating, especially when everyone keeps asking you. Tell me, when do you know how you are feeling?*

Student: Well, I know when I am happy, I laugh and smile. But sometimes when I laugh and smile, it isn't real, you know?

Counselor: When you laugh and smile, it may be more of what others expect of you, not a reflection of how you actually feel inside.

Student: Right, like if my friends are goofing off or doing dumb stuff in class, I don't always think it's funny.

Counselor: That incongruence between what you are feeling versus what emotions you display to others through facial expressions or laughter is a very deep insight! Even though you are struggling to name the specific emotion you are feeling, you can tell when you are not being authentic to yourself. Instead of trying to find a name for the emotion, tell me the sound it makes. If it's not laughter, maybe it's a sign (take a deep breath) or an AHHH.

Student: I think it would be a (takes a deep inhale) UGH!

Counselor: UGH! That's a great place to start.

As these deeper conversations about the student's experience occur, the school counselor must embrace compassion, verbalizing authentic expressions of understanding and empathy, so the student feels heard and connected to the school counselor.

Efficacy in treatment for most depressive disorders can be tackled through psycho education, family education, and psychotherapy, whereby more extreme cases may need consultation for medication management (Mullen, 2018). Psycho education and parent education are achievable through the school setting and speak to practices in ASE. Approaching parents about observed depressive symptoms can be a sensitive topic. However, by using ASE and forming a dialogical connection, the school counselor can navigate the process through curiosity, allowing the family to find commonality between behaviors observed at home and school and compassion for how distressing it can be to have a child struggle. These processes allow for connection to the school counselor, allowing student and family to create a working alliance that will promote betterment for the student, and auxiliary services within the environment are put into place. As families engage in these conversations, they are exposed to the modeled process the school counselor utilizes, absorbing its efficacy. In turn, they may utilize that process, leading to co-regulation. Similar approaches can be utilized with other mental health disorders as well.

Anxiety Disorders

Anxiety has become one of the most common disorders experienced by children and adolescents (Bhatia & Goyal, 2018; Walter et al., 2020). Furthermore, anxiety has become both a symptom in and of itself and a diagnosable disorder. For example, students often comment on how much anxiety they are experiencing. However, anxiety is often a term that defines an experience of several symptoms, such as tightness in your chest, sweaty palms, or lightheadedness – the dimensions of anxiety range from cognitive to affective and behavioral. Identifying diagnostic criteria does not diminish the individual experience. Rather it provides a defining term that validates what may be overlooked and provides access to help needed. Because of the multidimensional aspect of anxiety, there are numerous ways by which children and adolescents experience it.

It is more generalizable when anxiety is not identifiably occurring from a specific situation (separating from an attached person or social situation). *General anxiety disorder* occurs when a student experiences excessive anxiety more days than not for at least six months. This experienced anxiety must be so prevalent that students cannot engage in daily activities because of their preoccupation with worries related to school performance, relationships with peers or family, or feeling as though they are being treated differently than others (Bhatia & Goyal, 2018). Anxiety symptoms experienced by students have been correlated with numerous behavioral outcomes, such as truancy/attendance issues (Finning et al., 2019). The anxiety experienced is difficult to control. Students often report feeling restless, easily fatigued, having difficulty concentrating, irritability, muscle tension, and difficulty sleeping (A.P.A., 2022). While older children and adolescents more commonly experience general anxiety, younger children are more likely to experience anxiety related to a specific person or experience (Walter, 2020).

Separation anxiety can averagely affect preschool and young elementary school children, especially when experiencing a significant change in routine, such as starting schooling or even transitioning into a new school environment. Such transitions are considered developmentally appropriate responses and typically last a few days until a new routine is established.

The first condition of separation anxiety considers the developmental inappropriateness of excessive fear or anxiety in situations where there is separation from an attached individual, such as a child with a parent or guardian (A.P.A., 2022). The distress is accompanied by excessive fears from the anticipation of an upcoming separation, harm for those they are attached to, or fear for themselves experiencing an unfortunate event. These fears lead to refusal behaviors by refusing to leave home or school, to sleep away from home, or without being near attached persons. Younger children are most likely to experience separation anxiety, often experienced through somatic complaints with headaches, stomach aches, or generalized pain.

In some occurrences, separation anxiety can be a culmination of the experience of both the parent and the child. Should the attached parent also be experiencing symptoms of separation anxiety, they may unconsciously transfer some of that anxiety onto the child, leading to both parent and child experiencing a reinforcing pattern of behavior. For example, a student may feel excited about starting kindergarten. While happy for their child, the parent also experiences fear that they will not adjust to the environment successfully. These fears a common for all parents, but the amount of distress experienced and how said distress is managed leads to problematic outcomes. Messages of these fears may be unconsciously communicated to the child, leading to increased anxiety about the upcoming transition for them as well. The school counselor can intervene to aid in supporting both parent and student through this transition.

Counselor: Mrs. A suggested we connected today. What is going on?

Mother: We have been struggling to stay at school this past week. With everything being new, I think she is struggling to adjust.

Counselor: She is struggling setting into her new school environment. Tell me, what does drop-off look like to you?

Mother: Well, when we get to school, she starts to get nervous, like holding onto my hand very tight. When we get to her classroom, she usually stands behind me, peeking out at the other children putting their things away. All the other kids seem so well-adjusted. I don't think she's quite ready yet. When I try to leave, she grabs my leg and starts to cry. The teacher asked me to leave her and go, but how could I do that to her? I ask her if she wants to stay or not, and she says she wants to go home, so we leave.

Counselor: I see how both you and your daughter are experiencing feeling nervous about her new school. When she stands behind you and cries, you also feel upset, so you take her home.

Mother: Well, of course! I am not heartless. I do not want my child to think I do not care about their feelings.

Counselor: I understand that you want her to know you understand and support her feelings. What else might bringing her home each day be telling your child?

Mother: That I love her and don't want her to be upset.

Counselor: Yes, and what else? How much would you like her to have a successful school experience?

Mother: I want her to go to school and be happy.

Counselor: You want her to be at school and be happy. I absolutely want that for her too! Let's make that happen! What has worked before when you had to separate from one another?

As the mother and school counselor work together to find a solution to this problem, the school counselor can also gain valuable background information that can aid in understanding both the mother and her child's experience with this new transition. The dialogical connection demonstrates empathetic understanding through curiosity on behalf of the school counselor. Granted, the vignette shows things working out favorably. Nevertheless, if the mother had responded that she did not care for the school, the school counselor could shift the conversation to best support her in feeling supported with a plan that met their needs. Being open through curiosity and expressing that with dialogical creates a connection between the school counselor, the parent, and the student. While separation anxiety may be more commonly experienced by children and their parents, social anxiety becomes more prevalent as children age into adolescence.

As children become more socially aware of themselves, *social anxiety* is another term commonly used but not necessarily in diagnosable contexts. Social anxiety occurs through fear of social situations where one feels judged by others, such as in conversations with others, meeting new people, or being observed in public settings engaging in common behaviors (such as eating or drinking), or engaging in a performance or public speaking activity (A.P.A., 2013). Each of those situations can cause some distress; the experienced fear of those that experience social anxiety is considered out of proportion to the social context (A.P.A., 2013). For school-aged children, this may translate into temper tantrums, crying, shutting down/blank facial expressions, and refusal to speak. Because of the immense anxiety experienced in these situations, the student may avoid engaging in social settings (Golombek et al., 2020).

Overall, anxiety disorders are among students' most experienced disorders (Bhatia & Goyal, 2018; Walter et al., 2020). Research has identified emotional dysregulation as a potential risk factor for developing anxiety symptoms among youth (Schneider et al., 2018). Self-regulation is considered an internal capacity with ASE targets as an intervention approach. Understanding a risk factor related to the onset of such a prevalent mental health disorder can inform practice through preventative skill-building activities for the general school environment targeting executive functions and social and emotional learning, which target self-regulation skill sets. Examples of school-based educational curricula that target this capacity include evidence-based school counseling curricula such as the Student Success Skills program (Brigman & Webb, 2010).

Trauma and Stressor Related Disorders

Applicable for children six years and older, adolescents, and adults, trauma and stressors related disorder occurs first and foremost when there has been exposure to actual or threatened death, serious injury, or sexual violence either by directly experiencing or witnessing the event or learning the traumatic event occurred to a close family member or friend (A.P.A., 2022). Synonymous with ASE, this diagnosis relates to the experience of an event, or multiple events, that have significantly impacted the capacity by which a school-aged child can co-regulate within their environment.

In today's context, many people worldwide have experienced trauma from the COVID-19 pandemic and related outcomes. Trauma and stressful events are not reduced to fighting in a war. It can occur after the sudden loss of a loved one, leading to a change in life circumstances, loss of a job and related economic hardships, or even experiencing a car accident or complicated childbirth procedure. Like the other disorder criteria covered in this chapter, the diagnosis is the only common language to identify a significant struggle. The way we identify internal capacities to join and construct a supportive environment.

Symptoms of posttraumatic stress disorder (P.T.S.D.) have a significant impact on the daily functioning of school-aged children, interfering with social and cognitive functioning. Based on having this traumatic experience or repeated traumatic experiences, school-age children may experience recurrent memories typically expressed through play, frequent dreams, flashbacks, and prolonged psychological distress (A.P.A., 2022). The response to the traumatic event is so extreme that school-aged children avoid situations that may trigger thoughts, feelings, or memories of what had occurred (A.P.A., 2022).

Because the impacts of P.T.S.D. vary for children and adolescents, suggestions have been made to change diagnostic criteria (De Haan et al., 2020). Symptomologies can become muddied in matching an exact diagnosis when it comes to diagnosis in children and adolescents. As it currently stands, children experiencing P.T.S.D. also display signs of depression given low mood (De Haan et al., 2020). Furthermore, the DSM 5-TR criteria focus on cognitions, which speak directly to maladaptive thoughts that occur around the specific traumatic event, which in children may be expressed through play (A.P.A., 2022). While environmental stimuli are also considered in the experience of cognitions, the experience in and of itself is inherently deemed a weakness, maintaining and reinforcing a viewpoint that is essentially deficit-based.

An ASE approach to P.T.S.D. would include considerations of the strengths school-aged children experience. For example, identifying triggers can be important, but it is also valid to identify points of strength and tools students currently utilize to cope. While making the P.T.S.D. diagnosis can be essential to provide services rendered, the ASE counselor must remain conscious of how language is used to conduct assessments and consider including special interests, strengths, play preferences, and life or family goals. Such influences reframe the deficit of struggling with P.T.S.D. to a strength, identifying what works and using that as the foundation to establish a trusting relationship.

Mental Health Assessments and ASE

Schools across the country differ in the way they manage mental health diagnoses. Some may require a referral to an outside provider, while others may utilize the school-based mental health counselor. While the school counselor collects comprehensive data to inform diagnosis, the diagnosis occurs outside the school counseling office. School counselors must be familiar with interpreting valid and reliable modes of assessment commonly used to make a diagnosis. Such knowledge is essential when supporting a student and monitoring progress. General mental health screeners assess for multiple disorders. They include the Patient Health Questionnaire (P.H.Q.), the DSM-5 Online Assessment Measures, the Adverse Childhood Experiences questionnaire, the Pediatric Symptom Checklist, Youth Outcome Questionnaire, and the Strengths and Difficulties Questionnaire. These screeners can be used within pediatrician offices or as intake paperwork within a counseling agency. Should results indicate any conditions exist, further evaluation may be necessary to identify what the child is experiencing. From an ASE perspective, an assessment that is comprehensive and utilized perspectives from multiple sources speaks to the systemic impact of a child's behavior. The following list includes comprehensive assessments commonly utilized by child and adolescent psychologists: Behavior Assessment System for Children, Third Edition (B.A.S.C.-3); Child Behavior Checklist (C.B.C.L.); Conners Comprehensive Behavior Rating Scales; and Swanson, Nolan, and Pelham (S.N.A.P.-IV).

In addition to considering outcomes from assessments that include multiple systemic perspectives, ASE practitioners must consider environmental factors and assessment of students' perceived capacities (Bowers & Lemberger, 2016). Such assessments may include students' perceived connectedness to various stakeholders within their environment, measures of executive functioning skill sets, or social and emotional learning constructs. This practice speaks to the belief that mental health diagnosis is not a defining characteristic of the student. Further information about their capacity allows the school counselor to know how to support the student within the school setting best, utilizing various support personnel that can provide services, as seen in Chapter 3. Ideally, an ASE school would consist of all stakeholders working together in the environment towards continued academic growth, social and emotional progress, and career development.

Using ASE to Address School-Based Mental Health

Utilizing ASE as the theoretical foundation for intervention targeting school-based mental health occurs both at the individual and systems levels. By intervening, the skill sets learned will permeate into the greater school environment. In approaching a student individually, the first tenet centers around *curiosity*. The counselor is encouraged to join the student's reality by seeking understanding and information through inquiry and openness (Lemberger-Truelove & Bowers, 2019). By taking this stance, rapport is built with the student. Much of curiosity is communicated through a common language. Counselors need to utilize a common language with students. Such practice can be difficult when comparing diagnostic criteria to expressed experience. Through dialogue, the counselor can gauge the student's actual experience.

When it comes to establishing goals for individual counseling, ASE discourages using any specific learning or social outcomes influenced by the school or system itself (Lemberger-Truelove & Bowers, 2019). When working within the field of mental health, we are conditioned to utilize a reduction of distressful symptomologies identified within diagnostic criteria as a mode of goal setting. Such practices are encouraged by evidence-based treatments and insurance providers as conditions for reimbursement. However, these goals, established more so by the counselor than the student, are essentially dehumanizing, disregarding the student's personal goals and self-agency to effect change. Instead, the counselor must place their trust in the student to identify socially meaningful goals that reflect their understanding of their social circumstances (Lemberger-Truelove & Bowers, 2019).

Dialogue is essential when curiously engaging with students regarding their mental health concerns. The counselor must be aware of their power influences, making considerable effort to join with the student in a state of equality, honoring their perspective without imparting your own. These efforts speak to *compassion*, whereby the counselor practices social acceptance with conscious awareness of their judgments. This may be difficult when the power of diagnosis, which shapes the goal of curiosity centered around defining beliefs (e.g. cognitive behavioral approaches), has traditionally driven the counselor's practice (Lemberger & Bowers, 2019). Placing diagnosis aside, the counselor can utilize the validation tool to join the student's reality and display empathy to build trust. The drive behind curiosity is to understand influences and possibilities, speaking to the environment and students' internal capacities.

While intervening with the individual student is invaluable regarding mental health concerns, efforts towards environmental improvements are also encouraged to practice under the ASE approach. Considering the ASE conceptual map in Chapter 1, this practice utilizes *co-regulation*, the mediating factor between the student and the environment. Considering co-regulation, the counselor utilizes an inherent understanding of systemic influences mediating student behavior and how student behavior impacts systemic functioning. However, individual behavior is heavily influenced by personal and social influences beyond the counselor's frame of reference. In treating mental health, co-regulation forces the counselor to remember that the student and their behavior is more than a symptom of the diagnosis. Rather it is a myriad of environmental experiences and influences. In application, co-regulation is expressed through the counselor's dialogue with the student. Rather than inquiring about behavior, the counselor is mindful of situational circumstances.

Counselor: Last meeting, you discussed difficulty sleeping in your new home. How are you adjusting to your new living situation since your father lost his job?

Student: I am still having trouble. We are on a noisy road, and it's hard to make my brain turn off all the outside noise so I can get to sleep. I worry about everything – the noise, am I safe, is my family safe, what will happen to us? It is like my brain doesn't turn off.

Counselor: It sounds as though the noise doesn't allow your brain to turn off at night, and you think about everything that is going on with your life, which is completely understandable considering all that you and your family have encountered these past few months. It is very overwhelming.

Connectedness results from building trust through curiosity and compassion and practicing through co-regulation. Connectedness is considered the experience of sharing respect between school system members. While it foundationally influences a student's connection to the counselor, it also inadvertently impacts the school system. Students struggling with mental health-related concerns internally struggle to connect to others, regardless of prior associations or desires to engage in connection. Feeling as though someone understands, that they trust, and is willing to advocate for their needs within the school system can provide a sense of hope.

When intervening within the system, the shared aspect of connectedness can be promoted through psycho education on relevant and widespread external stressors experienced by students and the surrounding community. For example, topics on the impact of COVID-19, allowing students the space and opportunity to share some of the struggles or experienced strengths they had related to immense adversity, promote opportunities to allow students to connect as well as with their teachers and other administrators through shared experiences. The C.D.C., as well as outcomes from numerous empirical research (Lemberger-Truelove et al., 2015; Lemberger-Truelove et al., 2018; Bowers et al., 2018), identifies the importance of school connectedness as students who felt connected to adults or peers at school were less likely to have persistent feelings of sadness or hopelessness.

The culmination of all these efforts put forth by the counselor leads to *contribution*, whereby the counselor is making an intentional change towards social advocacy within the school environment. For example, the counselor may conduct training with teachers to understand warning signs of specific mental health-related symptoms but also place such within the context of the environmental struggles experienced by the community. Such training may lead to co-regulated effects on teachers, whereby in their effort to support students, they, in turn, become more aware of their mental health-related struggles, feeling further supported by the environment because of the genuine understanding of such experiences. By engaging in open dialogue whereby each experience is valued, members of the environment feel safe, connected, and accepted by one another.

Conclusion

Intervention to address mental health is critical within the school setting. Through a review of common mental health concerns seen within the school, practitioners can conceptualize using ASE to alter the view of diagnosis to include a more comprehensive view of the student that includes environmental factors and internal capacities. Discussing common disorders from the ASE perspective provided a lens to approach each mental health-related concern. Finally, the direct application was provided using the five C's of ASE: curiosity, compassion, connectedness, co-regulation, and contribution. While ASE serves as a systemic theoretical approach, it also embodies social justice initiatives to better aid the students we support.

References

American Psychiatric Association. (2013). *Diagnostic and statistical manual of mental disorders (DSM-5®)*. American Psychiatric Publishing.

American Psychiatric Association. (2022). Diagnostic and statistical manual of mental disorders, Text Revision (DSM-5-TR™). American Psychiatric Association publishing. Washington, DC, USA.

Arora, P. G., Collins, T. A., Dart, E. H., Hernández, S., Fetterman, H., & Doll, B. (2019). Multi-tiered systems of support for school-based mental health: A systematic review of depression interventions. *School Mental Health, 11*(2), 240–264.

Bhatia, M. S., & Goyal, A. (2018). Anxiety disorders in children and adolescents: Need for early detection. *Journal of postgraduate medicine, 64*(2), 75.

Bortolotti, L. (2020, July). Doctors without 'disorders'. In Aristotelian Society Supplementary Volume (Vol. 94, No. 1, pp. 163–184). Oxford University Press.

Bowers, H., & Lemberger, M. E. (2016). A person-centered humanistic approach to performing evidence-based school counseling research. Person-Centered & Experiential Psychotherapies, 15(1), 55–66. https://doi:10.1080/14779757.2016.1139502

Bowers, H., Whitford, D. K., & Maines, N. (2018). Effects of the Student Success Skills program with exceptional students: Influences and outcomes. The Journal of Humanistic Counseling, 57(3), 173–190.

Brigman, G & Webb, L. (2010). Student success skills: Classroom manual (3rd ed.). Boca Raton, FL: Atlantic Education Consultants

Bruno, A., Celebre, L., Torre, G., Pandolfo, G., Mento, C., Cedro, C., ... & Muscatello, M. R. A. (2019). Focus on Disruptive Mood Dysregulation Disorder: A review of the literature. *Psychiatry research, 279*, 323–330.

Center for Disease Control and Prevention. (2022). New CDC data illuminate youth mental health threats during the COVID-19 pandemic. www.cdc.gov/media/releases/2022/p0331-youth-mental-health-covid-19.html. Retrieved September 11, 2022.

Decosimo, C. A., Hanson, J., Quinn, M., Badu, P., & Smith, E. G. (2019). Playing to live: outcome evaluation of a community-based psychosocial expressive arts program for children during the Liberian Ebola epidemic. *Global Mental Health, 6*, e3.

De Haan, A., Landolt, M. A., Fried, E. I., Kleinke, K., Alisic, E., Bryant, R., ... & Meiser-Stedman, R. (2020). Dysfunctional posttraumatic cognitions, posttraumatic stress and depression in children and adolescents exposed to trauma: a network analysis. *Journal of child psychology and psychiatry*, *61*(1), 77–87.

Duan, L., Shao, X., Wang, Y., Huang, Y., Miao, J., Yang, X., & Zhu, G. (2020). An investigation of mental health status of children and adolescents in china during the outbreak of COVID-19. *Journal of affective disorders*, *275*, 112–118.

Finning, K., Ukoumunne, O. C., Ford, T., Danielson-Waters, E., Shaw, L., Romero De Jager, I., ... & Moore, D. A. (2019). The association between anxiety and poor attendance at school–a systematic review. *Child and adolescent mental health*, *24*(3), 205–216.

Ghandour, R. M., Sherman, L. J., Vladutiu, C. J., Ali, M. M., Lynch, S. E., Bitsko, R. H., & Blumberg, S. J. (2019). Prevalence and treatment of depression, anxiety, and conduct problems in US children. *The Journal of pediatrics*, pp. *206*, 256–267.

Golombek, K., Lidle, L., Tuschen-Caffier, B., Schmitz, J., & Vierrath, V. (2020). The role of emotion regulation in socially anxious children and adolescents: a systematic review. *European Child & Adolescent Psychiatry*, *29*(11), 1479–1501.

Hsieh, K. Y., Kao, W. T., Li, D. J., Lu, W. C., Tsai, K. Y., Chen, W. J., ... & Chou, F. H. C. (2021). Mental health in biological disasters: from SARS to COVID-19. *International journal of social psychiatry*, *67*(5), 576–586.

Kaufman, J. H., Seelam, R., Woodbridge, M. W., Sontag-Padilla, L., Osilla, K. C., & Stein, B. D. (2015). Student Mental Health in California's K–12 Schools: School Principal Reports of Common Problems and Activities to Address Them. In *Student Mental Health in California's K-12 Schools: School Principal Reports of Common Problems and Activities to Address Them* (pp. 1–6). RAND Corporation.

Koshollek, A., Wright, C., Henriques, C., Caldwell, M., & Hunt, Q. (2020). Suicide ideation, depression, and family structure in elementary students. *Journal of Family Strengths*, *20*(2), 8.

Lemberger, M. E., Carbonneau, K. J., Selig, J. P., & Bowers, H. (2018). The role of social–emotional mediators on middle school students' academic growth as fostered by an evidence-based intervention. *Journal of Counseling & Development*, *96*(1), 27–40.

Lemberger, M. E., Selig, J. P., Bowers, H., & Rogers, J. E. (2015). Effects of the Student Success Skills Program on executive functioning skills, feelings of connectedness, and academic achievement in a predominantly Hispanic, low-income middle school district. *Journal of Counseling & Development*, *93*(1), 25–37.

Lemberger-Truelove, M. E., & Bowers, H. (2019). An advocating student-within-environment approach to school counseling. *Theories of school counseling for the 21st century*, pp. 266–294.

Lemberger-Truelove, M. E., Carbonneau, K. J., Atencio, D. J., Zieher, A. K., & Palacios, A. F. (2018). Self-regulatory growth effects for young children participating in a combined social and emotional learning and mindfulness-based intervention. *Journal of Counseling & Development*, *96*(3), 289–302.

Liang, L., Ren, H., Cao, R., Hu, Y., Qin, Z., Li, C., & Mei, S. (2020). The effect of COVID-19 on youth mental health. Psychiatric quarterly, 91, 841–852.

McKune, S. L., Acosta, D., Diaz, N., Brittain, K., Beaulieu, D. J., Maurelli, A. T., & Nelson, E. J. (2021). Psychosocial health of school-aged children during the initial COVID-19 safer-at-home school mandates in Florida: a cross-sectional study. *BMC Public Health*, *21*(1), 1–11.

Meherali, S., Punjani, N., Louie-Poon, S., Abdul Rahim, K., Das, J. K., Salam, R. A., & Lassi, Z. S. (2021). Mental health of children and adolescents amidst COVID-19 and past pandemics: a rapid systematic review. *International journal of environmental research and public health, 18*(7), 3432.

Mullen, S. (2018). Major depressive disorder in children and adolescents. *Mental Health Clinician, 8*(6), 275–283.

Schneider, R. L., Arch, J. J., Landy, L. N., & Hankin, B. L. (2018). The longitudinal effect of emotion regulation strategies on anxiety levels in children and adolescents. *Journal of Clinical Child & Adolescent Psychology, 47*(6), 978–991.

Tang, S., Xiang, M., Cheung, T., & Xiang, Y. T. (2021). Mental health and its correlates among children and adolescents during COVID-19 school closure: The importance of parent-child discussion. *Journal of affective disorders*, pp. *279*, 353–360.

Wade, M., Prime, H., & Browne, D. T. (2020). Why we need longitudinal mental health research with children and youth during (and after) the COVID-19 pandemic. *Psychiatry research*, p. *290*, 113143.

Walter, H. J., Bukstein, O. G., Abright, A. R., Keable, H., Ramtekkar, U., Ripperger-Suhler, J., & Rockhill, C. (2020). Clinical practice guideline for the assessment and treatment of children and adolescents with anxiety disorders. *Journal of the American Academy of Child & Adolescent Psychiatry, 59*(10), 1107–1124.

8

ASE APPROACH TO CRISIS

Prevention, Response, and Recovery

Hannah Bowers Parker

Responding to the crisis in the school is an immense topic to cover and warrants its own text. Over the past year alone, numerous states have been riddled with natural disasters such as hurricanes, tornados, and fires. The year 2022 saw 18 weather/climate disasters that resulted in $1 billion in economic devastation and the death of 474 people (N.O.A.A. National Centers for Environmental Information, 2023). The occurrence of violent deaths through active school shootings or suicide is prevalent now more than ever. During the 2018–2019 school year, 1,508 youth homicides and 2,233 youth suicides occurred (National Center for Education Statistics, 2022). From 2020–2021, 93 school shootings occurred, resulting in 118 casualties, the most recorded in a year over 20 years. School counselors must be prepared for whatever crosses the threshold on any day. While ASE has been demonstrated as a tool in working with students, faculty, and administrators in various capacities to increase systemic functioning, it can also be used as a modality in crisis response.

What Is a Crisis?

With synonyms such as catastrophe, emergency, and disaster, a crisis is a time of intense difficulty, trouble, or danger, according to the Oxford English Dictionary. More specifically, a crisis includes a critical incident that may result in death and or serious injury to students, faculty, and staff (MacNeil & Topping, 2007). Because a school is considered an open system, it is susceptible to crises occurring internally and externally, while impacts may be experienced directly and indirectly. External crises can occur from the school globally or nationally. For example, the COVID-19 pandemic was a crisis experienced globally. The

DOI: 10.4324/9781003312871-8

practices and procedures within the school were significantly altered because of outside influences. Another example would be the September 11th terrorist attack on the world trade center. Many around the United States and abroad may remember where they were and what they were doing when they heard the news, whether at work or school. Some schools outside the affected area turned on television coverage, while others encouraged early dismissal so loved ones could be together.

There is also a situation whereby a crisis occurs outside of the school but closer to home. These community events may occur geographically within the same state or region. Consider natural disasters, whereby an entire community can be impacted by devastation, with some losing access to all their basic needs. Schools often serve as a community pillar, providing needy community members shelter, food, or other essentials. However, these disasters can also impact schools, losing supplies or physical structure. Students already experiencing an extreme disruption to daily living activities must shift to alternative educational formats.

When considering crises that could occur within the school setting, these span from impacting the eternity of the school system inward toward an individual student, at the school level, 93 school shootings occurred between the 2021–2022 school year, resulting in 118 casualties (National Center for Education Statistics, 2022). Schools such as Sandy Hook Elementary, Columbine High School, Marjory Stoneman Douglass High School, and Robb Elementary School are a few that serve as reminders that safety in a school setting is not a guarantee and threats can occur at any school level. A review of school-related shootings by the Federal Bureau of Investigation identified schools as the second most likely place to experience an active shooter incident (Blair & Schweit, 2014). School-related violence has a resounding impact throughout the school system, community, and nationally. Individually, a student can experience a crisis in isolation, experiencing thoughts and behaviors related to harming themselves or others. Students could also be experiencing active trauma, living in a home where they experience abuse and or neglect, managing the tragic loss of a loved one, or even managing highly tense social relationships or bullying with their peers exacerbated by social media's influence. In 2016, a sample of 45,287 children found 22.5% to be experiencing economic hardship, 21.9% experienced parental or guardian divorce or separation, 8.1% lived with someone who had a problem with drugs or alcohol, 7.1% lived with a family member who was mentally ill (Crouch et al., 2019). Less than 5% indicated being a victim, witnessing violence in their neighborhood, or being mistreated because of their race or ethnic group. Considering the context of these numbers, this data was collected in 2016 before massive social unrest, a recession plunging millions into economic hardship, and a global pandemic.

The process of executing crisis assessments and actions varies across faculty and staff throughout the school, taking measures to ensure the safety of all students. While these processes are usually grounded in policy and procedure created by district and state officials, sensitivity in carrying out such actions is essential. School counselors and school-based counselors are considered mental health experts on campus and are typically responsible for assessing suicidality, using results to create an action plan. However, these plans may differ by school. It is essential to understand your specific school's operations and the role of yourself and others when a crisis occurs. School crisis plans may centralize themselves around the safety of all school members, and considerations of mental health needs could be ignored. School counselors must advocate for the emotional well-being of their students, intervening with the principal and potential school district officials. Hence, all understand the impact of the crisis on students and the protective factors that can aid in managing traumatic situations.

Crisis Management Plan

Many players have a role and task in the school setting when a crisis ensues. A crisis management plan (C.M.P.) is ultimately decided upon by the school district, which is then enacted by faculty and staff members within the school system. Initially created within the private sector, C.M.P.s are applied to schools to manage crisis outcomes, including loss of safety to the school, impacting enrollment and staff attrition, and the overall psychological well-being of all staff, faculty, and students (Elbedour et al., 2020). It is imperative that school mental health staff, led by school counselors, are key players throughout the development and implementation of a C.M.P..

From an ASE perspective, the school counselor is uniquely positioned to consider all systemic players within the school, their roles, contributions, and related assets in managing crises. Furthermore, in creating the C.M.P., the school counselor can identify weaknesses impacting student preventative programming or professional development opportunities for faculty and staff. An investigation of disparities school counselors identified in the wake of the COVID-19 pandemic found increased student mental health concerns coupled with a lack of connection for students and caregivers, all within an environment where their administration lacked the understanding of the school counselor's role (Limberg et al., 2022). At a time when students needed more support, school counselors reported being inundated with non-counseling-related duties, leaving counseling departments overlooked when they are indeed trained professionals to manage these crises best.

Precrisis: Mitigation and Prevention

Without the occurrence of a crisis, schools are generally considered a safe place for many within the community. Parents are to feel confident placing their children in the care of others, believing no harm will come to them. The process of mitigation and prevention encourages the school counselor to assess the school environment, utilizing data to inform general questions such as:

- What are potential threats to school safety?
- What does school data tell us about potential risks?
- What steps need to be taken to minimize the identified risks?

From a systemic ASE perspective, these questions can be answered within the environmental dimensions of the school: global, national, communal, and internal.

Assessing Needs

Gaining a better understanding of the needs of all school stakeholders is essential in this process. Needs assessments often utilized by school counselors can be utilized to inform CMPs as well as commonly collected data points. Considering preexisting data points, school counselors can use attendance records to identify students struggling with attendance anxiety that may be related to experienced school-based trauma. As for needs assessments, school counselors can illicit feedback from all school stakeholders through qualitative and quantitative methods, sending out surveys or open responses that allow members to identify needed support areas. For ease of utilization, many of these assessments are multiple-choice, forcing students to identify predetermined options that may not fit their needs or experiences. This speaks to the agenda often pushed upon students, making assumptions about their needs and experiences. Utilizing the ASE approach, open-ended questions embrace curiosity. Table 8.1 provides the standard school counseling needs assessment question and is then reframed from the ASE perspective.

TABLE 8.1 Standard Needs Assessment VS ASE Needs Assessment

Standard Needs Assessment Question	*ASE Needs Assessment Question*
How much do you need the following services: - individual counseling - group counseling	When working with others, in what settings do you feel most comfortable?
What topics for classroom lessons would you find beneficial? - Growth Mindset - Communication and Social Skills	What do you find to be true about yourself? For example, do you see yourself as a good student, a good friend, or independent?
How can I support you?	What are you looking to change in your school experience?

Preventative Intervention

With an understanding of student needs, school counselors intervene in numerous modalities to best support students. While much of this text has focused on building the internal capacities of students, that is revisited here as crisis prevention is inherently built through strengthening internal capacities, which enhance their ability to manage stressful situations as they arise. While these internal capacities aid students in managing crises, needs assessment and comprehensive guidance counseling curriculum also aid the school counselor in identifying high-risk students and increasing intervention efforts.

Similar to recommendations for faculty and staff, the ASE school counselor may support students' experience of universal interventions that include reviewing safety protocols for all. This includes reviewing plans such as fire, tornado, or active school shooter drills. These experiences may be upsetting for students, providing the school counselor a unique opportunity to engage and process the experienced emotions within a classroom setting, small group, or individually. Within the classroom and small group atmosphere, connectivity is fostered between classmates as they come together to encourage the safety and well-being for one another. Should the crisis occur, students can ideally feel confident knowing what to do while feeling supported in their environment.

School counselors also utilize skill sets learned through classroom guidance and small group counseling activities to enhance protective factors that prevent individual crises. For example, the ASE grounded, evidence-based, comprehensive guidance curriculum, the Student Success Skills program, has impacted pro-social skills and decreased aggression among students when delivered in a classroom format (Mariani et al., 2015). Further outcomes from the classroom curriculum relate to students' self-reported increase of connectivity to classmates (Lemberger et al., 2015), whereas participation in the small group curriculum led to increased connectivity to people within the school (Lemberger & Clemens, 2012). Connectivity is one of the foundational tenets of ASE and a natural outcome of joint engagement and participation through meaningful topics whereby students learn the skill sets to form authentic connections with one another. Regarding prevention, connectivity is essential to address at-risk behaviors such as bullying, suicidality, or even the courage to identify safe sources of support to disclose potential abuses occurring outside the school system.

Professional Development

Mitigation and prevention also call for examining professional development and support offered to faculty and staff in responding to crises and the aftermath of recovery. Responses to the COVID-19 pandemic highlighted the essential need to enhance training for all faculty and staff on crisis management plans (Grissom & Candon, 2021). When considering concepts of co-regulation from ASE, strengthening internal capacities is more than just a prevention activity limited to supporting students. Professional development opportunities focused on supporting faculty and staff in strengthening their own internal capacities furthers their ability to engage in co-regulating engagement with students, aiding in the way the crisis is managed. Teachers participating in a mindfulness social-emotional learning consultation intervention were found to increase personal awareness and decrease reported stress and conflict within the student-teacher relationship (Molina et al., 2022). The ASE school counselor does not only intervene with students but also with faculty and staff. The following workshop example outlines ways to use the workshop to review the CMP and process faculty's emotional experience while contemplating the potential of experience a school-based crisis utilizing Brigman and colleagues' workshop lesson plan template (2022).

Planning: Using technology can be valuable in imparting information. Providing faculty with a copy of the C.M.P. and notes or a PowerPoint with a breakdown of the information provided within the workshop. Support resources should be included in these handouts. A technical presentation allows participants to track throughout.

Warm Up: Introduce the topic being discussed. Provide an outline of objectives for the meeting to ensure participant buy-in, helping them feel as though you are using their time effectively.

Ask Before Telling: Consistent with the ASE, participants are asked to share their thoughts and feelings about the school crisis. This open conversation allows the school counselor to hear specifically what faculty needs may be in this situation, gaining understanding and better able to tailor the workshop to best meet their needs.

Workshop Content: Addressing the topic related to the crisis. While the information is imparted, an ASE school counselor incorporates self-care techniques that can aid faculty in addressing these situations. Asking for feedback on these areas is crucial to ensure participants know that the modalities given are not fixed but rather flexible recommendations that can be taken.

Personalize and Practice: As mentioned within the workshop content, including the opportunity to personalize and practice the content is essential. After discussing aspects of the topic or reflecting on the potential crisis, the school counselor can facilitate meditation, pair and then share opportunities on personal self-care techniques.

Process and Summarize: After reviewing the information and engaging in experiential activities that promote the practice and individual meaningfulness, ask faculty what the experience was like or how you can use what you learned further personalizes the experience.

Evaluation: Once the workshop has concluded, asking faculty for feedback on their experience in an anonymous forum is essential. This provides the opportunity to revise materials, delivery, and or provide follow-up to all or some who may need additional support.

Communication is an essential component of a C.M.P.. It must be a core component of professional development training, so all faculty and staff understand their role and responsibility as a crisis ensues. From an ASE perspective, this training could also be an opportunity to practice mindfulness-based meditations that encourage faculty and staff to envision the crisis occurring, process those feelings, and learn new techniques to help manage the anticipated emotions that may be experienced. As the roles for each staff and faculty member are reviewed, there is an inherent opportunity to enhance the concept of contribution. Each member is responsible for playing an essential role that will contribute to the physical and psychological safety of one another. Engaging in these activities further establishes the connectivity between members of the system, understanding that each person plays a part and, should a crisis arise, they are engaging in the experience together.

Responding to Crisis

As a crisis occurs, a C.M.P.'s components must be attended to. Depending on the nature of the crisis and the level by which it is experienced, these protocols are typically grounded in communication and immediate action. Communication considers how specific information is shared with the public, parents, students, faculty, and staff, primarily emphasizing safety (Elbedour et al., 2020). Designating a staff member responsible for communication is key within the CMP, as well as whom they need to communicate with based on the type of crisis occurring. Understanding how people respond to crises is crucial as information is imparted during these times. The ASE school counselor can utilize role playing during professional development opportunities while addressing stress management techniques to validate and manage personal reactions to best accomplish their role.

Action protocols are grounded in the outcome that ensures students' and staff's physical and psychological safety (Brock et al., 2013). These plans are practiced with students, faculty, and staff regularly and vary based on the type of crisis occurring. For example, the response to a community crisis may include the school going on lockdown and students, faculty, and staff engaging in a safety protocol. Action protocols must be clearly communicated to all school members, practiced, processed, and disseminated to parents and community members who may find themselves on school grounds as a crisis occurs.

Action protocols and communication for communal and school crisis differs from a crisis at the individual level. Individual level crises include harm to self, harm to someone else, or known harm occurring to a vulnerable population (children, disabled individuals, or the elderly). Suicidality, abuse, and instability at home are a few crises that arise on an individual level. While the preventative measures mitigate some of these situations, even by notifying the school counselor who is more at risk for these potential behaviors, specific protocols must be followed should a student present as being in active crisis. For expressed thoughts or plans of suicidality, school counselors are considered the mental health expert in the school and are tasked with conducting a risk assessment. These assessments are usually standardized within the school district and a uniform practice across schools. Similarly, all adults within a school are typically deemed mandated reporters for child abuse or sexual abuse.

The ASE school counselor navigates these situations by attending the school and district protocol regarding risk assessments. However, the way the ASE school counselor presents in these assessments is unique. Through curiosity, the school counselor is non-judgmental, promoting open conversation in a top-down fashion that may encourage the student to be more truthful in their experiences. The school counselor can connect with the student through compassion, expressing understanding and validating emotional experiences. Where the change occurs is exploring what could be done differently and identifying opportunities for self-directed connection.

Counselor: While this isn't the usual context that we meet, I really do appreciate this time we have together. I have heard a few things before stepping in for this assessment, but I am much more interested in hearing what has occurred from your point of view.

Student: Last night, I was feeling really overwhelmed and was unable to complete my school assignments. On top of that, my friends are all fighting with each other and putting me in the middle of everything. When I got to school this morning, I don't know, I just couldn't keep it together. I told Mrs. A that things would be easier if I was dead and I just wanted to kill myself.

Counselor: I hear that you are overwhelmed with both school and your friends. The workload from school on top of being in the middle of your friends' conflict has become too much for you.

Student: Yes, I just want it all to stop. It would just be easier, you know? To not have to deal with all of it.

Counselor: It is a lot to manage, all of the things you have going on right now. Like you're at maximum capacity on what you can handle. Tell me, what are your beliefs about school and what kind of student you are?

Student: I am a good student, my parents expect me to get A's, B's are ok. I work hard and am in a lot of the advanced classes. It feels good when they are proud of me.

Counselor: I hear how you like to make your parents happy through earning good grades. I wonder, aside from your parent's perspective, how do you feel about the type of student you are?

Student: Sometimes I wonder if it is worth it. Like, I feel so competitive with my classmates and I'm like, why? Why is this so important? I feel like I work myself to death and rarely get to enjoy life because of it.

Counselor: While it feels good to achieve for your parents, you struggle to find balance in your life. You believe all you do is work schoolwork.

In this example, the school counselor would continue to use this method of discussion to future explore beliefs about peer relationships, identify protective factors, and further ask specifics related to the indicated suicidality. When asking specific questions about suicide, utilizing a straightforward method is most recommended, but creating the dialogical connection first is essential to ensure responses are authentic. Risk assessments are often a snapshot of the student's life, identifying social and cultural systems, family, community, and student peers. Results from these outcomes are communicated to parents and guardians with recommendations on the next steps.

Recovery

The response to crisis recovery highlights the importance of student mental health. Students who were seemingly able to complete tasks on time may no longer be able to attend to meeting basic needs. Others may have large reactions to a small setback. Response to crisis looks different for each individual and is not limited to only students. The effects of a crisis extend to all members of the school setting, including faculty and staff. While the physical and related emotional sensation of crisis, the memory of the event still lingers with the capability to elicit strong emotional responses. Recovery refers to rebuilding the community and returning to a sense of normalcy within the school system, even if it takes years (Cowan & Rossen, 2013). In addressing recovery post-crisis, the school counselor must advocate ensuring any student, faculty, or staff member needing mental health support has access to counseling services.

The foundational tenets of ASE believe that all feelings, thoughts, and responses to situations are valid and reasonable. Where change occurs is the reflection on how such repeated responses may limit potential. As applied to the crisis, experiencing fear during and following a traumatic incident is warranted. In a simplistic viewpoint, fear is a natural response to crisis situations that allow us to know instinctively that something is wrong, and we need to take measures to stay safe. Best practices within a C.M.P. call for immediate counseling services post-crisis. Post-trauma recovery efforts focus on positive relationships that support students' resiliency while focusing on the entirety of the school system, recreating a safe and supportive learning environment (Wolpow et al., 2009). These relationships can be built through classroom guidance, small group counseling, and individual counseling services administered by the school counselor or led by the school counselor.

When trauma occurs at the communal or school level, a mental health trauma response team will often be brought in to provide additional support. School counselors working from the ASE perspective welcome the support of others, using the opportunity to advocate for their students, faculty, and staff while consulting to ensure these new professionals can engage and connect with those in need. Mental health teams called in for crisis response services were more successful when collaborating directly with community members, such as the school counselor (Fruetel et al., 2022). The best advocacy post-trauma is providing services to all in need.

School counselors must be protective of how time is spent during crisis recovery. An investigation of the COVID response found that school counselors engaged in non counselor activities experienced the highest rates of burnout. In contrast, those focused on delivering direct counseling services (i.e., classroom guidance, small group counseling, individual counseling, and consultation) found school counselors to be compassionate and effective in their contribution efforts (Villares et al., 2022). The ASE school counselor must focus on the direct delivery of counseling related services, whether through advocacy of consultation and coordination of services and providing direct counseling through classroom guidance, small group counseling, or individual counseling.

These collaborative efforts taken by the school counselor may shift into online learning environments. Looking at responses to COVID-19, school counselors often shifted to engaging with students in online capacities. This was an opportunity to learn new software and technology to engage with students (Limberg et al., 2022). In this transition, school counselors were also found to increase collaboration efforts with teachers and other professionals, increasing role recognition of the school counselor and increasing the ability to support all school system members. The state of education and all students and faculty are still reeling within this post-pandemic era, which highlighted the use of technology and how it can be used in lieu of face-to-face instruction. As future crises occur, maintaining awareness of online platforms is crucial, and the shift in instruction can occur anytime.

Conclusion

The goal of an effective C.M.P. includes ensuring the physical and psychological well-being of all school stakeholders and allowing the school counselor to work from an ASE perspective to advocate for mental health needs. This approach provides a rationale for incorporating preventative intervention through direct services to all students and professional development for faculty and staff. From an ASE perspective, the school counselor is qualified to collaborate, train, and implement a C.M.P.. Creating a C.M.P. is often the organizational duty of the district. However, the school counselor is primed to provide insight into the psychological impact on students, faculty, and staff. Because of that insight, the school counselor advocates for the school system's psychological safety and provides considerations in the prevention, response, and recovery efforts outlined within the C.M.P..

Engaging preventatively starts with the needs assessment, allowing the school counselor to understand where at-risk behaviors may lie. Such assessments then inform the implementation of preventative programming. At the student level, that includes communicating about the C.M.P. and processing emotional reactions while utilizing evidence-based modality to increase internal capacities and, in turn, a sense of connectedness to others. Such intervention addresses crises from a communal, school, and individual level. Preventative intervention is also essential among faculty and staff from the ASE perspective. The school counselor is called upon to lead professional development opportunities with similar outcomes among staff and faculty as student outcomes: connectivity and compassion while promoting opportunities for co-regulation.

Students, faculty, and staff are to feel safe at school, assured that no harm will come their way. Unfortunately, the prevalence of incidents such as school shootings, pervasive bullying, or even exposure to self-harming behaviors such as cutting leaves all experiencing trauma even after the crisis has passed. The ASE school counselor must advocate that all impacted by the crisis can receive counseling services. Such efforts may include providing direct counseling services or coordinating efforts with outside crisis response teams to ensure recovery efforts can occur.

References

Blair, J. P., & Schweit, K. W. (2014). Texas State University and Federal Bureau of Investigation. US Department of Justice, Washington DC.

Brigman, G., Villares, E., Mullis, F., Webb, L. D., & White, J. F. (2022). *School counselor consultation: Skills for working effectively with parents, teachers, and other school personnel*. John Wiley & Sons.

Brock, S. E. (2013). Preparing for the school crisis response (pp. 19-30). New York: Routledge.

Cowan, K. C., & Rossen, E. (2013). Responding to the unthinkable: School crisis response and recovery. *Phi Delta Kappan*, *95*(4), 8–12.

Crouch, E., Probst, J. C., Radcliff, E., Bennett, K. J., & McKinney, S. H. (2019). Prevalence of adverse childhood experiences (ACEs) among US children. *Child Abuse & Neglect*, *92*, 209–218.

Elbedour, S., Alsubie, F., Al'Uqdah, S. N., & Bawalsah, J. A. (2020). School crisis management planning. *Children & Schools*, *42*(4), 208–215.

Fruetel, K. M., Duckworth, R. C., Scott, S. L., & Fenderson, E. N. (2022). Exploring the experiences of counselors responding to the crisis in rural communities. *Journal of rural mental health*, *46*(1), 40.

Grissom, J. A., & Condon, L. (2021). Leading schools and districts in times of crisis. *Educational Researcher*, *50*(5), 315–324.

Lemberger, M. E., & Clemens, E. V. (2012). Connectedness and self-regulation as constructs of the student success skills program in inner-city African American elementary school students. *Journal of Counseling & Development*, *90*(4), 450–458.

Lemberger, M. E., Selig, J. P., Bowers, H., & Rogers, J. E. (2015). Effects of the Student Success Skills program on executive functioning skills, feelings of connectedness, and academic achievement in a predominantly Hispanic, low-income middle school district. *Journal of Counseling & Development*, *93*(1), 25–37.

Limberg, D., Villares, E., Gonzales, S., Starrett, A., & Rosen, N. (2022). An investigation of how school counselors adapted their delivery due to COVID-induced disparities. *Professional School Counseling*, *26*(1b), 2156759X221105797.

MacNeil, W., & Topping, K. (2007). Crisis management in schools: evidence based. The Journal of Educational Enquiry, 7(1).

Mariani, M., Webb, L., Villares, E., & Brigman, G. (2015). Effect of Participation in Student Success Skills on Prosocial and Bullying Behavior. *Professional Counselor*, *5*(3), 341–353.

Molina, C. E., Lemberger-Truelove, M. E., & Zieher, A. K. (2022). School Counselor Consultation Effects on Teachers' Mindfulness, Stress, and Relationships. *Professional School Counseling*, *26*(1a), 2156759X221086749.

National Center for Education Statistics. (2022). Violent Deaths at School and Away From School and School Shootings. *Condition of Education*. U.S. Department of Education, Institute of Education Sciences. Retrieved Feb 25, 2023, from https://nces.ed.gov/programs/coe/indicator/a01.

NOAA National Centers for Environmental Information (2023) U.S. Billion-Dollar Weather and Climate Disasters. Retrieved Feb 25, 2023, from www.ncei.noaa.gov/access/billions/, DOI: 10.25921/stkw-7w73

Villares, E., Starrett, A., & Limberg, D. (2022). Exploring school counseling during the first wave of COVID-19. *Journal of Counseling & Development*.

Wolpow, R., Johnson, M. M., CPP, C., & Hertel, R. (2009). The heart of learning and teaching. *Olympia, WA: Office of Superintendent of Public Instruction (OSPI) Compassionate Schools*.

9

ASE AND THE DATA-MINDED SCHOOL COUNSELOR

Matthew E. Lemberger-Truelove

In the most recent edition of the American School Counselor Association National Model (A.S.C.A., 2019), school counselors are directed to deliver interventions supported by empirical evidence. School counselors are further challenged to capture and report their own evidence for the purposes of improving and marketing their comprehensive programs. This data-minded orientation is relevant to the Advocating Student-within-Environment (ASE) (Lemberger, 2010; Lemberger & Hutchison, 2014; Lemberger-Truelove & Bowers, 2019) as there is a nascent body of empirical evidence in support of the approach as contributory to student and educator outcomes. Yet as a personal liberatory and social justice approach to education and school counseling, the bases for ASE theory can both accommodate traditional empirical approaches while offering critical commentary on how empirical practices affect students and school systems.

Data captured in schools are symbolic representations of persons, things, and dynamics in systems. School systems and each person therein are profoundly complex. From a sympathetic perspective, data as symbols provides educators and other stakeholders mechanisms for understanding and informing action. For example, observing and describing students' responses to a teacher's pedagogical approach can aid a school counselor who provides consultation services intended to improve the class climate. Numbers and language symbols cannot necessarily capture or suspend the actual event, but it can provide the school counselor with insights into what occurred and elucidate important trends.

Unfortunately, unsophisticated collection and use of data can be incredibly harmful and dehumanizing. The biases of the person collecting the data can misrepresent students or the events in a school. Callow empiricists might neglect

DOI: 10.4324/9781003312871-9

structural inequities across groups of students and therefore misrepresent the unique challenges they face as compared to other groups of students. Consistent with the bases of ASE, which is an approach that is concerned with cultivating more perspicacious personal orientations that complement more just schooling environments, a data-minded school counselor must pursue symbols that are personally authentic and empowering while also challenging restrictive education systems.

To this end, in this chapter the reader will be presented with three foci for ASE-informed school counseling practitioners and scholars. First, readers will be offered a brief, philosophical primer related to the utility of ASE empirical practices and outcomes. Second, an overview of select empirical studies related to general school counseling and ASE-specific literatures will be presented. Finally, drawing from the first two foci, readers will be offered specific recommendations for empirical practices as consistent with ASE theory.

ASE and Empirical Scholarship

A.S.C.A. (2019) recommends that school counselors utilize data to support the academic and learning, personal and social, and career development of students, school personnel, and other relevant education stakeholders. Embracing an empirical perspective does not necessarily suggest that the school counselor passively accepts all data as veritable or valuable, just as a school counselor should consider data and related empirical messages with a healthy and protective skepticism. Orientated with a theory such as ASE, a school counselor might be able to leverage the useful qualities from data and empirical findings and challenge unhelpful narratives that potentially compromise students or school systems.

Adherents to ASE theory generally believe that empirical practices are potentially helpful, albeit often limited and occasionally harmful. Ideally, data, analyses, and interpretations can be useful in assessing occurrences in schools and in contributing to informed intervention and advocacy decisions. Furthermore, data can be used to expand counseling services in schools, especially in spaces where school counselors have been typically underutilized or maligned. Alternatively, data, analyses, and interpretations of results have been historically used as tautologies to pander to researcher predilections or to further marginalize the most vulnerable students, families, or educators. Even well-intended and yet callow attempts at scholarship cause harm by misrepresenting the perspectives and potentials of participants.

An ASE practitioner or scholar understands the potential benefits and limitations of empirical scholarship, be it quantitative or qualitative approaches. Often one research paradigm is privileged over the other based on the favors of the scholar. ASE proceeds from a pragmatic epistemological position; namely, all data are imprecise symbols intended to capture dynamic experiences in complex systems. Rigorous methodologies and procedures should be pursued but accomplishing such ends do not automatically suggest that the research is beyond scrutiny or more veritable. Instead, empirical scholarship cannot necessarily accomplish probabilities or trustworthiness; rather, the principal focus of empirical work pertains to expanding useful possibilities for students and school environments.

Consider the example of the standard psychological assessment. There are certain thresholds for reliability and validity that are considered appropriate, yet even a sound instrument cannot precisely capture respondent experiences. If a student were to complete a depression assessment and a prompt pertains to current experiences, does the student circling a given anchor ever fully encapsulate the unique experience of that student? Does commingling scores across multiple questions or multiple respondents necessarily close the gap between the response chosen based on the assessment anchors presented and the unique experience of sadness?

Given these types of assessments are derived from a positivist worldview, postmodern empirical approaches that utilize interviews or observation are often considered more nuanced. Yet these approaches also rely on symbols, in this case linguistic, to capture and suspend experience for the purposes of analyses (Lemberger, 2012). It appears all approaches are fraught with limitations in their ability to capture and report actual experiences, especially dynamic experiences that are contemporaneously complex, evolve over time, and vary across contexts or conditions.

Yet all is not lost. An ASE informed school counselor does not adopt empirical mindedness simply to assign value to a student or ascertain the truth about a school system. Instead, consistent with ASE practice in counseling, an ASE empiricist embraces the presupposition that all data are complex and generative. Rigorous results are meaningful, not as an end to themselves, but as a part of a larger mosaic of information related to peoples' experiences and circumstances in elaborate social systems. The use of the most elegant and appropriate methodologies is pursued not because they close the aperture towards truth, instead we do so for more pragmatic reasons. Just as ASE practice attempts to cultivate sapience (i.e. personal and social wisdom) in students, empirical practices and data can inspire scrutiny related to one's experience and the surrounding milieu. Further, empirically minded practitioners can connect with a greater variety of allies, using learned results from empirical practices to advocate for more helpful outcomes.

Just as data is subject to scrutiny, the results of empirical inquiry are also examined. Results and related interpretations affect systems. From an ASE perspective, it is essential that empirical results and interpretations of findings are contextualized relative to their fitness for students and schools. Returning to the example of the depression assessment, when results of assessment are shared with a student or guardian, the effect reflects the intent of the assessment and also the experiences and interpretations of the student or guardian. Akin to ASE epistemology, the experience of empirical data or results co-determines experience in reflexive ways; the student alters the results, and the results alter the student. Therefore, a school counselor inspired by ASE theory takes as much credence in the empirical data and results as one does the lived experience of the people they pertain to.

Similar to ASE counseling practice in schools, where intervention affects the student, and the student in turn affects the school system, or intervention that affects the system that in turn affects the student, empirical data and results affect each student and aspect of the school system. In differing but related ways, the student and school environment each affect data and results.

The ultimate aspiration of the ASE scholar or practitioner is advocacy for any given student or the total school environment. The acme of this aspiration is to demonstrate how the student and elements within the school system co-regulate; in this way, the purpose is not to pursue empirical outcomes that necessarily validate the efficacy of ASE, rather the intent of scholarship is to further inform the necessary changes in ASE so that it may evolve as students and school systems evolve.

School Counseling and Education Literature

School counseling is an evolving identity and practice profession with origins in vocational and educational guidance that has matured into a comprehensive student support profession with relevance to student learning and academic performance, personal and social development, career development, systems advocacy, and educator support (Dollarhide & Saginak, 2021; Gysbers & Henderson, 2001). From an ASE perspective, the school counselor has a non-dual identity that is equal parts educator and professional counselor (Levy & Lemberger-Truelove, 2021). This posture affects the training, professional practice behaviors, and anticipated outcomes for the professional.

The professional literature affiliated with professional school counseling has evolved as the profession has evolved over the recent decades. Generally speaking, the literature has reflected the push for evidence-based outcomes in education more broadly. Initially, the preponderance of the literature dealt with the roles and responsibilities of the school counselor, whereas more recently there has been a push for the inclusion of scholarship that illustrates how school counseling activities contribute to specific student and school outcomes.

School counselors can utilize these findings from the literature in a variety of ways. First, given many school counselors are maligned to indirect services, school counselors can present empirical evidence to advocate for the inclusion of more direct services. In a related way, the literature can assist the school counselor in prioritizing intervention approaches based on the composition and needs of a particular school. In addition to program advocacy, a school counselor can draw from the extant literature as a point of comparison relative to any outcome data that they might collect. In many ways, awareness of the literature can aid the school counselor in being more attentive to student needs and potential or anticipated effects on entire school systems.

School Counseling Literature

The school counseling literature provides practitioners and stakeholders with some evidence that direct services generally improve student or school related outcomes (Whiston & Quinby, 2009). In a meta-analytic analysis of approximately 150 school counseling studies performed over nearly 25 years, Whiston and colleagues (2011) found that students who direct counseling services reported outcomes approximately one-third of a standard deviation higher than those students who were not exposed to those services. Effect sizes for student participants were particularly high in the areas of discipline (d = .83), problem solving (d = .96), and career knowledge (d = .67), with significant but more modest outcomes on academic achievement (d = .16). These student outcomes were particularly apparent when school counselors utilized small group counseling activities (d = .41), with some evidence in support of whole class activities (d = .31) and minimal evidence in support of individual counseling services (d = .07).

Although school counselors are associated with desirable student outcomes, they are often under-utilized and get encumbered with ancillary or administrative tasks (Blake, 2020). Role confusion pertaining to school counseling is especially curious, as their contributions as an educator and a counselor can reflect and amplify educational processes and outcomes. Carrell and Hoekstra (2014) found that one additional school counselor reduces delinquent behaviors in all students and contributes to increases in male students' reading and math. They further found that school counselors have similar influences on achievement as compared to increasing the teacher quality for each educator in a school and are more than twice as influential on whole school outcomes such as employing a new teacher. Longitudinal and large-scale data drawn show that school counselors have desirable effects on areas such as student achievement, attendance, and discipline, particularly for culturally diverse, low-income, or academically challenged students (Domina et al., 2022; Mulhern, 2022). Considered together, the empirical evidence does provide some evidence that school counselors can affect students and school systems in profound ways.

Capitalizing on these trends in the literature, A.S.C.A. (2021) put forth the A.S.C.A. Student Standards: Mindsets and Behaviors for Student Success.

Colloquially known as the Mindsets and Behaviors, they are a series of 36 standards intended to inform school counselors on the knowledge, attitudes, and skills students should be able to demonstrate as a result of exposure to intervention. Each of the standards was drawn from allied literature and not necessarily tethered to specific empirical studies evaluating the intervention effects as influenced by school counselors. On the one hand, the standards provide school counselors with areas to focus intervention and anticipate specific school-related outcomes in the areas of students' learning strategies, self-management skills, and social skills. On the other hand, these standards challenge school counseling practitioners and scholars to link specific interventions with the outcomes outlined in the standards. Inferentially, school counselors should adopt a theoretical posture that is correspondent to these standards.

It should be noted, consistent with ASE theory and the intention of the A.S.C.A. Mindsets and Behaviors, there are a great number of diverse ways that a student can express mindsets and behaviors. For example, Standard B-LS 4. is "Self-motivation and self-direction for learning." It could be easily misinterpreted or misused as a single outcome, especially reflective of the motivation and learning values of educators or other adults. Instead, this standard should be understood in a mechanistic way from the student's perspective. Self-motivation can apply to the practice of learning a great variety of things, not limited to academic content but also cultural artifacts pertinent to the values of the student or their social systems.

ASE Literature

The first writings related to ASE theory (e.g. Lemberger, 2010) shows up in the literature more than a decade before the publication of the A.S.C.A. Mindsets and Behaviors (2021). This said, ASE and the Mindsets and Behaviors were both inspired by similar literatures, particularly pertaining to how supporting the development of certain student capacities can be supported such that they might mature in outcomes relevant for learning and personal-social outcomes.

In addition to the shared focus on student development, the language found in the A.S.C.A. Mindsets and Behaviors appear to be consistent with the epistemological (i.e. students and aspects of the school environment as interacting determinants of experience) and social justice foci. Specific to the A.S.C.A. Mindsets and Behaviors, it is suggested that "school counselors shape ethical, equitable and inclusive school environments that help all students achieve and succeed" (n.p.). There are likely to be nuanced differences between ASE and the A.S.C.A. Mindsets and Behaviors, yet school counselors might be able to draw inspiration from their shared agreements from the literature.

For example, ASE and to the A.S.C.A. Mindsets and Behaviors reflect the growing appreciation for social and emotional learning (S.E.L.) in schools. S.E.L. includes the development of knowledge, skills, and attitudes that contribute to healthy identities, manage emotions and contribute to the accomplishment of personal and collective goals, feel and show empathy for others, establish and maintain supportive relationships, and make responsible and caring decisions (C.A.S.E.L., 2022). In large reviews and meta-analyses of hundreds of students on diverse groups of students, S.E.L. practices are associated with various student outcomes including increased academic achievement, personal and social growth, and psychological and physical wellness (Durlak et al., 2011; Mahoney et al., 2018). In kind, there is developing support that SEL interventions also support classroom teachers' interactions with students and classroom management (Blewitt et al., 2020). This literature is intuitively consistent with school counseling broadly given that practitioners utilize various relational and empowerment strategies to support students and educators.

ASE theory draws from a more granular literature related to student capacity building. For example, a school counselor who is guided by ASE might be concerned with assisting the development of a student's executive functioning, which include the various processes necessary for goal-intended behaviors (Doebel, 2020). These self-regulatory operations include how the student monitors experience (in working memory), shifts attention, and inhibits emotional and cognitive responses (Miyake & Friedman, 2012). Another primary conceptual influence on ASE theory is the literature related to a student's feeling of connectedness to the school, which includes if the student feels safe, valued, and contributory (Witherspoon et al., 2009). A student's executive functioning and their feelings of connectedness are each uniquely associated with academic and behavioral outcomes desired in school environments (e.g. Jacob & Parkinson, 2015; Niehaus et al., 2012).

While at first blush these findings might not appear to be fully supportive of a liberatory and social justice practice such as ASE theory, S.E.L. and related concepts such as students' executive functioning and feelings of connectedness can be understood as the mental and relational operations necessary for development and response in turbulent schooling environments. For example, students who hail from economically challenged communities can inhibit full collapse into the cycles of oppression and commit to learning and social outcomes more commensurate with uncontaminated goals. Similarly, students who connect with key stakeholders might be able to better leverage their resources and challenge typical impediments to success. While in some way this places a profound burden on the students as self-advocates, it does place students as the arbitrators of their own outcomes. Also, assuming an ASE-inspired counselor co-regulates the development of these capacities and further challenges systems to value their expression in school contexts, it is feasible that entire educational systems can change to accommodate the capacity of students.

More than conceptual inferences to guide practice, there is an emerging literature that substantiates the implementation of ASE theory. These findings are consistent with the S.E.L. focus found in the A.S.C.A. Mindsets and Behaviors and further links S.E.L. operations with students' academic achievement outcomes. Also, each of the current ASE-related studies were completed in ethnically diverse and economically challenged school environments, therefore providing some inferential evidence that ASE is culturally responsive and social justice focused. Finally, more recent empirical studies have focused on how the delivery of ASE interventions affect classroom teachers. Commingling the results of student- and teacher-focused studies does provide some inferential evidence in support of key theoretical themes including the importance of co-regulated schooling relationships and the primacy of reflexive interventions contributing to more apposite co-determinants of experience in school environments.

ASE and Social and Emotional Learning Outcomes. Student Success Skills (S.S.S.) is a suite of manualized school counseling interventions that are consistent with the theoretical assumptions and practice behaviors of ASE theory (Villares et al., 2011; Webb et al., 2019). The S.S.S. program has been endorsed by the Collaborative for Academic, Social, and Emotional Learning (C.A.S.E.L.) as one of the preeminent S.E.L. intervention approaches (2015). S.S.S. is constituted of multiple training and practice protocols, tailored for differing student ages, native languages, and settings (e.g. classroom, small group). Each protocol includes activities intended to support students' cognitive skills (e.g. goal setting, progress monitoring, and memory), social skills (e.g. listening, problem solving), and self-management skills (e.g. attention, motivation, and anger regulation) (Brigman et al., 1999). Reviews of the S.S.S. program have evinced positive outcomes on students' academic achievement and social skills related to S.E.L. (Vilares et al., 2012).

There have been several S.S.S. studies that specifically cite the affiliation with ASE theory and demonstrate how the approach might contribute to S.E.L. outcomes in students. In the first published ASE study, investigators evaluated the effects of exposure to the S.S.S. small group protocol as delivered to 53 inner-city, fourth and fifth grade African American students (Lemberger & Clemens, 2012). Compared to the control group, those students who participated in the S.S.S. small group intervention reported significant changes in metacognitive skill and feelings of connectedness, in addition to positive change in teacher-reported executive functioning.

In five randomized controlled trials of the S.S.S. classroom protocol, researchers found significant treatment effects on S.E.L. pertinent outcomes. Three of these studies considered changes in a sample of predominately Hispanic, low-income middle school students, and results included significant treatment effects in students' changed executive functioning and feelings of connectedness to school (Bowers et al., 2015; Lemberger et al., 2015; Lemberger et al., 2018). More recently, in a study of more than 4,300 culturally diverse fifth grade students, Webb and colleagues (2019) found treatment effects for students' behavioral engagement, disruption, assertion, cooperation, and test anxiety skills. Finally, Bowers and colleagues found that teachers reported positive changes in kindergarteners' executive functioning and social, emotional, and academic-related behaviors improved after exposure to five weeks of the S.S.S. program.

ASE and Academic Achievement. Many of the S.S.S. studies utilizing ASE theory also included academic achievement outcomes to further demonstrate the potential usefulness of the approach. A primary example was the Lemberger and colleagues (2018) study of 193 predominately Hispanic 7th graders who were randomly assigned to participate in the classroom version of the S.S.S. program. Results from a multi-level growth analysis across four testing periods showed that students in the treatment conditions increased in reading and mathematics achievement at a greater rate as compared to their peers in the control group. In fact, students in the treatment condition grew at a rate greater than expected on state norms for the various achievement tests, suggesting that the intervention had some direct influence on closing the achievement gap for participating students. Even more impressively, the slope of academic growth persisted in each of the months after the intervention period, therefore suggesting that the students internalized and expressed generalized capacities as consistent with theoretical assumptions of ASE theory.

In the first ASE related study to not use some version of the S.S.S. program, Lemberger-Truelove and colleagues (2021) trained school counselors to deliver a novel theory-influenced intervention to 109 randomly assigned middle school students in an ethnically diverse Title I school. Significant treatment effects were observed in students' changes in stress tolerance, social curiosity, executive functioning (i.e. shift, plan and organize, and task monitoring), and academic achievement (i.e. mathematics, science, English, and social studies). In a qualitative follow-up (Ceballos et al., 2021), student who participated in the ASE intervention reported experiences of changed emotional expression, enhanced self-control, and greater connectedness and mindfulness.

ASE and Teacher Outcomes. The student experience is the primary focus in ASE theory, but students are understood in relationships to their school environments. Classroom teachers have an earnest influence on classroom climate, including how school affects social and academic development (Rucinski, Brown, & Downer, 2018). A.S.C.A. (2019) recognizes the interrelatedness of students and teachers, therefore suggesting indirect services such as collaboration and consultation that school counselors can provide to educators that are intended to support school-related adults and have distal effects on students. From an ASE perspective, each intervention must be delivered in a way that affects students and members of the school community as interacting determinants. Ideally, this requires the school counselor to deliver interventions to students and classroom teachers simultaneously, or sequentially to both as appropriate. Occasionally when parallel intervention is impossible, an ASE influenced intervention can be delivered to the student or teacher autonomously but only insofar as the counseling activities reinforces the mutuality of experience.

Historically, teaching can be a highly demanding and stressful vocation (von der Embse et al., 2019), especially in the current epoch given the unique pressures in response to the global pandemic, social unrest, and economic and environmental uncertainty (Santamaría et al., 2021). Given that school counselors are charged with supporting the social and emotional development of the whole school, they can deliver consultation services that can benefit the teacher in myriad ways while also offering positive influence on how one interacts with students (Brigman et al., 2021). Recent ASE related studies have demonstrated how school counselors can contribute to teachers using consultation and how such services might contribute to co-regulated outcomes between teachers and students.

In a study of 30 secondary educators teaching in Title 1 schools, randomly assigned participants who engaged in an ASE school counseling consultation intervention reported growth in select mindfulness dispositions (i.e. acting with awareness) and decreases in teacher-reported stress and conflict in the student-teacher relationship (Molina et al., 2022). In another ASE informed school counselor consultation study, Lemberger-Truelove and colleagues (in press) considered how nine teachers of 149 students in a Title 1 school were affected by a six-week 30 to 45 minute once a week consultation session focusing on S.E.L. teacher skills, emotional reactivity and communication skills, teacher mindfulness, and school social justice advocacy. Utilizing hierarchical regression analyses on matched pairs of teachers and middle school students, results indicated changes in teachers' perceptions of the student-teacher relationship predicted students' perception of the same relationship. Additionally, participation in the consultation intervention predicted changes in two curiosity scales and small but statistically significant changes in teacher stress over three data collection periods.

Many of the initial ASE empirical studies included teachers in the intervention but did not necessarily capture process or outcome data (e.g. Bowers et al., 2015; Lemberger et al., 2015; Lemberger et al., 2018). Inferentially, the student level findings in these interventions that touched both students and teachers, coupled with the recent consultation studies aimed specifically at teacher participants, begin to depict the potential of ASE theory to affect influential elements found in the broader school environment. While these findings are optimistic, fully actualized ASE studies, with process and outcome data captured for both students and teachers as co-regulated co-determinants of experience in school systems, are still elusive.

Recommendations for Practice and Scholarship

As school counselors, we are always empirically minded. Whether drawing from one's anecdotal experiences or influenced by the results of a highly systematic study, information drives response. This perspective is consistent with ASE theory in that experience is equal parts co-determined and co-regulated by individuals and their surrounding systems. With this perspective, school counselors can utilize empirical practices and outcomes in a variety of ways.

Many school counselors are prohibited from the delivery of direct services intended to support students and other school persons because of misunderstandings related to the roles and responsibilities of profession. Relatedly, many administrators who influence school counselors are not exposed to the evidence related to the profession, including how school counselors affect personal, social, academic, and career outcomes (Dollarhide et al., 2007). In response, school counselors can consider and report the findings found in the previous paragraphs of this chapter or from other sources in the academic literature. Many of the findings are quite startling and counterintuitive, including but not limited to the achievement effects on students compared to afterschool tutoring or additional teachers (e.g. Carrell & Hoekstra, 2014; Mulhern, 2022).

A school counseling practitioner or scholar can utilize prior findings to educate influential administrators and other school stakeholders. For example, I (Matthew) have shown many district and school administrators the various tables in our study that showed the influence of a school counseling intervention on state sanctioned academic achievement tests (Lemberger et al., 2018). Almost universally, administrators were galvanized for related interventions to be performed in their schools after witnessing the effects of a mere five-week intervention using existing school counseling resources. It is easy to simply blame administrators for assigning school counselors with inappropriate duties; but unless that administrator is presented with compelling evidence to dedicate resources, it seems unlikely that that administrator would invest in counseling services in schools.

Drawing from the successes found in the literature can be a powerful first step in changing the complexion of school counseling programs. Given the sparse resources often provided to school counselors, it would be wise to utilize theories and practices with empirical support in school specific contexts. For example, school counselors can consider findings catalogued by The Ronald H. Fredrickson Center for School Counseling Outcome Research & Evaluation at the University of Massachusetts (www.umass.edu/education/center/school-counseling) or generic archives related to evidence based intervention outcomes in schools (e.g. the Collaborative for Academic, Social, and Emotional Learning [C.A.S.E.L.] [https://casel.org], and What Works Clearinghouse from the Institute of Education Sciences [WWC] [https://ies.ed.gov/ncee/wwc/]). Each of these organizations offer various resources related to evidence-based interventions that school counselors can utilize to support students, educators, or other school-related individuals.

Many of the interventions described in these archives are either inspired by theories other than ASE or seemingly atheoretical. ASE theory can be an overlay on these interventions or, alternatively, the inclusion of novel theory can potentially compromise the integrity of the original intervention. When a school counselor adopts an evidence-based intervention, theory can be a guide in choosing the most fit intervention out of the various possibilities or theory could be used to support the total school system beyond the limits of a single intervention protocol.

In addition to informing the choice of intervention, school counselors can use a theory such as ASE to identify research and program evaluation questions. There are boundless types of data that a practitioner or scholar can capture, but theory can focus the choices to those most germane to educational contexts. Specific to ASE theory, a school counselor might be interested in pursuing research questions that pertain to how the student is affected by a teacher, or the inverse. An example research question might be, "How does changes in a teacher's feelings of connectedness to students predict students' self-report of classroom climate?"

Related to how theory might direct research questions, theory can also specify the types of concepts captured as data points. These are constructs or themes that after analyses can help the school counseling practitioner or scholar make sense of the empirical results. Practitioners and scholars are informed and guided by prior understandings. Theory can help identify trends or ideas that culminate in the research questions one pursues or how one interprets findings.

Information related to these themes are often found in the extant literature. Whether one is attempting to complete a formal empirical study for publication in a peer-reviewed academic journal or commit to program evaluation for the purposes of reflection, improvement, and dissemination to stakeholders, the school counselor is influenced by the existing knowledge in the field. Theory can help the school counseling practitioner or scholar wade through the plentiful literature and make sense of narratives related to constructs. In a similar way, theory can help guide one's use of the literature as one completes the empirical procedures. As an example, the main purpose of a literature review is to inform about the relevant literature and, moreover, provide enough information to substantiate the methodological choices of the authors. Also, the literature review should provide the ground from which the results will be explicated and contrasted in the interpretation of the results (often in the form of a Discussion section in a manuscript).

Related to identifying a construct, theory might help the school counselor make prudent decisions related to data collection. For an ASE inspired school counselor, familiarity and credence in the importance of feelings of connectedness to school might lead one to seek out a valid and reliable instrument that captures students' related beliefs and experiences. Given the importance of connectedness for ASE theory, a school counselor might use the *Child and Adolescent Social Support Scale* (C.A.S.S.S.) (Malecki et al., 2000). The C.A.S.S.S. instrument has been used in a variety of school specific studies, including ASE intervention work (e.g. Lemberger & Clemens, 2012). A school counselor practitioner and scholar can compare and contrast present findings with prior findings and make some inferences about the efficacy of the intervention.

Critical reflection of empirical findings is potentially helpful to a great variety of individuals. For example, if a school counselor constructs a self-study that closely reflects an intervention described in an academic journal and gets differing outcomes, theory can help that counselor interpret how or why the findings differed. For example, it might be possible that the demographics deviated from the initial study or the intervention fidelity was not maintained faithfully; therefore, the school counselor can begin to formulate more appropriate and sophisticated interpretations of the findings.

In addition to introspection, research findings have external relevance. Returning to ASE theory, advocacy is intentionally placed as the first word of the theory. Data and results can be used to advocate for expanded school counseling services or, more importantly, they can be used to demonstrate the conditions necessary for students and school environments to thrive.

An exciting empirical approach called youth participatory action research (Y.P.A.R.) appears to be consistent with the spirit of ASE school counseling theory (see Anyon, Bender, Kennedy, & Dechants, 2018). Cammarato and Fine (2008) suggested that Y.P.A.R. extends the critical research tradition of participant action research to include children, particularly those who have experienced harmful societal forces. Unlike classical empirical approaches where the research team pursues inquiry *onto* the subject or environment, Y.P.A.R. is a study *within* the subject and environment. From the inception of the research project, youth are encouraged to work with the researchers and partnering educators to identify useful research questions, procedures, and outcomes. The intention of Y.P.A.R. is more than informative, rather, it is concerned with research that contributes to change in social systems. Student researchers engaged in Y.P.A.R. deconstruct the information in a manner that contributes to their critical awareness and liberated action. There are several potentially helpful conceptual writings targeting school counselors who are interested in Y.P.A.R. approaches (e.g. Cook & Krueger-Henney, 2017; Smith, Davis, Bhowmik, 2010).

From an ASE perspective, people are affected by experience, especially experience shared between various people in collective environments. Using data and results from analyses can affect perceptions and misperceptions and inspire more intentional and helpful behaviors. This is the foundation of ASE, providing people with opportunities to be enriched through inquiry and connections shared as a consequence of these experiences.

References

American School Counselor Association. (2019). *ASCA National Model: A framework for school counseling programs* (4th ed.). Alexandria, VA: Author.

American School Counselor Association. (2021). Mindsets and behaviors for student Success: K-12 college–and career-readiness standards for every student. Alexandria, VA: Author.

Anyon, Y., Bender, K., Kennedy, H., & Dechants, J. (2018). A systematic review of youth participatory action research (YPAR) in the United States: Methodologies, youth outcomes, and future directions. *Health Education & Behavior, 45,* 865–878. http://dx.doi.org/10.1177/1090198118769357

Blake, M. K. (2020). Other duties as assigned: The ambiguous role of the high school counselor. *Sociology of Education, 93*(4), 315–330. https://doi.org/10.1177/0038040720932563

Blewitt, C., O'Connor, A., Morris, H., Mousa, A., Bergmeier, H., Nolan, A.,…. Skouteris, H. (2020). Do curriculum-based social and emotional learning programs in early childhood education and care strengthen teacher outcomes? A systematic literature review. *International Journal of Environmental Research and Public Health, 17*(3), 1049. https://doi.org/10.3390/ijerph17031049

Bowers, H., Lemberger, M. E., Jones, M. H., & Rogers, J. E. (2015). The influence of repeated exposure to the Student Success Skills program on middle school students' feelings of connectedness, behavioral and metacognitive skills, and reading achievement. *Journal for Specialists in Group Work, 40*(4), 344–364. https://doi.org/10.1080/01933922.2015.1090511

Bowers, H., Lemberger-Truelove, M. E., Whitford, D. K. (2020). Kindergarteners are ready to learn: Executive functioning and social-emotional effects for a pilot school counseling intervention applying Advocating Student-within-Environment theory. *Journal of Humanistic Counseling 59*(1), 3–19. https://doi.org/10.1002/johc.12126

Brigman, G., Lane, D., Switzer, D., Lane, D., & Lawrence, R. (1999). Teaching children school success skills. *The Journal of Educational Research, 92*(6), 323–329. https://doi.org/10.1080/00220679909597615

Brigman, G., Villares, E., Mullis, F., Webb, L. D., & White, J. F. (2021). *School counselor consultation: Skills for working effectively with parents, teachers, and other school personnel.* John Wiley & Sons.

Cammarota, J. & Fine, M. (2008). Youth participatory action research. In Cammarota, J. & Fine, M. (Eds.) *Revolutionizing education* (pp. 1–12). New York: Routledge.

Carrell, S. E., & Hoekstra, M. (2014). Are school counselors an effective education input? *Economics Letters, 125*(1), 66–69. https://doi.org/10.1016/j.econlet.2014.07.020

Ceballos, P. L., Lemberger-Truelove, M. E., Molina, C. E., Laird, A., & Carbonneau, K. J. (2021). Culturally diverse middle school students' perceptions of a social and emotional learning and mindfulness school counseling intervention. *Journal of Child & Adolescent Counseling, 7*(2), 72–86. https://doi.org/10.1080/23727810.2021.1948809

Collaborative for Academic, Social, and Emotional Learning (CASEL) (2015). *Effective social and emotional learning programs* (Middle and High School Edition). Chicago: Author.

Collaborative for Academic, Social, and Emotional Learning. (2022). *What Is the CASEL Framework? A framework creates a foundation for applying evidence-based SEL strategies to your community*. Retrieved from https://casel.org/fundamentals-of-sel/what-is-the-casel-framework/

Cook, A. L., & Krueger-Henney, P. (2017). Group work that examines systems of power with young people: Youth participatory action research. *The Journal for Specialists in Group Work, 42*(2), 176–193. https://doi.org/10.1080/01933922.2017.1282570

Doebel, S. (2020). Rethinking executive function and its development. *Perspectives on Psychological Science, 15*(4), 942–956. https://doi.org/10.1177/1745691620904771

Dollarhide, C. T., & Saginak, K. A. (2021). *Comprehensive school counseling programs: K-12 delivery systems in action* (3rd Ed). Pearson Higher Ed.

Dollarhide, C. T., Smith, A. T., & Lemberger, M. E. (2007). Critical incidents in the development of supportive principals: Facilitating school counselor-principal relationships. *Professional School Counseling, 10*(4), 360–369. https://doi.org/10.5330/prsc.10.4.k111116677917913

Domina, T., Akos, P., Bastian, K. C., & Godwin, J. (2022). The impact of school counselor resources in elementary and middle grades. *Professional School Counseling, 26*(1a), 1–12. https://doi.org/10.1177/2156759X221086746

Durlak, J. A., Weissberg, R. P., Dymnicki, A. B., Taylor, R. D., & Schellinger, K. B. (2011). The impact of enhancing students' social and emotional learning: A meta-analysis of school-based universal interventions. *Child Development, 82*(1), 405–432. https://doi.org/10.1111/j.1467-8624.2010.01564.x

Gysbers, N. C., & Henderson, P. (2001). Comprehensive guidance and counseling programs: A rich history and a bright future. *Professional School Counseling, 4*(4), 246.

Jacob, R., & Parkinson, J. (2015). The potential for school-based interventions that target executive function to improve academic achievement: A review. *Review of Educational Research, 85*(4), 512–552. https://doi.org/10.3102/0034654314561338

Lemberger, M. E. (2010). Advocating Student-within-Environment: A humanistic theory for school counseling. *The Journal of Humanistic Counseling, Education and Development, 49,* 131–146. https://doi.org/10.1002/j.2161-1939.2010.tb00093.x

Lemberger, M. E. (2012). A return to the human in Humanism: A response to Hansen's Humanistic vision. *Journal of Humanistic Counseling, 51*(2), 164–175. https://doi.org/10.1002/j.2161-1939.2012.00015.x

Lemberger, M. E., Carbonneau, K., Selig, J. P., & Bowers, H. (2018). The role of social-emotional mediators on middle school students' academic growth as fostered by an evidence-based intervention. *Journal of Counseling and Development, 96*(1), 27–40. https://doi.org/10.1002/jcad.12175

Lemberger, M. E., & Clemens, E. V. (2012). Connectedness and self-regulation as constructs of the Student Success Skills program in inner-city African-American elementary students. *Journal of Counseling and Development, 90*(4), 450–458. https://doi.org/10.1002/j.1556-6676.2012.00056.x

Lemberger, M. E., & Hutchison, B. (2014). Advocating Student-within-Environment: A humanistic approach for therapists to animate social justice in the schools. *Journal of Humanistic Psychology, 54*, 28–44. https://doi.org/10.1177/0022167816652750

Lemberger, M. E., Selig, J. P., Bowers, H., & Rogers, J. E. (2015). The influence of the Student Success Skills program on the executive functioning skills, feelings of connectedness, and academic achievement in a predominately Hispanic, low-income middle school district. *Journal of Counseling and Development, 93*(1), 25–37. https://doi.org/10.1002/j.1556-6676.2015.00178.x

Lemberger-Truelove, M. E., & Bowers, H. (2019). An Advocating Student-within-Environment approach to school counseling. In C. T. Dollarhide & M. E. Lemberger-Truelove (Eds.), *Theories of school counseling for the 21st century* (pp. 266–294). Oxford.

Lemberger-Truelove, M. E., Ceballos, P. L., Molina, C. E., & Carbonneau, K. J. (2021). Growth in middle school students' curiosity, executive functioning, and academic achievement: Results from a theory-informed SEL and MBI school counseling intervention. *Professional School Counselor, 24*(1b): 1–8. https://doi:10.1177/2156759X211007654

Lemberger-Truelove, M. E., Molina, C. E., Carbonneau, K. J., & Smith, M. J. (in press). Effects of a school counselor consultation intervention on middle school teacher-student relationships, student curiosity, and teacher stress. *Professional School Counselor.*

Levy, I. & Lemberger-Truelove, M. E. (2021). Educator-counselor: A non-dual identity for professional school counselors. *Professional School Counselor,* 24(1b): 1–7. doi: 10.1177/2156759X211007630

Mahoney, J. L., Durlak, J. A., & Weissberg, R. P. (2018). An update on social and emotional learning outcome research. *Phi Delta Kappan, 100*(4), 18–23. https://doi.org/10.1177/0031721718815668

Malecki, C. K., Demaray, M. K., & Elliot, S. N. (2000). *The Child and Adolescent Social Support Scale.* DeKalb, IL: Northern Illinois University.

Miyake, A., & Friedman, N. P. (2012). The nature and organization of individual differences in executive functions: *Four general conclusions. Current Directions in Psychological Science, 21*(1), 8–14. https://doi.org/10.1177/0963721411429458

Molina, C. E., Lemberger-Truelove, M. E., & Zieher, A. K. (2022). School counselor consultation effects on teachers' mindfulness, stress, and relationships. *Professional School Counseling, 26*(1a), 1–9. https://doi.org/10.1177/2156759X221086749

Mulhern, C. (2022). Beyond teachers: Estimating individual guidance counselors' effects on educational attainment. Institute of Education Sciences, Harvard University. http://papers.cmulhern.com/Counselors_Mulhern.pdf

Niehaus, K., Moritz Rudasill, K., & Rakes, C. (2012). A longitudinal study of school connectedness and academic outcomes across sixth grade. *Journal of School Psychology, 50*(4), 443–460. https://doi.org/10.1016/j.jsp.2012.03.002

Rucinski, C. L., Brown, J. L., & Downer, J. T. (2018). Teacher–child relationships, classroom climate, and children's social-emotional and academic development. *Journal of Educational Psychology, 110*(7), 992–1004. https://doi.org/10.1037/edu0000240

Santamaría, M. D., Mondragon, N. I., Santxo, N. B., & Ozamiz-Etxebarria, N. (2021). Teacher stress, anxiety and depression at the beginning of the academic year during the COVID-19 pandemic. *Global Mental Health, 8*, e14, 1–8. https://doi.org/10.1017/gmh.2021.14

Smith, L., Davis, K., & Bhowmik, M. (2010). Youth participatory action research groups as school counseling interventions. *Professional School Counseling, 14*(2), 174–182.

Villares, E., Frain, M., Brigman, G., Webb, L., & Peluso, P. (2012). The impact of Student Success Skills on standardized test scores: A meta-analysis. *Counseling Outcome Research and Evaluation, 3*, 3–16. https://doi.org/10.1177/2150137811434041

Villares, E., Lemberger, M., Brigman, G., & Webb, L. (2011). Student success skills: An evidence-based school counseling program grounded in humanistic theory. *The Journal of Humanistic Counseling, 50*(1), 42–55. https://doi.org/10.1002/j.2161-1939.2011.tb00105.x

von der Embse, N., Ryan, S. V., Gibbs, T., & Mankin, A. (2019). Teacher stress interventions: A systematic review. *Psychology in the Schools, 56*(8), 1328–1343. https://doi.org/10.1002/pits.22279

Webb, L., Brigman, G., Carey, J., Villares, E., Wells, C., Sayer, A., Harrington, K., & Chance, E. (2019). Results of a randomized controlled trial of the student success skills program on grade 5 students' academic and behavioral outcomes. Journal of Counseling and Development, 97(4), 398–408. https://doi.org/10.1002/jcad.12288

Whiston, S. C., & Quinby, R. F. (2009). Review of school counseling outcome research. *Psychology in the Schools, 46*(3), 267–272. https://doi.org/10.1002/pits.20372

Whiston, S. C., Tai, W. L., Rahardja, D., & Eder, K. (2011). School counseling outcome: A meta-analytic examination of interventions. *Journal of Counseling & Development, 89*(1), 37–55. https://doi.org/10.1002/j.1556-6678.2011.tb00059.x

Witherspoon, D., Schotland, M., Way, N., & Hughes, D. (2009). Connecting the dots: How connectedness to multiple contexts influences the psychological and adademic adjustment of urban youth. *Applied Developmental Science, 13*(4), 199–216. https://doi.org/10.1080/1088869090328875

10

EXAMPLE ASE SCHOOL COUNSELING BEHAVIORS

Matthew E. Lemberger-Truelove

Advocating Student-within-Environment (ASE) school counseling theory is primarily concerned with creating the conditions for students to thrive in K12 education contexts (Lemberger, 2010; Lemberger & Hutchison, 2014). The individual student is conceptualized as an amalgamation of various personal and social ingredients. Therefore, student development can be accomplished by cultivating characteristics inbuilt to the student and by succoring features in the environment. In this chapter, we will introduce a few example behaviors school counselors can utilize at the individual level and an example of an intervention approach intended to support the broader school environment.

The ASE counseling behaviors provided in this chapter are only a small sample of many expressions that a school counselor can use to support a student or other members of the school community. The practice of ASE can be accomplished using manualized intervention protocols, semi-structured activities, spontaneous counseling dialogue aimed at an individual or groups of people, or advocacy behaviors pointed at features in and beyond the immediate school context. What is consistent across the various types of intervention behaviors is a certain ASE orientation. An ASE orientation is receptive to the various experiences, interpretations, and possibilities germane to the individual while maintaining that all individual experiences are bound to a vast kaleidoscope of influencing systems. The orientation is also optimistic and empowering, yet earnest in a commitment to personal development that is complemented by change in the various social structures that affect students. Finally, an ASE orientation is relevant to everyday wisdom and pragmatic behaviors; the process and the outcome of school counseling are compatible,

DOI: 10.4324/9781003312871-10

therefore counseling practice must reflect the lives, values, and aspirations of the various people served.

Individual Advocacy Behaviors

In practice, counseling behaviors inspired by one counseling theory can seem compatible with counseling behaviors inspired by other (even diametrically opposite) counseling theories. This is not terribly surprising given many western counseling theories were intended to support clients in similar settings (i.e. often clinical psychological treatment environments). Also, most contemporary counseling theories generally emerged from corresponding cultural and philosophical influences (e.g. post-enlightenment conceptions of an autonomous and volitional self, mind-body dualism). In many ways, even though ASE theory is specific to school environments and operates from nascent philosophic assumptions, the practice can be compatible with several classical theoretical approaches, especially when working directly with a certain individual in a school context. This is not to suggest that ASE is technically eclectic, sans a distinct epistemological and practice foundation; instead, ASE theory can draw from customary counseling behaviors and filter out in unique ways that are uniquely relevant to students in school environments.

The ways that counseling behaviors emerge from the various counseling theories are often subtle and only discerned through a deep scrutiny. ASE theory shares beliefs and behaviors with many classical approaches but is nonetheless different enough to be conceptualized and implemented as a standalone approach. In the box below, three of the most prominent counseling paradigms are introduced as a way to compare and contrast with ASE theory.

Counseling Theory Comparison

Humanistic counseling (e.g. person-centered, existential, gestalt, experiential) assumes the innate goodness in people who are endowed with responsibility and the free will to pursue personal and social wellness (Schneider, Pierson, & Bugental, 2014). The practice of humanistic counseling generally pertains to the here-and-now experiences of the client as supported by a counselor who prizes authentic therapeutic rapport.

Cognitive-behavioral counseling (C.B.T.) (e.g. rational emotive behavior, cognitive, third wave, behavior modification) is a suite of approaches that suggest that people hold and express cognitive distortions (thoughts, beliefs, and attitudes) and their associated behaviors that can result in disturbed symptoms or broader core pathologies (Dobson & Dozois, 2019). The practice of C.B.T. includes spontaneous and structured interventions that typically pertain to challenging irrational or maladaptive thoughts, feelings, or behaviors and replace these irrational assumptions with more coherent expressions.

Post-modern counseling approaches (e.g. narrative, relational-cultural, constructivist) are based on the philosophical belief that there are multiple truths, often affiliated with subjective personal positions and/or distributed social influences (Anderson, 2015). Post-modern practices encourage flexible interpretations of experience while challenging potentially oppressive and harmful environmental conditions.

Advocating Student-within-Environment (ASE) theory pertains to school counseling and adherents aim to amplify students' and other school stakeholders' capacities while simultaneously pursuing more hospitable and contributory school climates. ASE is similar to humanistic approaches given its concern with relationship building and here-and-now experiences; it is compatible with C.B.T.'s use of metacognition to untether personal and social influences that affect student and systems outcomes; and ASE is germane to the multiplicity of identity and options, as consistent with post-modern approaches. What distinguishes ASE as a theory for practice is the requirement that all interventions are reciprocal at the individual and systems level and, second, the non-dual assumptions of self and volition. Consequentially, ASE is generally more focused on preventative and advocacy behaviors, as compared to classical counseling theoretical approaches that are chiefly concerned with responding to the psychology of the individual.

Many classical theories are readied with specialized techniques that emerge from the philosophical assumptions endemic to each of these approaches. Further, counseling theories can alter how trans-theoretical skills are expressed. Two of the most foundational counseling behaviors that are present virtually every counseling theory includes a reflection of a client's feelings and open-ended questions. The following examples elucidate how these general counseling behaviors are expressed differently based on their influencing counseling theory:

Reflecting Feelings

Humanistic counseling:

Example 1: As we are talking about your parents, I can see the profound grief that you're experiencing (*empathy*). This is more than a memory, but a feeling that you carry with you even now in this room after all these years (*here-and-now; experiential*).

Example 2: I noticed you pulled backed when I said that; fearful of what you're experiencing now as we talk about what you experienced in the past (*here-and-now; immediacy & authentic experience*).

Cognitive behavioral counseling:
Example 1: Witnessing the grief of others (*activating event*) reminds the struggles you endured after your own parents passed away, and now you believe that you will never escape the feelings of despair (*beliefs*), which in turn compels you to limit your interactions with other people in your life (*consequence*).

Example 2: You attach shame to your experiences of grief; a belief which has haunted you for decades (*Core belief)*

Post-modern counseling:
Example 1: The grief still persists from the loss of your parents; some days are better than others (*deconstruction; dominant story; externalizing*). This illustrates that you are more than your grief, you are someone who can suffer deeply and also someone who experiences deep joy (*re-authoring*).

Advocating Student-with-Environment:
Example 1: You're experience of grief (curiosity and connectedness) affects you deeply (compassion) and in different ways across different circumstances (co-regulation).

Example 2: The loss you experienced is associated with a feeling of distress, yet sadness is coupled with this profound passion to support your family members as they are also grieving (contribution).

Questions:

Humanistic counseling:
Example 1: How does reflecting on the past affect you in this moment? (*here-and-now; experiential*)

Example 2: You've endured much and I witness your resilience. In a similar way, I wonder what you learned about yourself? (*meaning*)
Example 3: You work hard to maintain your composure, but what is your fidgeting knee tell us if it could speak? (*somatic here-and-now*)

Cognitive behavioral counseling:
Example 1: (downward arrow) 1) Can you tell me what you experienced when you were taking the test? (*minor mode*) 2) Okay, so felt anxious because you had the impression that you were not performing well after much preparation. If true, from your perspective, what does this experience tell you about yourself as a learner? (*protoschema*) 3) So you interpreted this one anxiety laden experience as reflective of your total ability as a learner. How might you then describe yourself as a learner generally? 4) You have this circular experience, you believe that you are incapable of learning even when

preparing, which leads to anxiety in performance situations, contributing to undesirable learning outcomes and now this larger belief that you are unable to learn or demonstrate your learning? (*core belief*)

Post-modern counseling:
Example 1: I wonder how someone else might interpret this experience in class. Think of the most charitable person you know, if she or he knew how anxious you were in class how might they interpret your performance after studying so many hours? (*externalizing*)

Example 2: Let's not disregard this recent episode, but let's also not focus only here. Could you describe to me some occasions when you had a different experience in a similar situation? (*exceptions*)

Advocating Student-with-Environment:
Example 1: What aspects from your classroom experiences most affect how you participate as a student? (*curiosity, co-regulation, and contribution*)

Example 2: Who in class is most helpful when you are struggling? (*co-regulation*)

Example 3: How might you notice when your attention starts to get distracted? (*co-regulation*) What things typically occur in class when you start to experience distraction? (*curiosity*)

To further illustrate how ASE theory employs reflections of feelings and questions to support the development of children, I (Matthew) was supervising my five-year-old son and his four-year-old cousin. After a few normal disagreements, my son said that he wanted to play by himself, assumingly to avoid further conflict. This greatly disappointed my nephew who apparently felt rejected and angry, as he said, "If you don't play with me, I am going to hit you." My response to my nephew was something like the following:

Matthew: I see that you're quite angry when Atom (my son) said that he wanted to play alone. You were so upset that you said you're going to hit him.
Nephew: Yes, I am so angry at Atom.
Matthew: I wonder if you can tell me all of the different things that you can do when you get this angry?
Nephew: (listed about three strategies his parents had formerly introduced)
Matthew: That's a lot of ways to express anger; I wonder which ones might make you feel just a little bit better?"

In this short example, ASE concepts such as co-regulation and the prior determinants of experience are evident. Rather than discounting either child's feelings, experiences, or desires, the intention of my response was to recruit from those prior determinants and refocus them in a manner that is more consistent with each child's intended outcome. At the same time, each child is situated in a relationship with the other child, therefore personal desires must be distributed and reconsidered as they are compliant to the desires and actions of others.

From an ASE perspective, each individual counseling intervention is conceived and practiced from a systems perspective. It is essential that the school counselor does not approach the individual student, educator, or other stakeholder with a fixed or hierarchical perspective. Even when utilizing one of the various behaviors or aphorisms associated with ASE theory, these counseling behaviors are considered opportunities for the recipient to consider and integrate, adjust, or even disregard as it pertains to one's development within their given systems. Further, individual intervention is never assumed to offer a definitive or fixed cause or resolve, rather the intent of counseling is to perpetuate growth that can evolve within dynamic personal and social systems. This orientation can be captured in the following ASE aphorism: "I alone didn't create my circumstance, but I can affect how I internalize and express myself."

Systemic Advocacy Behaviors

To illustrate how a school counselor can support student development through influence at the environment (systemic) level, we present a series of school counselor led consultation sessions that are aimed at supporting classroom teachers from an ASE perspective. Consultation is when a school counselor delivers content to one person or group with the intention that that person or group will utilize the content to support another person not generally involved in the initial consultation activities (Baker et al., 2009). The practice of consultation suggests that the content can be amplified to various individuals and settings, as the person engaged in the actual consultation activities will be subsequently exposed to various individuals. Stated otherwise, the value in the content and the reach of the school counselor is amplified beyond the contact with a single recipient; instead, the efforts of the school counselor have the potential to reverberate through the consultee repeatedly.

Consultation is one of many strategies that a school counselor might utilize to advocate for more facilitative school environmental conditions. There are certainly other approaches to advocacy, not limited to when a counselor participates in political advocacy that might shape education and public policy. A school counselor can also advocate by engaging community partners who might become active allies in schools. Another example of advocacy is when a school counselor raises awareness about structural inequality and the mistreatment of people. While each of these advocacy activities are invaluable, consultation is uniquely orientated to empowering members of the social system to act on behalf of the needs of students and school systems. This feature of consultation is particularly consistent with the spirit of ASE theory, as consultation has the potential to result in reciprocal benefits for the consultee and students. Further, consultation is by its nature generative and adaptive, and it can adjust over time and across circumstances relative to how the content is internalized and actualized by the consultee.

It is for these reasons that consultation was chosen as one exemplar ASE practice. ASE can be delivered in various ways – such as individual counseling with a student, teacher, guardian, etc. or group counseling in and out of classrooms – but consultation most clearly reflects the ASE position that cultivating personal capacities can affect total systems. To this end, this chapter includes a five-consultation session unit that was used and empirically tested in an economically challenged middle school (Lemberger-Truelove et al., 2023). Findings from the consultation intervention delivered by nine middle school classroom teachers (and their 149 students) included significant change in teachers' perceptions of the teacher-student relationship that predicted students' perception of the same relationship. Results from the study also demonstrated similar co-regulated changes in two curiosity scales and a small change in teachers' stress tolerance from the pre- to post-test data collection periods. These results provide some inferential evidence that the ASE approach can affect personal development (for the teacher consultees) and system change (the relationships shared between teachers and students).

It is important to note that there are some unique features to this particular consultation example. First, the words provided below are semi-scripted and therefore more directive as compared to many other ASE interventions. ASE theory is generally complaint to direct and indirect practices (e.g. psycho educational or spontaneous counseling sessions), yet in practice ASE is predominately student- or teacher-centered whereby the person served dictates much of the content and process. In the case of the consultation example used in this chapter, a more directive approach was identified to better illustrate the concepts and should not be confused as the ideal or even standard approach to practice. Second, these consultation sessions were delivered exclusively to classroom teachers and yet the acme ASE intervention would include something like these sessions delivered to teachers and complementary sessions delivered to students in classrooms. Hopefully a school counselor can cultivate a reciprocal and dynamic climate shared between students, educators, and other members of the school community. Third, any intervention requires priming the participants, relationship building, and follow-up, all inferred in the current example but not fully elaborated in the text. For example, each of these sessions includes a mindfulness activity that can be confused with forced self-care activities often pushed onto teachers without their discretion. Certainly, mindfulness and ASE in general aspire toward a greater feeling of equanimity, but that is not the primary intent; instead

> The consultation intervention included a mindfulness lesson in each session, but the particular mindfulness activities were not necessarily focused on stress reduction but chiefly concerned teachers' awareness of experience and intentional teaching behaviors.
>
> *(Lemberger-Truelove et al., 2023, p. 7)*

Again, the general purpose of ASE is to elucidate how experiences are internalized, embodied, and then shared; moreover, ASE pertains to how we are more than passive recipients of experience, and with intentional intervention we can co-determine new possibilities.

Session One

School Counselor

Thank you for coming today, I know your time is valuable, and I hope that the time that we share over the following five weeks will be worth the investment, with clear benefits to you and your students. These are incredibly challenging times for educators and our meetings might provide you an opportunity to explore how these challenges have affected you and further explore new insights and responses to challenges in and beyond the classroom.

Our work together is not therapy in the classical sense, rather this is consultation. Consultation is intended to support a person who will in turn use those experiences to support someone else. In our case, hopefully what we do here between you and me will have direct effects on your experiences in the classroom and how you support your students' development. This said, almost all effective consultation reflects the processes and outcomes of therapy, including the disclosing of personal information or the experience of intense emotions. With this in mind, it is essential that we establish some ground rules for our active participation in these sessions.

First, including this session, there will be five 30-minute consultation sessions. In these sessions we will establish a generic structure that I will facilitate, but much of the content will be dictated by your experiences and disclosures. We will begin each session with a brief breathing exercise intended to help focus our attention here and engage a mindset of mutual openness and growth. Then we will ask if there are any persistent or concerning professional experiences that you'd like to discuss. In the absence of anything specific, I have some prepared language devices inspired by research on social and emotional learning practices in school settings.

Either using your experiences or these imported language devises, we will spend some time exploring how your initial impressions are valid and how alternative responses might add new ways to approach your experiences with others. Second, in each session we will spend a few minutes discussing tangible strategies to improve the social and working conditions as an educator. Rather than commiserating on unattainable goals for change, we will try and narrow on immediate and attainable outcomes with measured implications you can experience directly and utilize immediately. Then, we will spend approximately ten minutes each week engaged in a brief mindfulness activity. In this activity, we will use our breath to consider the various thoughts that arise, explore our reactions to these thoughts, and on occasion encourage curiosity and diverse responses to future experiences.

Finally, privacy is vital to the success of this consultation experience. Because we are in small groups with me and your peer teachers, I cannot promise total secrecy, but it is important that we make a formal commitment to keep what is said in here between us and in this context only, into perpetuity. As the lead consultant, my commitment to confidentiality is an ethical and legal requirement; anything you mention during our time together will be confidential, that is it is private and I will not share anything stated with other staff, faculty, or administrators on campus. I will uphold confidentiality and would request you do the same to keep the integrity of our work together. However, in cases of child abuse, neglect, exploitation or intent to harm another person or yourself, I am required by law to report it to the appropriate authority. Are there any questions?"

Teachers

(Response).

School Counselor

Before we begin, I want to provide you with an opportunity to ask any questions about any of the introductions, including the duration and structure of sessions, issues pertaining to confidentiality, or the nature of consultation. Any questions or thoughts?

Teachers

(Response)

School Counselors

Given what we have discussed, are you willing to consent to participation in these consultation sessions? We can revisit this commitment at any point.

Teachers

(Obtain verbal consent).

School Counselor

As mentioned, I would like for each of us to begin this meeting with a brief breathing exercise intended to focus our attention here together. With this in mind, I encourage you to close your eyes and simply bring your awareness to your breath. Make no effort to change your natural breathing at this point, simply notice that you are breathing. Notice that this breath sustains your life and is something shared between you and the world around you. Try not and judge the quality of your breath, again simply experience it for the next ten or so seconds.

(Provide the teachers about ten seconds)

Okay, perfect. Keep your eyes closed and continue to breathe in a natural way. It has been said, "As long as you are breathing, there is more right with you than wrong, regardless of what is going on in your life."

While maintaining an awareness on your breath, I now invite you to take five intentional, deep breaths. If comfortable, take approximately a second or more to inhale, a second or more to fully exhale, and then just a short instance between each of the five breaths. Continue to be present with this deeper breathing, adding no additional mental reflection or commentary; simply sustain an open attention to your breath.

Once you are complete with these five breaths, slowly return to this moment by opening your eyes and engaging back into your typical breathing patterns.

Breathing is incredibly powerful and yet often neglected. It is astounding that our noses are situated right next to our brains, especially that front location called the prefrontal cortex, which is generally associated with how we regulate our experiences and make intentional decisions. This will set the tone for our experiences, namely accepting the inhale-breath as reflective of the various influences that are present in our world, the exhale-breath as how we share our reactions with the world, and the brief pause in between as our quick and yet essential opportunity to reflect and create the next moment with intentionality and grace.

Let's take no more than three minutes to share what it was like to breath together, whether you have done things like this in the past or not is not necessarily important, we are interested in the present experience of doing it there together.

(Three to five minutes of teacher disclosure)

School Counselor

Breathing is both an individual and group activity. It is especially apparent in these times that breathing is shared between people. In this way, it is appropriate that we take about five minutes total and introduce ourselves and at least one thing we hope to get from these five consultation sessions. I will begin by modeling and then I invite you to disclose as you feel fitting.

(Provide five minutes for the teachers to share)

Thank you.

School Counselor

For our first meeting, the content will be a bit different as compared to what will occur for the next four meetings. In the subsequent meetings, I anticipate that much of the content will be driven by what you bring for us to discuss whereas today I want to briefly set the tone for the philosophy and practice behind this form of consultation. We will use this content to inform our work together.

Let's start with a little thought experiment: Think about your thoughts before you think them. (Give the teachers about five seconds to contemplate)

Of course, this is an impossibility, you cannot think about a thought before you think it. All thoughts are this way, we are experiencing thoughts as a reflection after their inception. It feels as if we are creating thoughts before they occur, but this is an impossibility; rather we are observing them after they manifest. And if true, then where do they come from, these thoughts?

(Give the teachers about 20 seconds to reflect and respond)

Let's play with this idea a bit longer with another experiment. Take just about 15 seconds to simply pay attention to your thoughts. Whatever the content, any thought is fine. Simply capture it. Try not to attach any evaluation or judgment about the rightness or wrongness; simply capture the thought.

(Give the teachers about 20 seconds to reflect and respond)

Thank you for giving these thought-experiments a try. I am going to now take a couple of minutes to unpack how they pertain to our work together.

With our thoughts, we often conflate the consequences of our thoughts with the causes of our thoughts. For example, in doing the thought experiment with you, my thought(s) was(were) (insert example), but upon deeper reflection that thought was informed by my personal background, the language I use, how my current day is going, values and hopes, and myriad other contributing influences.

When we experience only the consequence of a thought, we often inadvertently reduce it to the perceived cause. There is some function in this, as humans we try to make predictions based on prior causes and how they might likely lead to predictable consequences. But there is a shadow side, we tend to get rather algorithmic and rigid in our thinking, often missing the various causes or multiple consequences.

In action, this means we react, rather than respond. To react is to act again. There is a lot of wisdom and functionality in this. It is efficient, we don't have to exhaust a lot of effort to be influenced by a prior cause or react in a familiar way. But as a habit, simply reacting can also limit us.

Last exercise before we transition to our final two activities. Briefly write down one example of something that has affected your stress as a teacher in the recent past, preferably today or in the last week.

Try not to write any evaluations or judgments about these experiences, simply write them as objective experiences. Use no more than a single sentence. After this is complete, take just a few minutes to sketch out as many of the things that contributed to this event or experience. Oscillate between things that you contribute to this experience and things outside of yourself. And then write out some of the things that preceded and contributed to these causes. Take about three minutes to accomplish this task. (Verbally provide them an example from your life while they write)

Now, look at your sketches. See how each consequence is reasonable given the causes; this isn't to suggest that the consequence is right (or wrong), good or bad, but how it follows coherently between causes and effects. Now look at the list and see if there is one or more causes that can be altered; this doesn't mean that it was right or wrong, good or bad; rather it is simply something that you have the ability to easily manipulate without much effort or sacrifice. It can be as provocative as having a completely different instigating cause or as subtle as having a different perspective on the same cause.

Today, as you are confronted with novel experiences and thoughts, take a moment to briefly engage in this practice. "How am I reacting, what prior causes (personal and environmental) influence me to react this way? And while I accept my *reaction* as reasonable, I also accept that I can *respond* differently and contribute to a new possible outcome; noticing however small or influential those new outcomes might be."

To help you do this, I encourage you to consider using this phrase as a reminder, "Don't doubt my ability, try a different strategy."

I want us to briefly transition to our second content portion. Each session we will do something like the prior portion to support you in how you experience things internally and then we will do something to help influence your environment. It is wrongheaded to think that things will improve by simply altering one's orientation. As a teacher, your feelings of stress are real as are the things that contribute to these feelings. Students can be stressful. Administration or peers can be stressful. Policy can be stressful. Even our lives outside of our jobs can affect the stress we experience in our work. Stress is a natural physiological and psychological experience.

I want us to think of one thing that affects our stresses as educators, something that is particular to our school. Let's not judge it as good or bad at this point, let's simply identify it. Let's identify something that we think has various causes but consequences that affect our performance and experience as teachers. Over the next four weeks we are going to explore the causes and consequences of this stressor and pursue specific behaviors, together as a team, to make the school culture a little better, less stressful, and more connected.

(Take five minutes to explore and commit)

Thank you. While we might not be able to completely change the working conditions, we might be able to alter some aspects that might in turn contribute to more helpful learning and working conditions. Just as earlier we used the phrase "don't doubt my ability, try a different strategy" to affect our internal thoughts, I offer another one for how we as a team might approach our work in advocating for a stronger school culture: "Little by little, bit by bit, we are improving every day." Pursuing, noticing, and accomplishing a series of small and yet important improvements is a way of affecting causes leading to new consequences in and beyond our shared school environment.

Finally, I want us to take five minutes to close with our first formal mindfulness exercise. You might have some prior experiences with mindfulness, whether formal practice or things you have heard or read about. Consistent with our prior activity, I am going to ask you to not import any judgment or impressions related to prior experiences with mindfulness, instead I encourage you to approach this opportunity as novel as is possible. I am going to read my mindfulness script and support you as much as is possible.

School Counselor

ASE MEDITATION 1

As teachers, we rely on our intuitions and rapid recall and expertise. There are myriad people and events, always pining for our attention. Teachers are human, beautifully so; and like all humans, our capacity to be fully intentional is often limited.

The great developmental psychologist Alison Gopnik commented that young children are like lanterns who distribute light broadly so to witness and have access to as many things as possible, for the more experiences at one's disposal, the greater number of things we can draw from to operate on own worlds later in life. This is different than adults, who are like flashlights, focusing light to specific apertures with targeted intention. We do this to be efficient because we'd be overwhelmed if we were constantly accumulating and processing disturbed experiences. As teachers, we must be like lanterns and flashlights, oscillating between the expanse of curiosity and creativity and intentional focus.

In our practices together, we are going to play around with these ideas, that is oscillating between expanding our awareness and curiosity and bringing back specific and useful details into intentional focus. To do this, we are going to use some practices associated with mindfulness, tailored specifically to working with children especially as an educator and in a school environment. Many of you have had experiences with mindfulness, and while these past experiences with mindfulness might range from helpful to challenging and while such past experiences will certainly affect your experiences with our exercises together, it might be helpful to suspend memory as much as is possible, begin anew with our work together now, as a lantern garnering new opportunities.

This first practice will be rather short. But I encourage you to consider the transferability of these short practices, especially in your busy day as a teacher. It is often suggested that one must practice many hours to become an expert, and while there is much wisdom in practice; in the current context, we are simply practicing attention to one's experiences, and there is no greater expert on you than you. These short practices are designed so that you can get back to you, be the expert of you, especially when the environment around you can be challenging and even stressful.

Our practice today will be especially brief and each week we will add a bit more time and focus. This week we will play around with the concept of personal and social curiosity. For our purposes, we will define curiosity as the pursuit of new information or experiences, where novel and surprising outcomes are anticipated and prized.

If you are standing, please take a seat or if you are already seated, take a moment to become aware of the sensation of sitting. It is generally helpful to sit as comfortably as you can, in whatever way that keeps you tranquil and yet attentive.

As you focus your gentle awareness on sitting. Perhaps take a few deep breaths. Become aware of the sensations of breathing. You need not force anything. Simply observe. Notice where you feel the breath most clearly; it could be the tip of the nose, possibly the rise and fall of the abdomen or chest. Where you identify the sensation of your breath is personal and it can change as you continue to attend.

15 seconds

Breath is always with us. There is no need to alter the quality of your breathing for this exercise. Simply observe it. Notice all aspects of the breath, including the initial contact of the air outside of you to your skin, follow where it moves to in your body, and as it exits, and the pauses between breaths.

Continue to breathe in a normal and comfortable manner and notice any thoughts, feelings, or sensations that might arise. Regardless of the content of these inner mental experiences, open up to them with curiosity. They are neither good nor bad, right nor wrong, simply attend to these thoughts. You might ask yourself, are there many thoughts, a single theme of thoughts, or maybe something like both myriad thoughts inspired by a single theme. Simply breathe and appreciate that you are the sole expert of your inner experiences.

Take a moment to inquire into the genesis of these inner mental experiences. Did you think of them before you thought them? More likely, you observed them after they are perceptible. Notice the relationship between the sensations of sitting and breathing, the sensation of attending to oneself in a curious way, and the cascade of thoughts that capture us.

When thoughts or feelings creep in, simply acknowledge them with brief momentary curiosity and then return to the breath.

When comfortable, comfortably expand your awareness back to the surroundings. To the counselor you are working with and the room that surrounds you.

The distinguished psychologist Lisa Feldman Barrett offers the following wisdom: "In every waking moment, your brain uses past experience, organized as concepts, to guide your actions and give your sensations meaning. When the concepts involved are emotion concepts, your brain constructs instances of emotion." (Barrett, 2017, p. 31).

This brief practice we shared is an introduction in how one might interrogate how the brain uses our mind to organize and respond to our experiences. As teachers, especially during these inauspicious times, with many personal, professional, and social threats, it might be helpful to be curious about the infancy of our experiences, especially our emotions. While capturing our emotions will not necessarily remove or even alter the characters of these threats; it is possible that our curiosity is the first step in engaging in responding with flexibility and intention, rather than reacting.

This week you will find yourself back in your familiar classroom. While it might be infeasible to dedicate five to ten minutes to capture your breath as we did; do invest in three to five intentional breaths with curiosity, interrogate where any thoughts might have come from, and return to the classroom with intention and compassion for oneself and others.

School Counselor

As we close, I want to encourage you to think about one thing that stood out and affected you today in our session. Commit to one very specific behavior that you can use this strategy immediately. How will you know when to use this strategy, how will you know if it was helpful, and if helpful how will you reinforce and celebrate your commitment or if it didn't help how can you try a different strategy?

Finally, I want to encourage each of you to consider downloading an app called "Healthy Minds Program," that is free for either Apple or Android. While not necessarily required, it is a great research-supported program that is consistent with the practices we will be doing and therefore likely deepen the outcomes of our efforts here. Thank you again and I greatly look forward to seeing you again this time next week.

Session Two

School Counselor

As we begin our work today, I want to briefly start by asking if you have any questions about the composition of these consultation sessions or revisit the confidentiality promise and limitations.

Teachers

Allow one minute (or more if needed based on the teachers' queries)

School Counselor

Similar to last week, I would like for each of us to begin this meeting with a brief breathing exercise intended to focus our attention here together. With this in mind, I encourage you to close your eyes and simply bring your awareness to your breath. Make no effort to change your natural breathing at this point, simply notice that you are breathing. Notice that this breath sustains your life and is something shared between you and the world around you. Try not and judge the quality of your breath, again simply experience it for the next ten or so seconds.

(Provide the teachers about ten seconds)

Teacher Self-Advocacy

School Counselor

Today I want to introduce the concept of radical curiosity and offer some very specific strategies informed by the empirical and conceptual literature pertaining to social and emotional learning to help us accomplish this radical curiosity. The hope is that we can apply these radical curiosity strategies, resulting in new insights and new more desirable outcomes.

Curiosity is a "drive state for information" (Kidd & Hayden, p. 450); as a practice, curiosity is a non-evaluative expression of inquisitiveness about a person and/or circumstance. In this way, the outcome of curiosity is not the acquisition of an unchanging or even ideal end, rather a persistent openness to ongoing development. For example, "What did you accomplish?" is only minimally curious whereas "How did you experience your accomplishments?" is more inquisitive and generates greater curious reflection. In both brief prompts, you can receive specific information about the accomplishment but only in the latter question does the prompt encourage elaboration beyond an isolated circumstance.

To be curious, it is often helpful to interrogate some of the things that contribute to our own inner conversations. This process of interrogation requires first, self-awareness, and then, second, self-management. Self-awareness is becoming more aware of our culture, thoughts, feelings, and potential whereas self-management is how we intentionally affect our emotions, thoughts, and actions to achieve goals, coping with stress, and preserving.

Let's practice two language devises to generate curiosity through self-awareness and -management, namely a reflection of feeling and an open-ended question.

(Encourage one teacher to interface with another)

A reflection of feelings is identifying the emotional experience of another person and sharing it with this person to demonstrate empathy, understanding, and connection. This requires you to accurately receive and articulate the emotion and couple it with a causal anchor affiliated with the person's emotional experience. Here are a couple of examples:

- Janelle, you are feeling frustrated because the number of responsibilities you have as a teacher seems to exceed your time or resources.
- I can see how happy you are when you work really hard and identify one of many possible solutions that might work for you.

A second skill to generate curiosity is a non-evaluative, reflective question. These open-ended questions should be more than a request for information, rather a way to evince that you are curious about the other person's lived experience:

- What is it like for you to be experiencing these frustrations as a relatively new teacher?
- How did the A.P.s statement affect your remainder of the day in class?

- When you are feeling motivated, what are some typical things that inspire these feelings?

Let's take a couple of minutes and practice these reflections and questions a few times.

(Allow two minutes for each teacher to practice one or two each, with you offering non-evaluative help if requested)

These language strategies can be used for our own internal dialogue but also can be used as conversation devices when we interact with students, colleagues, or parents. Let's take a few minutes as a group and utilize each of these two skills. Pair up and come up with some event that occurred today in school. It can be something troubling or even something banal and ordinary. With your partner, rather than trying to figure out an immediate solution, try and use both reflections of feelings and open-ended questions to demonstrate curiosity. I am here to help should you need it.

(Allow approximately five minutes)

School Environment Advocacy

Okay, great. Let's shift our attention from our group to our broader school context. Last week we spoke about a possible event or phenomenon that is present in the school environment or culture; something that as a team we might be able to influence. Let's take a few minutes to discuss some possibilities and using our concept of radical curiosity, and the skills of reflection and questions, what are some specific behaviors that we can do to start the process of climate change in the school?

Mindfulness Activity

I want us to take about ten minutes and participate in our second formal mindfulness exercise. I am going to read a script and I encourage you to follow along as you find it comfortable and helpful.

ASE MEDITATION 2

Welcome back. We genuinely hope that you found some value in the practice last week; in fact, we hope that the value inspired you to practice beyond these mere ten minutes we share together. As a counseling professor, I tell my students that the measure of effective therapy is not found merely in the experiences during the 50-minute session but rather how that 50-minutes affects all of the minutes, hours, and days between and beyond sessions.

Last week we did a brief exercise of paying attention to your inner experiences, noticing how thoughts and feelings seem to emerge, and then evolve into other thoughts or feelings. We also briefly encouraged you to notice any evaluations that get overlaid on top of these transitory mental experiences. By distinguishing an experience from an evaluation, we might be able to better regulate our experiences, discern what is acceptable, and act more intentionally and connect to others.

This week, we are going to take this practice one step further and encourage you to interrogate these inner experiences, note the complexity of prior mental and environmental influencers that contributed to the manifestation, and how to retain that balance between accepting our inner experiences are natural expressions. In short, we accept that all responses are feasible, but reacting in the same way over and over again potentially limits our choices and consequences.

Last week, when walking my eight-year old daughter to school she asked, "Daddy, is it okay to be scared?" And I responded something like, "Of course, everyone gets scared from time to time. It is your body's way of telling you it feels threatened or unsure. Being scared can be a very helpful feeling to keep us safe. What is not helpful is that we behave the same way to everything that makes us scared. Sometimes when we are scared we need to run away, other times we need to protect ourselves, and sometimes it is okay to simply note that you felt something and that fear will soon go away and become something else."

This brief story reflects a helpful practice of differentiating reacting from responding. To re-act is to act again, in a habituated way. To respond is to consider, however briefly, with complexity, acceptance of oneself, and discernment of various possibilities. As a teacher, we experience a litany of emotions, often influenced by prior determinants outside of our conscious awareness and control. It is okay to feel how we do in response to circumstance, but it is also permissible and even helpful to come prepared with a diversity of responses to circumstance. In fact, research suggests that the more that we anticipate prior determinants of experience, note that there are multiple determinants to any one or more experiences, and practice flexible responses, we generally have more internally useful ends.

Remember, our initial experiences are valid, but not fixed. Similarly, our evaluations we overlay experience have a basis in prior influences. As a practice, we can break them apart and interrogate them for more intentional and helpful outcomes; but ultimately, they are both simply the content of consciousness. We can observe them and by doing so, we are more likely to create new determinants of experience.

If you are standing, please take a seat or if you are already seated, take a moment to become aware of the sensation of sitting. It is generally helpful to sit as comfortably as you can, in whatever way that keeps you tranquil and yet attentive.

As you focus your gentle awareness on sitting. Perhaps take a few deep breaths. Without too much effort, bring to memory any salient feeling that you experienced today. Whatever first comes to mind is perfect and you need not sift through multiple possibilities.

Press down on this recollection for a couple of seconds. Where were you at? What was happening? Was anyone else involved? At this stage, effortlessly suspend any evaluation of the experience or anything related to it; simply bracket your attention to the facts about how you experienced whatever it is.

In a similar way, take a few seconds and recall any events however small or influential that contributed to the experience you noted. Even the most seemingly banal or insignificant experiences just observe your recollection. For example, returning to the story of my daughter and her inquiry about fear. Prior experiences might include being afraid the night before, messages she heard other say about being scared, what it means to disclose and inquire with her father. As a teacher, you might have recalled something challenging or inspiring in the classroom or with an administrator. There are proximal determinants like the relationships that contributed to the experience or there might be more distal and abstract determinants of experience like your values associated with being a teacher that led you to the profession. Simply note all of them, quickly and without evaluation… all while retaining a gentle unforced pattern of breathing.

15 seconds

As you reflect on these causal agents of experience, did any standout? Any surprise or affirm you? You can extend this beyond yourself and your determinants of experience. For example, if a student, parent, colleague or admin was a part of your memory, what prior determinants affected them and in turn contributed to your experience? Suspend evaluation, simply breathe and with each breath note that these are possible determinants that affect how we respond to circumstance.

Ten seconds

Our initial memory, the feelings and evaluations attached to them are not necessarily separate, as they are all content of our conscious experience. But it can be helpful to disentangle their hold on us by pulling them apart, interrogating how causes contribute to consequences, noting that there are various causes, and how we privilege certain causes.

In accepting our thoughts and feelings, we are not passively accepting harmful things that happen to us. In a similar way, we don't accept that only helpful things will occur all of the time. Instead, we accept that our experiences are legitimate but the practice of breathing and reflection might contribute to more intentional, curious, flexible, and socially helpful outcomes. And when it doesn't immediately contribute, it makes us more likely to try something different until we do. Don't doubt one's ability, try another strategy.

Continue to breathe in a normal and comfortable manner and notice any thoughts, feelings, or sensations that might arise.

When thoughts or feelings creep in, simply acknowledge them with brief momentary curiosity and then return to the breath.

When comfortable, comfortably expand your awareness back to the surroundings. To the counselor you are working with and the room that surrounds you.

This week you will find yourself back in your familiar classroom. While it might be infeasible to dedicate five to ten minutes to capture your breath and interrogate every experience as we just did together, but commit to something that is more feasible. Is 15 seconds worth a different outcome? Five seconds to breathe, five seconds to reflect on possible prior influences, and five seconds to consider how curious, flexible, and connected outcomes might manifest from your investment.

Thank you again for your practice and for all of the important work that you do as an educator. These are dubious times. The purpose of these exercises is not to downplay the challenges you have as a professional teacher or to trivialize any event that happens in a school, but instead it they are intended to empower you in the midst of any challenge and honor the accomplishment of experience.

Closing

Return back to the group when comfortable. As we close, I want to encourage you to think about one thing that stood out and affected you today in our session. Commit to one very specific behavior that you can use this strategy immediately. How will you know when to use this strategy, how will you know if it was helpful, and if helpful how will you reinforce and celebrate your commitment or if it didn't help how can you try a different strategy?

Session Three

School Counselor

Last week we talked about the concept of applied curiosity, that is how as educators we might interrogate our own inner ways of processing experiences but also extending this introspective process outward to others. Researchers consistently find that expressing respectful curiosity tends to lead to better relationships and a variety of valued student and teacher outcomes like improved achievement, lower stress, and stronger classroom climates.

To start this week, we will try and be curious with you about your experiences as an educator. Let's take a moment and identify something that is affecting your experiences as an educator. These need not be negative experiences, but don't feel inhibited to bring up something that you feel comfortable talking about but might be compromising your experiences. Take no more than 30 seconds, what first comes to mind is fine.

(Spend about five minutes listening, validating, and exploring their stories. Use the reflective listening skills explicated in Session Two and ASE counseling skills listed in the Chapter 10 of this book.)

Building from curiosity, this week we are going to add to our concepts by adding co-regulation.

Co-regulation is the interface of two or more self-aware, intentional individuals who draw from various cultural, social, and personal sources to inform and influence behavior (McCaslin, 2009). For example, a self-regulated individual can monitor, predict, shift, and direct one's internal and external experiences, whereas co-regulation extends beyond one's inner experiences and places total experience in a broader social and historic context. "What have you done to improve yourself" is different than "How have you pursued your goals given the influences of (insert circumstance)?"

For our main activity today, we are going to bump up our Mindfulness segment.

Mindfulness Activity

ASE MEDITATION 3

Last week we did a brief exercise where you were encouraged to consider how any single experience has diverse and complex determining factors that all contributed to the experience. Nothing simply happens, but events occur out of numerous and often elusive prior influences. In a similar way, you were encouraged to attend to various possibilities that might arise from any circumstance. Our initial feelings can be completely valid; in fact, given the prior determinants, how we react to situations is plausible. This said, simply because something is plausible doesn't mean that it is inevitable. By having a flexible perspective about prior causes and diverse possibilities, we can be confronted by challenges, but also influence new more desirable outcomes.

This week, we are going to take this practice one step further and encourage you to consider how our inner dialogues affect our inner experiences or the experiences we have with others.

Returning to the lesson last week, we started by discerning facts about experiences from our inner evaluation of those experiences. That inner evaluation is baked into what it is to be a human, so we cannot likely turn it completely off (nor do we want to, as it can be protective or even lead to evaluations of gratitude and joy); but we do want to be more intentional about how we are affected by our inner stories.

For example, I was recently working with a teacher who was struggling with a student who was challenging in class, often interrupting the lessons with outbursts. We can accept that these behaviors are troubling, for you as teacher, for his peers in the classroom, and even for the student himself. We can also accept that there were probably prior causes for these behaviors, our reactions, and the effects on the classroom. In this case, the student was dealing with his parent's divorce, persistent violence in his neighborhood, among other things. By accepting these as possible influences, we can respond differently to this kid. Rather than reacting simply to the disruptions in class, we might respond with empathy. This doesn't require us to necessarily fix or even mention any of the causes, but by responding with compassion we might create new outcomes for all parties involved.

Please start by taking a seat and finding a comfortable and yet alert position. The goal here is to be comfortable and yet alert.

As you focus your gentle awareness on sitting, perhaps take a few deep breaths. Identify where the breath enters and then settles in your body. Continue to breathe naturally, noticing your unique breathing signature; notice any sensations in your body, or maybe more salient are thoughts that come to mind. Simply observe these experiences as they come and then naturally fade. It is curious that these inner experiences seem to come; note that they have an origin, birthed out of the sum total of your history and biology. There is nothing right or wrong about your experiences or history, simply note that these current sensations are present with you now.

Take a few more seconds and merely observe experiences as they arise.

Now, let's shift focus and provoke a specific type of experience, all while maintaining the same orientation of openness and acceptance.

Take a moment and try and generate a memory of a recent challenging conversation. Don't toggle through various memories or thoughts, simply land on the first one that comes to mind. Continue to breathe and use your breath as a way to accept that your experiences were valid given your history, personage, biology; also breathe with an openness that this validity doesn't foreclose you from different ways of experiencing yourself or others.

As you continue to attend to intentional breathing, again quickly and without elaboration, bring the experience to mind. Suspend the evaluations you have, but bring your awareness to your PROCESS. See yourself suspending your initial reaction. With a deep breath, witness yourself observing in an instant, "this conversation has a history, it occurred this way because of prior causes." Say to yourself, "I am going to respond in a way that creates connection in this conversation, where all participants will feel acceptance, safety, encouragement, and respect."

Our default ways of communicating are not necessarily wrong or harmful. Again, we accept that they have a history. But they do tend to be focused inward, privileging our perspective. As counterintuitive as it seems, we have a greater influence on others, in almost all circumstances, when we broach interactions with acceptance, safety, encouragement, and respect.

This need not take much time. What we are doing today is pairing our breathing with this orientation of acceptance, safety, encouragement, and respect. What occurs over time is that when we focus on our intentional breathing, this orientation will more likely be generated without much effort.

For approximately 20 seconds, breathe and attend to your process of connecting with others. Try not to blame, evaluate, or even look for causes or justifications. Simply note that there are causes and accept them. Then shift this acceptance to an orientation preoccupied with acceptance, safety, encouragement, and respect for self and others.

15 seconds

In accepting our thoughts and feelings, we are not passively accepting harmful things that happen to us. In a similar way, we don't accept that only helpful things will occur all of the time. Instead, we accept that our experiences are legitimate but the practice of breathing and reflection might contribute to more intentional, curious, flexible, and socially helpful outcomes. And when it doesn't immediately contribute, it makes us more likely to try something different until we do. Don't doubt one's ability, try another strategy.

Continue to breathe in a normal and comfortable manner and notice any thoughts, feelings, or sensations that might arise.

When thoughts or feelings creep in, simply acknowledge them with brief momentary curiosity and then return to the breath.

When comfortable, comfortably expand your awareness back to the surroundings. To the counselor you are working with and the room that surrounds you.

This week you will find yourself back in your familiar classroom. While it might be infeasible to dedicate five to ten minutes to capture your breath and interrogate every experience as we just did together, but commit to something that is more feasible. Is 15 seconds worth a different outcome? Five seconds to breathe, five seconds to reflect on possible prior influences, and five seconds to consider how curious, flexible, and connected outcomes might manifest from your investment.

Thank you again for your practice and for all of the important work that you do as an educator. We are completely aware that these mere activities cannot supersede the incredible number of stressors you have as a teacher. We also acknowledge that many of the tribulations we experience are influenced primarily by others. The point of these exercises is not to be compliant but instead to make oneself more aware, accepting, and intentional in how we respond to an ever-challenging world.

(Spend five minutes using their specific stories and asking them to practice co-regulated language. Use the example to help them reframe the language [i.e. "What have you done to improve yourself" is different than "How have you pursued your goals given the influences of (insert circumstance)?"]).

Encourage the teachers to strategize how co-regulated language might affect their inner experiences? In a similar way, encourage them to ponder how it might affect others (e.g. students, colleagues).

School Environment Advocacy

Last week we spoke about a possible event or phenomenon that is present in the school environment or culture; something that as a team we might be able to influence. Let's take a few minutes to discuss some possibilities and using our concept of radical curiosity, and the skills of reflection and questions, what are some specific behaviors that we can do to start the process of climate change in the school?

Closing

As we close, I want to encourage you to think about one thing that stood out and affected you today in our session. Commit to one very specific behavior that you can use this strategy immediately. How will you know when to use this strategy, how will you know if it was helpful, and if helpful how will you reinforce and celebrate your commitment or if it didn't help how can you try a different strategy?

Thank you again for your dedication. We have a spring break approaching. I wonder if there is one thing that each of you can dedicate specific practice, starting immediately, and reoccurring each day, just one thing be it the practice of radical curiosity or co-regulated language, how might you practice this and how will you recognize if it is affecting you?

See you when you get back.

Session Four

School Counselor

Welcome back. We have returned from a break and as we begin, I wonder if there are any experiences or insights that occurred over break that you might want to be included as content for our time together today?

Teachers

Allow one minute

School Counselor

Similar to each of the previous weeks, I would like for each of us to begin this meeting with a brief breathing exercise intended to focus our attention here together. With this in mind, I encourage you to close your eyes and simply bring your awareness to your breath. Make no effort to change your natural breathing at this point, simply notice that you are breathing. Notice that this breath sustains your life and is something shared between you and the world around you. Try not and judge the quality of your breath, again simply experience it for the next ten or so seconds.

(Provide the teachers about ten seconds)

Teacher Self-Advocacy

Before break, we talked about how many of our experiences are co-determined by a number of internal and external forces. How we respond to these experiences is how we co-regulate; that is, how we draw from these myriad internal and external resources and make the decisions in an intentional manner.

This week, we are going to extend this a bit by introducing the concept of connectedness. In some ways, we are all connected to these co-determinants of experience. For example, this particular consultation experience that we are sharing now is affecting you and me in ways that would not have occurred had we chosen to be in a different setting. But connectedness goes a bit further than co-determination; just as co-regulation is our efforts to act intentionally in concert with our personal and social influences, connectedness is how we experience and pursue acceptance, safety, encouragement, and respect between ourselves and others.

Let's take about five minutes and explore each of these constituent parts of feeling connected.

1 In what ways do you feel accepted or encouraged in your role as a teacher? Are there ways that your acceptance is compromised? Please consider specific examples.
2 In what ways do I consistently make others feel accepted or encouraged, including colleague teachers, students, and others?
3 What things contributes or compromises your current school environment in the areas of safety and shared respect?

The scholarship pertaining to feelings of connectedness in school are pretty compelling, as such feelings are associated with teacher stress, burnout, and persistence; for students, connectedness is affiliated with achievement, school behavior, and mental wellness. While we cannot control others feelings of connectedness, in the spirit of co-determination of experience, the literature is also clear that our feelings of connectedness can affect others. With this in mind, I wonder if we can come up with a simple, valuable (to you) goal to amplify the feelings of connectedness in your classroom?

(One minute)

School Environment Advocacy

Over the past few weeks we have talked about ideas to improve the school climate; particularly things that I might be able to do or advocate for as a school counselor, working in tandem with you as teachers. Inspired by your goals for highlighting connectedness in your classrooms, what further things might be improved upon in the broader school or education climate to affect your experiences of acceptance, safety, encouragement, and respect? What is one possible thing that we could do immediately to affect you and how you operate in the system?

Mindfulness Activity

I want us to take about ten minutes and participate in our fourth formal mindfulness exercise. I will read the script and participate in any way that feels comfortable and relevant.

ASE MEDITATION 4

Welcome back. Like you, the teachers and counselors involved in this project, I am coming back from spring break. I love these two words combined. Spring suggests new life. It also reminds me of a spring that coils into tension and then releases, jumping forward as if pursuing some intentional goal with passion. Break reminds us of the importance of resting and resetting, particularly after springing forward towards any goal. This message of springing towards goals and taking the time to break is an important lesson for us educators.

In our last mindfulness activity, we performed an exercise on attending to our thoughts, bracketing out any evaluations that get smuggled into our internal narratives, and pursuing more personally and socially meaningful outcomes.

This week we are going to pivot from introspection to how we interface with others. We cannot control other people, nor do we really want to (although it would occasionally be convenient or helpful!!!). But we do want to be intentional in how we affect them, as our intentions are likely to have some influence, which in turn will affect how they interface with us and further affect our inner experiences. In this way, our experiences are both connected and yet somewhat controllable.

Please start by taking a seat and finding a comfortable and yet alert position. The goal here is to be comfortable and yet alert.

As you focus your gentle awareness on sitting, perhaps take a few deep breaths. Identify where the breath enters and then settles in your body. Continue to breathe naturally, noticing your unique breathing signature; notice any sensations in your body, or maybe more salient are thoughts that come to mind. Simply observe these experiences as they come and then naturally fade. It is curious that these inner experiences seem to come; note that they have an origin, birthed out of the sum total of your history and biology. There is nothing right or wrong about your experiences or history, simply note that these current sensations are present with you now.

Take a few more seconds and merely observe experiences as they arise.

Now, let's shift focus and provoke a specific type of experience, all while maintaining the same orientation of openness and acceptance.

Take a moment and try to bring to your awareness a person in the school environment who makes you feel accepted, safe, encouraged, and respected. This person could be a colleague or even a student, but someone who you feel unreserved reverence for… now imagine that this person can somehow intuitively experience your current esteem and I want you to witness how it affects them. Witness the joy and appreciation in their response to your impressions about them.

15 seconds

Standing beside this person who you have identified and honored, conjure up the image of another person, someone in school who doesn't know their worth but you see their brilliance and importance. Using the same power of intuition, this person can also somehow experience all of the hope, compassion, and support you now experience on their behalf. Take just a few moments to observe how their prior manner changed as a consequence of your feelings towards them.

15 seconds

Finally, standing beside these two featured people, now bring to mind someone in school who challenges or even frustrates you. Continue to breathe in a normal and comfortable manner and notice any thoughts, feelings, or sensations that might arise. When thoughts or feelings creep in, simply acknowledge them with brief momentary curiosity and then return to the breath. Try not to couple your prior evaluation of this person with your current experience, simply note the prior history of challenge and return to your breath and open awareness. (Ten seconds) Now, look at all three people standing in a line in your mind; use the successes you invested in the initial two individuals and offer the same support and compassion to this third person. (Ten seconds) Notice if there is any changes in how you experience this person when you think of them with unmitigated compassion.

Take about one minute and see yourself standing in front of all three individuals, imagine yourself investing connectedness and compassion to each of these people for the entire duration.

Take just a moment and reflect on how this mental exercise affected your perspective. Take one final moment to extend this same compassion and connection to all beings in the school or people who affect people in your school.

When comfortable, comfortably expand your awareness back to the surroundings. To the counselor you are working with and the room that surrounds you.

This week you will find yourself back in your familiar classroom. While it might be infeasible to dedicate five to ten minutes to capture your breath and interrogate every experience as we just did together, commit to something that is more feasible. Is 15 seconds worth a different outcome? Five seconds to breathe, five seconds to reflect on possible prior influences, and five seconds to consider how curious, flexible, and connected outcomes might manifest from your investment.

> Thank you again for your practice and for all of the important work that you do as an educator. We are completely aware that these mere activities cannot supersede the incredible number of stressors you have as a teacher. We also acknowledge that many of the tribulations we experience are influenced primarily by others. The point of these exercises is not to be compliant but instead to make oneself more aware, accepting, and intentional in how we respond to an ever-challenging world.

Closing

Return back to the group when comfortable. As we close, I want to encourage you to think about one thing that stood out and affected you today in our session. Commit to one very specific behavior that you can use this strategy immediately. How will you know when to use this strategy, how will you know if it was helpful, and if helpful how will you reinforce and celebrate your commitment or if it didn't help how can you try a different strategy?

Session Five

School Counselor

Welcome back. We have made it to week five of this project!!! Congratulations. I genuinely hope that this has been as valuable to you as it has been for us as counselors. I have learned a lot and I hope that the experiences here in some way can translate into the total school environment. With that in mind, as we get started, I hope to use this last meeting as an opportunity to reflect on any developments, continued areas for personal and school growth, and looking forward to specific goals and resources.

School Counselor

As we have done in each of the previous weeks, I would like for each of us to begin this meeting with a brief breathing exercise intended to focus our attention here together. With this in mind, I encourage you to close your eyes and simply bring your awareness to your breath. Make no effort to change your natural breathing at this point, simply notice that you are breathing. Notice that this breath sustains your life and is something shared between you and the world around you. Try not and judge the quality of your breath, again simply experience it for the next ten or so seconds.

(Provide the teachers about ten seconds)

Teacher Self-Advocacy

Throughout the previous four weeks, we have talked about a number of topics, some based on your experiences as educators and others include some things that we have introduced from the empirical literature. Major themes include considering prior determinants of your experiences as teachers and even what contributes to the experiences of others. We have discussed and practices ways to co-regulate our responses to experience. For this week, it might be helpful to allow you to list some of the things that you have found helpful or some of the things that you are still working on.

(Using ASE-inspired active listening and reflecting skills, engage in approximately five minutes, including validating, expanding, and creating concrete plans for how to continue to grow.)

What topics were helpful? In what ways did these topics specifically affect you personally or your classrooms?

Were there any specific behaviors that were inspired by your experiences here in this project? In what ways might these behaviors be something you can retain and even amplify for the remainder of the academic year?

It is helpful for many people to celebrate our successes, even if they appear small and insignificant, they can have a profound and exponential effect on systems. Consider the phrase, "Little by little, bit by bit, I am improving every day." Small insights or large revelations here (or elsewhere) don't just affect one experience or relationship, but have the potential to be generalized broadly in one' personal and professional life.

Also considering the incremental nature of growth, we can become aware of the importance of compassion for self and others. Compassion is the steady and composed concern with either persistent or circumstantial feelings of suffering; com as a prefix means "to be with" and passion as the anchors highlights the "strong emotional connection." Being a teacher is sometimes challenging. We are deeply connected to it, because we value the content areas where learning occurs and we value students as learners. Sometimes, we are so tied to the outcome of learning that the passion exceeds the being-with requirement. Let's take a few moments today and work through how we can act compassionately with ourselves and others. What are some specific challenges that are still present in our school or your specific classroom? How can you reframe the challenge as a passion? And, what specific behaviors would accomplish "being with?"

School Environment Advocacy

Over the past few weeks we have talked about ideas to improve the school climate; particularly things that one might be able to do or advocate for as a school counselor, working in tandem with you as teachers. Inspired by your goals for highlighting connectedness in your classrooms, what further things might be improved upon in the broader school or education climate to affect your experiences of acceptance, safety, encouragement, and respect? What is one possible thing that we could do immediately to affect you and how you operate in the system?

Mindfulness Activity

ASE MEDITATION 5

Thank you for making it this far!!! When you committed to this project, you had only a modest notion of what would occur and yet here we are!!! Hopefully from those modest beginnings you have found one or more things helpful.

As humans, we generally crave seeing things to resolution. Like the storybooks from our youth, if there was a beginning there certainly must be an ending. As adults, life doesn't always feel so sequential; even with the various habits we maintain, the arch of time appears to march onward.

If true, absolute resolution seems elusive. In its absence, to persist, we must accomplish some type of compassion for self and the other peoples in our lives. Compassion is the steady and composed concern with either persistent or circumstantial feelings of suffering; this is captured in the word construction itself; the prefix com refers to "being with" and passion is any "strong emotional connection" to someone or thing.

This week we will focus on the practice of compassion. If experiences are predicated by prior determinants, no one can be fully responsible and yet because we are passionate about our experiences, we are responsible to have the greatest influence on the outcomes.

As you focus your gentle awareness on sitting, perhaps take a few deep breaths. Identify where the breath enters and then settles in your body. Continue to breathe naturally, noticing your unique breathing signature; notice any sensations in your body, or maybe more salient are thoughts that come to mind. Simply observe these experiences as they come and then naturally fade. It is curious that these inner experiences seem to come; note that they have an origin, birthed out of the sum total of your history and biology. There is nothing right or wrong about your experiences or history, simply note that these current sensations are present with you now.

Take a few more seconds and merely observe experiences as they arise.

Now, let's shift focus and provoke a specific type of experience, all while maintaining the same orientation of openness and acceptance.

With each in-breath, say to yourself, as if rehearsing for the great play that is one's own life, "be with" and then with the deep and yet comfortable out-breadth, "give out." Be with. Give out.

(30 seconds)

This mental rehearsal coupled with the breathing is intended to codify the experience of patience and curiosity that you might associate with these exercises with the intentions to be truly and deeply with yourself and others, and then the intention to give out compassion to yourself in others as co-determinants of experience. Continue to breathe; be with, give out.

(15 seconds)

This action of breathing reflects the words themselves and illustrates how we are affected by others and how we affect others. This manner of thinking illustrates the importance of compassion. If our aspiration is to live a quality life, we must be with and give out to self and others. We breath in what all people and non-people in the world give us, and we give out through breathing. Just like our minds, what we bring in and what we give out affects the qualities of experience.

(15 seconds)

Thank you for your commitment to these practices for the last month and a half. We genuinely hope that you found some value. Certainly, exploring how your mind works in these brief exercises is insufficient given the fast pace and complexity of our lives, but hopefully these mere activities offered some examples of what is possible when you are curious (about self and others), co-regulate, connect, and act with compassion. Further, we hope that these exercises inspire you to find other related support, as your work as a teacher is invaluable and you genuinely deserve these types of support.

Closing

These five weeks have been inspiring and enlightening. As we close, I want to encourage you to think about one thing that stood out and affected you today in our session. Commit to one very specific behavior that you can use this strategy immediately. How will you know when to use this strategy, how will you know if it was helpful, and if helpful how will you reinforce and celebrate your commitment or if it didn't help how can you try a different strategy?

One thing is not trivial. Thank you again for all that you do.

References

Anderson, H. (2015). Postmodern/poststructural/social construction therapies: Collaborative, narrative, and solution-focused. In T. Sexton & J. Lebow (Eds.), Handbook of family therapy, 4th ed. (pp. 182–204). New York: Routledge.

Baker, S. B., Robichaud, T. A., Dietrich, V. C. W., Wells, S. C., & Schreck, R. E. (2009). School counselor consultation: A pathway to advocacy, collaboration, and leadership. *Professional School Counseling, 12*(3), 200–206. https://doi.org/10.1177/2156759X0901200301

Barrett, L. F. (2017). How emotions are made: The secret life of the brain. New York, NY: Houghton Mifflin Harcourt.

Dobson, K. S., & Dozois, D. J. A. (Eds.). (2019). *Handbook of cognitive-behavioral therapies* (4th ed.). The Guilford Press.

Kidd, C., & Hayden, B. Y. (2015). The psychology and neuroscience of curiosity. *Neuron, 88*(3), 449–460. https://doi.org/10.1016/j.neuron.2015.09.010

Lemberger, M. E. (2010). Advocating Student-within-Environment: A humanistic theory for school counseling. *The Journal of Humanistic Counseling, Education and Development, 49,* 131–146. https://doi.org/10.1002/j.2161-1939.2010.tb00093.x

Lemberger, M. E., & Hutchison, B. (2014). Advocating Student-within-Environment: A humanistic approach for therapists to animate social justice in the schools. *Journal of Humanistic Psychology, 54,* 8–44. https://doi.org/10.1177/0022167816652750

Lemberger-Truelove, M. E., Molina, C. E., Carbonneau, K. J., & Smith, M. J. (2023). Co-regulation effects of a school counselor consultation intervention on middle school teacher-student relationships, curiosity, and teacher stress. *Professional School Counselor, 27*(1a), 1–10. https://doi.org/10.1177/2156759X231153380.

McCaslin, M. (2009). Co-regulation of student motivation and emergent identity. *Educational Psychologist, 44*(2), 137–146. https://doi.org/10.1080/00461520902832384

Schneider, K. J., Pierson, J. F., & Bugental, J. F. (Eds.). (2014). *The handbook of humanistic psychology: Theory, research, and practice*. Sage Publications.

INDEX

Taylor & Francis eBooks

www.taylorfrancis.com

A single destination for eBooks from Taylor & Francis with increased functionality and an improved user experience to meet the needs of our customers.

90,000+ eBooks of award-winning academic content in Humanities, Social Science, Science, Technology, Engineering, and Medical written by a global network of editors and authors.

TAYLOR & FRANCIS EBOOKS OFFERS:

- A streamlined experience for our library customers
- A single point of discovery for all of our eBook content
- Improved search and discovery of content at both book and chapter level

REQUEST A FREE TRIAL

support@taylorfrancis.com